BRITISH PRIME MINISTERS: POLITICS AND POLITICAL LEADERSHIP IN NUMBER 10

KEVIN THEAKSTON

Contents

   Acknowledgements

1. Introduction   1
2. Winston Churchill (1940-45 and 1951-55)   16
3. Clement Attlee (1945-51)   32
4. Anthony Eden (1955-57)   52
5. Harold Macmillan (1957-63)   67
6. Alec Douglas-Home (1963-64)   85
7. Harold Wilson (1964-70 and 1974-76)   99
8. Edward Heath (1970-74)   114
9. James Callaghan (1976-79)   127
10. Margaret Thatcher (1979-90)   142
11. John Major (1990-97)   158
12. Tony Blair (1997-2007)   171
13. Gordon Brown (2007-10)   185
14. David Cameron (2010-16)   199
15. Theresa May (2016-19)   214
16. Boris Johnson (2019-22)   234
17. Evaluating British prime ministers   255
18. Afterword on Liz Truss (2022)   278

Acknowledgements

This book in part comes out of, and brings together material from, lectures and seminars I have given in teaching a course (a third year BA Politics module) about British prime ministers at the University of Leeds. I am happy to acknowledge how much I have learned from the many enthusiastic students who took different versions of my course over the years. Various research projects, academic presentations and publications of mine have fed into that teaching, and also into this book. The relevant publications are listed below, some of them produced with hugely talented co-authors - Chris Byrne, Robert Crowcroft, Mark Gill, Nick Randall and Andrew Roe-Crines - from whom I have also learned a great deal about British politics and prime ministers.

- (2021) 'Edward Heath and the challenge of "the impossible leadership situation"', in: Andrew Roe-Crines and Tim Heppell (eds.) *Policies and Politics Under Prime Minister Edward Heath*, London: Palgrave Macmillan, 317-354 (co-authored with Chris Byrne and Nick Randall)
- (2020) *Disjunctive Prime Ministerial Leadership in British Politics: from Baldwin to Brexit*, London, Palgrave (co-authored with Chris Byrne and Nick Randall)
- (2021) 'Theresa May's disjunctive premiership: choice and constraint in political time', *British Journal of Politics and International Relations*, 23 (4): 699-716 (co-authored with Nick Randall and Chris Byrne)
- (2018) 'Understanding the power of the prime minister: structure and agency in models of prime-ministerial power', *British Politics*, 14 (4): 329-346 (co-authored with Chris Byrne)
- (2017) 'Evaluating British prime ministerial performance: David Cameron's premiership in political time', *British Journal of Politics and International Relations*, 19 (1): 202-220 (co-authored with Nick Randall and Christopher Byrne)
- (2015) '"Doing God" in number 10: British prime ministers, religion, and political rhetoric', *Politics and Religion*, 8 (1): 155-177 (co-authored with Andrew Crines)
- (2015) 'The oratory of Winston Churchill', in: Richard Hayton and Andrew Crines (eds.) *Conservative orators from Baldwin to Cameron*, Manchester: Manchester University Press, 30-46

- (2013) 'The fall of the Attlee Government, 1951', in: Timothy Heppell and Kevin Theakston (eds.) *How Labour Governments Fall*, London: Palgrave Macmillan, 61-82 (co-authored with Robert Crowcroft)
- (2013) 'Evaluating prime ministerial performance: the British experience', in P. Strangio, P. 't Hart and J. Walter (eds) *Understanding Prime-Ministerial Performance: Comparative Perspectives*, Oxford: Oxford University Press, 221-241
- (2012) 'David Cameron as prime minister', in: Timothy Heppell and David Seawright D (eds.) *Cameron and the Conservatives*, London: Palgrave, 194-208
- (2012) 'Winston Churchill, 1945-51', in: Timothy Heppell (ed.) *Leaders of the Opposition from Churchill to Cameron*, London: Palgrave, 7-19
- (2011) 'Gordon Brown as prime minister: political skills and leadership style', *British Politics*, 6 (1): 78-100
- (2011) 'The Postwar Premiership League', *Political Quarterly*, 82 (1): 67-80 (co-authored with Mark Gill)
- (2010) *After Number Ten: Former Prime Ministers in British Politics*, London, Palgrave
- (2007) 'What Makes for an Effective British Prime Minister?', *Quaderni di Scienza Politica*, volume 14: 39-61
- (2006) 'After Number Ten: What do former prime ministers do?', *Political Quarterly*, 7 (4): 448-456
- (2006) 'Rating 20th-Century British Prime Ministers', *British Journal of Politics and International Relations*, 8 (2): 193-213 (co-authored with Mark Gill)
- (2005) Prime ministers and the constitution: Attlee to Blair', *Parliamentary Affairs*, 58 (1): 17-37
- (2004) *Winston Churchill and the British Constitution*, London, Politico's
- (2002) 'Political Skills and Context in Prime Ministerial Leadership in Britain', *Politics and Policy*, 30 (2): 283-323

Kevin Theakston

Leeds, February 2023

Chapter 1

Introduction

This book is about British prime ministers from the era of Winston Churchill and Clement Attlee through to the time of Boris Johnson and Liz Truss, looking at how they became party leaders and got the top job in government; what they stood for and tried to achieve in terms of ideological purpose and policy goals; their political skills and style and governing methods; and the context, situation and challenges they faced in Number 10. It covers, therefore, eight decades of British politics and recent/ contemporary history from 1940 to 2022, a period involving major changes in terms of party politics, ideology, political institutions, the country's international position, the economy, society, and the mass media – all of which impacted on the role, power and success or failure of prime ministers as political and governmental leaders.

As a first step, it may be useful briefly to sketch some background on how prime ministers get and lose the job (see Brazier 2020). Formally, prime ministers are appointed by the monarch; by convention, the monarch invites the person most likely to command a majority in the House of Commons; that person is usually the leader of the largest party in the Commons, elected by the people. The monarch's role is normally unproblematic. In an earlier period, King George V did play a more active role in the choice of prime ministers in 1923 and 1931. The clear election winners thrown up in a two-party system normally make the choice a more obvious, virtually rubber-stamping, one. But there was some controversy over the choice of Alec Douglas-Home as the successor to Harold Macmillan in 1963 at a time when the Conservative Party leader 'emerged' through murky inner-party consultations and top-level politicking rather than being elected (see chapter 6). There were also the 'hung' parliaments of February 1974 and 2010 when the monarch was carefully kept out of things while the politicians manoeuvred and bargained until there was a clear leader for the Palace to 'send for'.

There are twentieth century cases of the prime minister not being leader of the biggest party in wartime or in a coalition (in the 1930s), but none since late 1940 (for his first few months, Churchill was prime minister but not actually leader of the Conservative Party). Labour leaders have always been elected – up to 1980 by MPs only; afterwards by an electoral college involving the unions, party members and parliamentarians (the system used to elect Tony Blair in 1994); and more recently by a one-person-one-vote election by party members and affiliated and registered supporters. From 1965 Conservative leaders were elected by MPs, and after 1998 the wider membership was given a role in choosing between the top two candidates selected by the votes of MPs (the system used to elect David Cameron in 2005 and Boris Johnson in 2019, as well as Liz Truss in 2022). Labour in 2007 and the Conservatives in 2016 short-circuited their full election procedures, resulting in something approaching 'coronations' for Gordon Brown and Theresa May respectively, as was also the case with the selection of Rishi Sunak as Conservative leader and prime minister in 2022. Studies of party leader elections generally conclude that the key factors affecting party choice(s) include ideology, governing competence, parliamentary skills, the ability to enthuse and/or unite the party, and electability (Stark 1996; Quinn 2012). However, different criteria may be more or less important to different groups in the 'selectorate' (party activists supposedly being more concerned about ideology, for instance, and parliamentarians wanting to keep their seats and perhaps prioritising electability), and all this may also be influenced by whether the party is in government (when perceived executive competence may be the vital factor, and there may be a desire to avoid a lengthy contest) or in Opposition after an election defeat.

Governments are ultimately made and broken by the electorate; prime ministers too. But of the sixteen prime ministers featured in this book, while six first entered office following a general election victory (Attlee, Wilson, Heath, Thatcher, Blair and Cameron), ten formally succeeded to Number

2

10 mid-term (Churchill, Eden, Macmillan, Douglas-Home, Callaghan, Major, Brown, May, Johnson and Truss). Three of the latter group - Douglas-Home, Callaghan and Brown - lost office at the next general election, while Eden, Macmillan, Major and Johnson subsequently won general elections during their time in Number 10, and May called an early election and lost her majority but remained in office. For his part, Churchill lost the first general election he fought as PM in 1945 but came back into office again after a stint in opposition and winning re-election in 1951. Harold Wilson, in 1974, was the last British party leader to return to Number 10 after hanging on through a period in opposition.

There is no constitutional requirement for an incoming mid-term 'successor' prime minister to call an immediate (or early) election to get a personal mandate – it is a matter of political judgement, and one that they have often seemed to get wrong. It is notable that the long-tenure prime ministers (Wilson, Thatcher, Blair) are the repeated general election winners, while the mid-term successor PMs often have short and unhappy tenures (though Major clocked up six and a half years).

In terms of personal backgrounds (see table 1.1), the Conservative prime ministers before 1964 were notably aristocratic and upper class (Churchill, Eden, Macmillan and Douglas-Home). Since then more middle-class and even working-class figures have risen to the top, with Cameron and perhaps also Johnson representing something of a reversion to the older elite type (though neither personally were from traditional aristocratic families). Three of the sixteen PMs from Churchill to Truss did not attend university at all, while twelve had been at Oxford. The average age on becoming PM was 55, after an average of around 21 years previous parliamentary experience (counting Douglas-Home's 15 years as an MP and 12 in the Lords). Blair and Cameron had no prior ministerial experience at all; the others had climbed the ministerial ladder (though Major very rapidly). Luck and chance events were important in reaching the top for some: Wilson and Blair got their chances after death of the then-Leaders of the Opposition; Macmillan benefitted from the collapse of Eden's health in the

3

aftermath of the disastrous Suez intervention; Thatcher unexpectedly leapfrogged over better-placed rivals in 1975 after Heath was destroyed by electoral failure; Thatcher's sudden and brutal toppling opened the way to the relatively 'unknown' Major; May's succession in 2016 also came about unexpectedly suddenly and dramatically, while her failure opened the way to Johnson succeeding in his second attempt at the top job. A smooth succession to a long-time 'heir apparent' is historically fairly unusual in British politics.

Most - in fact, nearly all - exits from No. 10 are involuntary in one way or another. Seven of this group of prime ministers were in effect evicted by the electorate: six in general elections (Attlee, Douglas-Home, Heath, Callaghan, Major and Brown) and another quit after losing a referendum (Cameron). Churchill finally resigned in 1955 (aged 80), under considerable pressure from ministers concerned about his deteriorating performance and their party's prospects if he led them into another election. Eden, as noted earlier, resigned on health grounds but would anyway have found it virtually impossible to continue for long after the failure of his Suez (mis)adventure. Macmillan quit on health grounds too, though after a period when his authority had been on the slide. Only Wilson finally retired at a time of his own choosing in 1976 without any political pressure on him to go (though he too had lost a general election in 1970, at the end of his first stint in Number 10). Five leaders were in different ways forced out by their party: Thatcher in a formal leadership challenge; Blair in a more drawn-out process of attrition and guerrilla warfare; May brought down by the Conservatives' Brexit civil war; Johnson brought down by a combination of impropriety, scandal and incompetence; Truss quit before she could be voted out by her MPs.

It is worth bearing in mind that there is no constitutional definition of the British prime minister's role nor any authoritative specification of the office's functions, powers and responsibilities. They are largely a matter of convention and usage, not statute, and are thus to a large degree flexible and subject to variation and change over time. The prime minister's formal powers include prerogative powers, exercised by the

4

premier on behalf of the monarch (such as the power to appoint or dismiss ministers, or to prorogue parliament).

One prime minister quipped he felt, at least initially, he had 'nothing to do' as a way of drawing a contrast with the job of a minister running a big departmental machine (Callaghan 1987: 403). It was the difference between playing an instrument and conducting an orchestra said another premier (Harold Wilson quoted in Jones 1985: 214). Functions, responsibilities and demands on the office and its holders have expanded over time – as various 'audits' by Peter Hennessy (2000) have indicated – but that brings overload as much as extra 'power' in any straightforward sense. The prime minister is by tradition First Lord of the Treasury and also usually Minister for the Civil Service but does not now normally take charge of any government department – though in the past prime ministers sometimes combined the role with holding office as Foreign Secretary, Chancellor of the Exchequer, or other posts.

Official guidance on the Prime Minister's role is limited. The official *Cabinet Manual* (first published in 2011) described the prime minister as head of the government, chief adviser to the Sovereign, and chair of the Cabinet. The prime minister is thus responsible for appointing/dismissing ministers, orchestrating the Cabinet committee system, and the overall organisation of the executive and allocation of functions between ministers and departments. The Cabinet is described in the *Cabinet Manual* as 'the ultimate decision-making body of government', while the prime minister is said to 'usually take the lead on significant matters of state' (Cabinet Office 2011).

The advent of coalition government in May 2010 impacted formally and politically on powers and responsibilities normally regarded as belonging to the prime minister alone. Under the *Coalition Agreement for Stability and Reform*, the prime minister (David Cameron) was obliged to consult and agree with the deputy prime minister (Nick Clegg, leader of the Liberal Democrats) over the appointment, reshuffling and sacking of ministers; in practice Clegg selected his party's ministers. The allocation of posts between the parties in the coalition operated on a 'one-in, one-out' rule to maintain the agreed balance between the two coalition partners. The premier's patronage power in all governments is subject in practice to political constraints but that was a new formal limitation. A similar limitation on the PM's normal discretion was in relation to the establishment of Cabinet committees, the appointment of their members, and the framing of their terms of reference, which had to be agreed between the prime minister and the deputy prime minister. Principles and expectations were also spelt out about the functioning of government, including requirements for consultation and discussion among ministers, and clearing certain issues if necessary through the Coalition Committee (though in practice a less formal group, the 'Quad', was used) to ensure both parties agreed. These rules and limitations terminated with the end of the coalition in 2015.

Two other issues about the power of the prime minister are worth briefly noting. The first relates to the PM's traditional power to call an election. The passage, under the Coalition, of the Fixed-term Parliaments Act in 2011, abolishing the prerogative power to dissolve parliament, was at the time widely seen as a very significant surrender of prime ministerial power. However, Theresa May easily secured the parliamentary vote to call an early general election in 2017, while Boris Johnson was initially stymied when he tried to call an early election in 2019 but found a way round the legislation – the key factor being whether opposition parties would support an election. The Fixed-term Parliaments Act was repealed in 2022, restoring the prerogative - i.e. prime-ministerial - powers in this area. The second issue involves the power to commit British troops to military action, which was traditionally authorised by the prime minister using royal prerogative powers. But after Blair allowed MPs to vote in 2003 on the action in Iraq it was suggested there was a new convention that a prior parliamentary approval was needed, and indeed in 2013 Cameron abandoned plans to deploy military forces in Syria after losing a vote in the Commons. However, plans to legislate on this subject were dropped in 2016, and May took military action against the Syrian regime in 2018 without a prior explicit parliamentary vote. In reality it would be difficult for a prime minister and government to engage in military action without parliamentary backing or support, but there are no clear constitutional obligations here.

For all the differences of personality and personal style in the period from Churchill to Johnson, the job of prime minister is not one which has been invented or re-invented from scratch every time a new prime minister has walked through the door of Number 10, as Anthony King (1991) long ago pointed out. There are clear expectations – the 'basics' of the role. First of all, as *head of government*, the prime minister must form a government and keep it running by appointing/dismissing ministers, chairing the Cabinet, managing the system of Cabinet committees, overseeing the machinery of government, being minister for the civil service, and taking overall responsibility for the security and intelligence services. The prime minister must also manage the relationship between the monarch and the government. Secondly, the prime minister can never neglect the *party leader* aspects of his/her role as the party's chief strategist, communicator and campaigner, ultimately in charge of the party machine. The prime minister is thus highly partisan, but is also, thirdly, a *national leader* making symbolic public appearances, representing the UK at international meetings, and being in some sense a 'trustee of the constitution' (Theakston 2005). In all this, as King (1991: 34) noted, there is no formal requirement for policy leadership in government by the prime minister. Historically, some prime ministers have concentrated largely on political management, fighting fires and arbitrating political and personal disputes, with policy mainly formed by departments, ministers and the Cabinet. Others focused on a few specific policy areas (often foreign and/or economic policy). Only a few strove to personally shape and direct their government's policies on a broad front (Thatcher being an extreme example there). Preventing fragmentation in government, focusing priorities and defining/guarding a coherent overall strategy are perhaps the most important tasks a prime minister should do (and no-one else really can) – but are also, as we shall see, the most difficult to perform well (see: Weller 1985, 2018).

British political science academics have frequently downplayed the personal factor when trying to understand and explain the role, powers and impact of the prime minister in the government system and as a political leader. There are innumerable political biographies and historical studies of British prime ministers and their governments, but these have been unduly neglected as a basis for comparison, generalisation and analysis. In marked contrast to the many American studies of the presidential leadership role and the impact of personality on that office, there is, it has been argued, a 'dearth of systematic studies on the individual characteristics of [British] prime ministers and on the personal components of leadership' (Foley 2000: 246). However, that gap has started to be filled in recent years as academics working on the British prime minister have begun to produce studies exploring different aspects or approaches to prime-ministerial leadership, including the notion of 'statecraft' (Buller and James 2012; James 2018), 'leadership capital' (Bennister et al 2017) and 'political time' (Byrne et al 2020), and have also been auditing and assessing prime ministers' political skills and leadership styles in terms borrowed from US presidential studies (Theakston 2007, 2011; McMeeking 2021).

The traditional but somewhat limited academic debate about 'prime ministerial versus Cabinet government' has mostly been argued in terms of the broad long-term development of the office of prime minister and related institutional processes, and has not usually placed a central emphasis on the personalities of prime ministers and the circumstances or situations they have faced (Barber 1991: 126). The office of prime minister is perceived to be highly institutionalised, located at the apex of a system of centralised government, consisting of disciplined political parties, a strong executive controlling parliament, and lacking significant checks and balances. Thus, Richard Rose (1980: 44) emphasised the role expectations and imperatives of office, organisational requirements and constraints, and maintained that 'political circumstances are more important than personality.' 'Personal style influences how a prime minister carries out the demands of office, but it does not determine what is to be done', he argued. While some writers have suggested that the interaction of personality, personal style, and circumstances are crucial in determining the role and power of the prime minister (King 1969: ix-x; Blake 1975; Barber 1991: 131-33), the argument has not usually been developed in an in-depth and systematic manner.

Influential mainstream political science accounts of the British premiership have tended to regard individual prime ministers' personalities, political skills and leadership styles as variables of secondary significance, if they are seen as relevant at all. Studies of the wider 'core executive', for instance, depict it as complex, fragmented, and not susceptible to personal direction or control from Number 10 Downing Street in any straightforward sense. The role of the prime minister in this system is analysed in terms of interdependence, networks, and resource exchange. Martin Smith (1999: 14) accepts that a prime minister's 'personality and style does affect both the policy process . . . and decisions', but argues that 'it is only one factor among many. Personality is not the predominant explanation of the operation of the core executive.' The core executive model emphasises institutions, structure, and context. It allows some limited and variable scope for the agency of individual actors and their choices and strategies—Smith (1999: 74, 105) conceding that a prime minister's resources and role do have an individual/personal dimension—but structural/ institutional factors are given much more explanatory weight.

Those writers who have argued that Britain is now a de facto 'presidential' system, or one that is developing along quasi-presidential lines, have also put the main burden of the explanation less on the personal characteristics and preferences of individual prime ministers than on a wider set of political trends, mass media pressures and institutional developments. As Michael Foley (2000: 25) argued: 'prime ministerial leadership has undergone changes of such profundity that they amount to a qualitative shift in the type of leadership which is now viable in British government. These changes are far deeper in substance than the personality and temporary circumstances of any one incumbent . . . [The] significance of such formidable figures as Margaret Thatcher and Tony Blair in the premiership rests less with their particular qualities as individual leaders and more in

9

the way they bring to the surface a set of underlying and irreversible dynamics in the character of the British political system.'

The possibilities, the limitations, and the functioning of the premiership have been seen in rather different terms by historians. As Eccleshall and Walker (1998: xiii) commented: 'political science models, while often illuminating, cannot explain those aspects of prime ministerial behaviour which derive from individual personality traits and the quality of temperaments under pressure. As political circumstances and fortunes fluctuate so the strengths and weaknesses of prime ministerial personalities and their particular approaches to the office [are] .. . revealed.' Similarly, Peter Hennessy (2000: 36-37) sees a key role for choice and individual flexibility: 'History deals each new incumbent a certain hand, the bundle of customs and conventions, practices and expectations that go with the office . . . The legacy of the past has a definitive shaping effect, but not so powerful a constraining impact. Because the constitution or the law actually prescribe so little by way of functions, a Prime Minister can make of the job a very great deal of what he or she wishes, provided other circumstances (size of majority, state of the economy, passivity of Cabinet colleagues, personal health and energy) allow it.'

While institutionally and constitutionally the office may be slow to change, the way in which successive prime ministers do the job can vary very significantly indeed, as this book will show. As Anthony King (1991: 42-43) explained: 'first, there is variety *between* and *among* different prime ministers. Different people bring different personalities to the job; they have different goals; they adopt different styles; and they find themselves operating in different political environments. Second, there is variety *within* the lifetime of a single premiership. This variety can be deliberate on the part of a prime minister (Thatcher's governing style became more dominant as she became increasingly confident and determined); or, more commonly, it can be dictated from outside by changed circumstances, as a prime minister's personal standing, electoral prospects and professional reputation change through time' (emphasis in original). 'The prime ministership in Britain is remarkably malleable', King maintained (1991: 34). Asquith (prime minister 1908-16) once famously wrote that, 'the office of the Prime Minister is what its holder chooses and is able to make of it', or as King (1991: 35) rephrased it: 'the power of the prime minister is what a prime minister wants, and is able, to get away with.'

This book discusses the experience of the sixteen Conservative and Labour prime ministers who have held office in Britain from 1940 through to 2022, exploring the scope for, forms of, and constraints upon prime ministerial leadership in the modern system. Focusing on prime-ministerial personality alone would admittedly be a limited and inadequate basis for understanding the behaviour and assessing the power and impact of top politicians. But neither can nor should prime ministers be conceived of as nameless, faceless, institutionally-determined actors. The individual prime minister has to be understood in his or her institutional setting and political and economic context.

Thus the argument of this book is that the prime ministerships and the achievements and failures of British leaders from Churchill to Truss can only be understood by analysing these factors:

1. the circumstances in which the individual advanced to the leadership of his/her party and the government (the party factor having an ongoing importance throughout a premiership);

2. the aims—strategic and tactical—pursued by the prime minister (what is the PM trying to achieve in terms of ideological purpose and policy goals?);

3. the political skills and style of the prime minister (including the professional politician's arts, the governing methods and techniques used to manage Cabinet and Whitehall, and the practice of statecraft in a broad sense); and

4. the operating environment or context faced (in the widest sense and including the economic situation; international constraints; media pressures; electoral and

public opinion trends; the parliamentary arithmetic; the pressure of events; etc).

Prime ministers face a complex and dynamic operating environment, some features of which they can—over time—influence, but never fully control. Within that situation they seek to achieve certain objectives (short- and long-term), using a range of methods and deploying the various political resources and skills they possess. Whether their time in office and their statecraft are successful depends on the relationship between aims and strategies, skills and methods, and the wider context.

References

Barber, J. (1991). *The Prime Minister Since 1945.* Oxford: Blackwell.

Bennister, M., Worthy, B., and 't Hart, P. (2017). *The Leadership Capital Index: a New Perspective on Political Leadership.* Oxford: Oxford University Press.

Blake, R. (1975). *The Office of Prime Minister.* London: British Academy.

Brazier, R. (2020). *Choosing a Prime Minister: The Transfer of Power in Britain.* Oxford: Oxford University Press.

Buller, J. and James, T. (2012). 'Statecraft and the Assessment of National Political Leaders: the Case of New Labour and Tony Blair', *British Journal of Politics and International Relations.* 14 (4) 534-555.

Byrne, C., Randall, N., and Theakston, K. (2020). *Disjunctive Prime Ministerial Leadership in British Politics: From Baldwin to Brexit.* London: Palgrave Macmillan.

Cabinet Office (2011). *The Cabinet Manual.* https://assets.publishing.service.gov.uk/government/ uploads/system/uploads/attachment_data/file/60641/ cabinet-manual.pdf

Callaghan, J. (1987). *Time and Chance.* London: William Collins.

Eccleshall and Walker, G. (1998). *Biographical Dictionary of British Prime Ministers.* London: Routledge.

Foley, M. (2000). *The British Presidency.* Manchester: Manchester University Press.

Hennessy, P. (2000). *The Prime Minister: The Office and Its Holders Since 1945.* London: Allen Lane.

James, T. (2018). 'Political leadership as statecraft? Aligning theory with praxis in conversation with British party leaders', *British Journal of Politics and International Relations.* 20 (3): 555-572.

Jones, G. (1985). 'The Prime Minister's Power', in A. King (ed), *The British Prime Minister.* Second edition. London: Macmillan.

King, A. (1969). *The British Prime Minister.* London: Macmillan.

King, A. (1991). 'The British Prime Minister in the Age of the Career Politician. *West European Politics.* 14 (2): 25-47.

McMeeking, T. (2021). *The Political Leadership of Prime Minister John Major: A Reassessment Using the Greenstein Model.* London: Palgrave Macmillan.

Quinn, T. (2012). *Electing and Ejecting Party Leaders in Britain.* London: Palgrave Macmillan.

Rose, R. (1980). 'British Government: the job at the top', in R. Rose and E. Suleiman (eds). *Presidents and Prime Ministers.* Washington DC: American Enterprise Institute.

Smith, M. (1999). *The Core Executive in Britain.* London: Macmillan.

Stark, L. (1996). *Choosing a Leader: Party Leadership Contests in Britain from Macmillan to Blair.* London: Palgrave Macmillan.

Theakston, K. (2005). 'Prime Ministers and the Constitution: Attlee to Blair', *Parliamentary Affairs*, 58 (1): 17-37.

Theakston, K. (2007). 'What Makes for an Effective British Prime Minister?', *Quaderni Di Scienza Politica.* 14 (2): 227-249.

Theakston, K. (2011). 'Gordon Brown as Prime Minister: Political Skills and Leadership Style', *British Politics.* 6 (1): 78-100.

Weller, P. (2005). *First Among Equals: Prime Ministers in Westminster Systems.* London: Allen & Unwin.

Weller, P. (2018). *The Prime Ministers' Craft*. Oxford: Oxford University Press.

Table 1.1 PMs' backgrounds and careers

Table 1.1	Tenure	Class origins	Education	Years as MP before PM	Previous Cabinet experience (posts/years)	Age when first PM
Winston Churchill	1940-45, 1951-55	Aristocrat	Public school, Sandhurst	38	Trade, Home Office, Admiralty, Munitions, War Office, Colonies, Chancellor of Exchequer (19)	65
Clement Attlee	1945-51	Upper middle class	Public school, Oxford	23	Lord Privy Seal, Dominions Sec., Deputy PM, Lord President of the Council (5)	62
Anthony Eden	1955-57	Upper class	Public school, Oxford	31	League of Nations Affairs, Dominion Affairs, Sec. Of State for War, Foreign Secretary (13)	58
Harold Macmillan	1957-63	Upper class	Public school, Oxford	31	Minister Resident in Mediterranean, Air Secretary, Housing, Defence, Foreign Sec., Chancellor of Exchequer (9)	63
Alec Douglas-Home	1963-64	Aristocrat	Public school, Oxford	27 (15 as MP, 12 as peer)	Commonwealth Relations, Leader of H. of Lords, Foreign Secretary (8)	60
Harold Wilson	1964-70, 1974-76	Lower middle class	Grammar School, Oxford	19	Board of Trade (4)	48
Edward Heath	1970-74	Skilled artisan/ lower middle class	Grammar School, Oxford	20	Chief Whip. Labour, Foreign Office, Trade (5)	54
James Callaghan	1976-79	Working class	State school	31	Chancellor of the Exchequer, Home Secretary, Foreign Sec. (8)	64
Margaret Thatcher	1979-90	Lower middle class	Grammar School, Oxford	20	Education (4)	54
John Major	1990-97	Skilled artisan/ lower middle class	Grammar School	11	Foreign Secretary, Chancellor of Exchequer (3)	47
Tony Blair	1997-2007	Middle class	Public school, Oxford	14	Nil	43
Gordon Brown	2007-10	Middle class	State High School, Edinburgh	24	Chancellor of Exchequer (10)	56
David Cameron	2010-16	Upper middle class	Public school, Oxford	9	Nil	43
Theresa May	2016-19	Middle class	Private/GS/state schools, Oxford	19	Home Secretary (6)	59
Boris Johnson	2019-22	Upper middle class	Public school, Oxford	11	Foreign Secretary (2)	55
Liz Truss	2022	Middle class	State school Oxford	12	Environment Sec., Justice Sec., Chief Sec. Treasury, International Trade Sec., Foreign Secretary (8)	47

Chapter 2

Winston Churchill (1940-45 and 1951-55)

Winston Churchill always had a strong sense of himself as a man of destiny. As a teenage schoolboy he had claimed to foresee 'great upheavals, terrible struggles; wars such as one cannot imagine' in which he would have a 'high position' and 'save London and England . . . [and] the Empire' (Roberts 2018: 22-23). In his early twenties a palm-reader predicted: 'he would pass great difficulties but reach the top of his profession.' 'I trust you may be right in your forecast', he replied (Roberts 2018: 63). The first biography of Churchill, published in 1905 when he was only a 30-year old first-term MP described him as a future prime minister (Roberts 2018: 97). But it took another 35 years and a world war to finally make him prime minister in 1940, after an extraordinary political roller-coaster journey full of advances, setbacks, successes, disasters and bitter controversy. He may then have kept Britain in the war and avoided defeat but – as he recognised and later lamented – could not hold back the decline and loss of his country's power and Empire.

Party Leadership
Starting as a Conservative, becoming a Liberal, and then 're-ratting' back to the Tories in the 1920s, and often hankering after political realignments or coalitions, Churchill was never a dyed-in-the-wool 'safe party man' with deep fixed loyalties. This was something which made other politicians, who were much more tribal, suspicious of someone who at different points in his career often seemed, for all his great gifts, a maverick, opportunistic, careerist, unreliable and lacking in judgement.

Churchill had been in the political wilderness for fully a decade before the outbreak of war in 1939 – isolated, at odds with his party leadership over issues like Indian self-government, the abdication crisis and appeasement, and being seen at the time as something of a political has-been or a failure (Rhodes James 1970). But the war allowed him another political comeback and he re-entered the Cabinet. He was not the leader of the majority party in the House of Commons when he first became prime minister in May 1940, after the resignation of Neville Chamberlain following a dramatic backbench rebellion in parliament. Churchill was not Chamberlain's first choice as his successor, and nor did ruling 'Establishment' circles, the King or the bulk of Conservative MPs want him. They would have preferred the Foreign Secretary, Lord Halifax, but at the crucial moment Halifax lacked the stomach to seize the ultimate prize and ruled himself out.

Chamberlain actually remained Conservative Party leader and sat in the small War Cabinet until he resigned due to ill health in October 1940 (he died a month later). Only then did Churchill become Conservative Party leader - but many Tories could not forget his past and continued to doubt his commitment to the interests of their party. He headed an all-party coalition 1940-45 – a genuinely national government - with Labour politicians in senior ministerial posts, including Clement Attlee the Labour leader as deputy prime minister, some Liberals in office, and a range of non-party technocrats, businessmen and administrators given important ministerial assignments too.

As Conservative leader, Churchill was never a good party manager or a party tactician, taking little interest in party organisation, which he left to others, and being pretty remote from the backbenchers, among whom there were undercurrents of discontent about his approach (Ball 2001). 'He has always been much too interested in himself to run a party', complained one Tory MP (Theakston 2012: 14). His leadership style was more the 'celebrity virtuoso soloist' than the 'leader of the orchestra', is how historian Keith Robbins (1992: 156) put it. He was for long periods after the war very much a part-time or absentee Leader of the Opposition (writing his war memoirs and giving speeches around the world), leaving much of the donkeywork of leading the opposition in parliament, overhauling the run-down party organisation, and devising new policies to others. It could even be argued that Conservative recovery after the 1945 general election defeat happened under Churchill rather than because of him (Theakston 2012).

Interested in promoting anti-socialist unity, at one point Churchill even suggested that the Conservative Party should change its name to the Union Party and pressed for an alliance with the then-small Liberal Party – neither idea going down well with his own party. Back in power in 1951, he offered the Liberal leader a ministerial post, but his party would not agree. As former Liberal himself, Churchill was proud of his association with pre-1914 welfare reforms (Addison 1993), while his status as the great war-leader, his strong anti-communism, and his love of tradition pleased the Tory right. But on economic and social policy it was the centre and left of the party under his leadership that he allowed to make the running, and his 1951-55 government did not undo or set the clock back on the Attlee settlement (Addison 1993).

Ideology and Aims

As wartime prime minister Churchill had a clear goal and objective and only one thought in mind – the total defeat of Nazi Germany and its allies. With a single-minded focus, he was utterly devoted to winning the war and very largely concentrated on military matters, strategy and international diplomacy to the exclusion of 'home front' issues, which he left to other ministers, also paying little attention to planning for the post-war scene. In that sense, in wartime, he had a driving sense of mission, clear aims and a strong sense of purpose. As prime minister again after 1951 he had another big, central aim on the international front – seeking a summit meeting to reduce the tensions of the cold war.

But in domestic politics Churchill was always more of a reactive and pragmatic party leader and prime minister, and not vision-driven or ideological. As Paul Addison (1993: 397) once put it, Churchill was more interested in politics than in policy. 'I do not believe in looking about for some panacea or cure-all . . . which we should try to sell in a hurry like a patent medicine to all and sundry', he once declared at a Tory party conference (Theakston 2012: 10). 'It would not be wise', he warned, 'to bind ourselves to a rigid programme' (Addison 1993: 395). He always wanted to keep options open and was generally rather dubious about the bright ideas and new schemes dreamed up by the party backroom staffs and policy thinkers. He did little personally to shape in a positive way the direction the Tory party took after its 1945 defeat when, in opposition, it slowly came to terms with the mixed-economy, welfare-state big-government reforms of the Attlee government, but in the end he was willing to make the changes of party policy and image necessary to win.

Political Style and Skills

Churchill's personal style and methods as prime minister were in some ways unusual and eccentric, but in institutional and constitutional terms he was pretty traditionalist as regards the premiership and the Cabinet system in Britain. 'The office of prime minister is not a dictatorship', he once said, 'certainly not in peacetime.' 'Most people feel the prime minister is always responsible; he should insist on getting his own way', he explained to Lord Moran, his personal doctor. But he continued, 'that is not my idea. I don't think he should be an autocrat. I never was, even in the war. Of course I had great powers, my relations with Roosevelt and things like that ensured this. But the Cabinet ought to have their say' (Theakston 2004: 207).

'All I wanted was compliance with my wishes after reasonable discussion' Churchill famously wrote in his war memoirs (Theakston 2004: 195). But while he was certainly a powerful, resolute and dominating prime minister, he always sought to maintain the principle and the reality of collective responsibility, carrying his Cabinet colleagues with him. 'I am a great believer', he said, 'in bringing things before the Cabinet', to 'get it argued by the Cabinet'. Although there were few big issues on which he was overruled by his colleagues during the war that was not because he was a dictator - Roosevelt and Stalin, he once said, 'could order; I had to convince and persuade' (Theakston 2004: 194). Later, in his second, much more low-key premiership in the 1950s, he operated very much as the chairman of the Cabinet where all the big issues were argued out and settled.

The notion of the prime minister and Number 10 developing a 'media strategy' like a modern leader would have been incomprehensible to Churchill, though he did have close personal relations with key 'press barons'. He had not had a prime-ministerial press secretary or media/public-relations adviser during the war and in 1951 took some persuading before he finally consented to the appointment of a press aide who – symbolically – did not have an office in Number 10 itself. But he operated in a very different media environment from that of today's political leaders. He never gave a television interview at all while PM and was not an enthusiast for television - indeed was highly suspicious of it, but it was not really a significant political presence while he was at the top. He performed instead in parliament, on the hustings at great public meetings, and on radio (with broadcasts playing a big role in election campaigns at that time and reaching huge audiences). He always took the House of Commons immensely seriously, even during the war, never forgetting that it was a parliamentary revolt that had made him prime minister. Immensely respectful of the traditions of parliament and the constitution, he punctiliously kept MPs informed about the major events and developments of the war, keeping little back – even when the news was bad.

He would, of course, have to be ranked as one of the great political communicators for the powerful and majestic oratory of his famous wartime speeches. He mobilised the English language, it was once said, and sent it into battle. Some of his phrases are now part of the national vocabulary and the collective historical memory. He transmitted his resolution to the nation and his showmanship, rhetoric and charisma projected and inspired confidence and determination. His wartime speeches were, says Paul Addison (2005: 169), those of 'a great parliamentary democrat, leading, informing and instructing a nation.' He never downplayed dangers and setbacks, believing that leaders had to tell the truth wherever possible. He had a feel for words and great artistry in their use, but also worked extremely hard at his speech-making. However, he was not a good impromptu speaker and was somewhat inflexible and ponderous in his debating style. His set-piece parliamentary speeches could sometimes be too lengthy and stylised to be effective. His oratory could seem old-fashioned in style, language and content. And while he always liked a good House of

Commons ding-dong argument, some Tories privately felt that he was liable to go over the top. After 1945, the more pedestrian Attlee – dry, astringent, precise, unemotional, matter-of-fact – could often cut him down to size and score tactical debating victories. Later, as prime minister the second time around, 1951-55, he could sometimes still rise to the occasion but as a platform and parliamentary performer was by then uneven and past his best (Theakston 2015).

Churchill is often portrayed as operating in a hugely personal, informal and idiosyncratic manner that did not really amount to a 'system' of management and would be given poor marks by any management studies handbook, and there is much in that view. But in fact some of his organisational arrangements were highly effective. No British prime minister has been so involved in supervising military strategy and defence decision-making as was Churchill. He had witnessed Lloyd George's failure to control the generals in the First World War, and as prime minister himself he was determined to gather the reins of control into his own hands and establish civilian control over the military (Cohen 2002). He appointed himself Minister of Defence, set up a Defence Committee of the Cabinet and a personal military secretariat, and dealt directly with the chiefs of staff through staff conferences. He had plenty of tough arguments with them, and a stormy relationship with the Chief of the Imperial General Staff and his foremost military adviser, General Sir Alan Brooke, who would stand up to him, argue back, and managed to deflect him from some of his crazier schemes. But he never overruled the chiefs of staff on a purely military matter.

Whereas a peacetime British Cabinet usually has 20-25 ministers or more, Churchill's wartime War Cabinet varied in size between only five and eight minsters, with an underpinning structure of committees drawing in other ministers and officials dealing with particular areas of policy or tricky issues. Although he had his suspicions of the civil service as an institution – and in 1940 immediately cleared out from Downing Street Horace Wilson, Chamberlain's right-hand-man in Whitehall – Churchill worked well with senior permanent officials such as Cabinet

Secretaries Edward Bridges (in the war) and Norman Brook (after 1951), and with his small civil service private office staff in Number 10 (Wheeler-Bennett 1968; Colville 1981). He also set up in his wartime premiership the Prime Minister's Statistical Section, headed by his personal friend and adviser 'the Prof' (the Oxford scientist, F. A. Lindemann, later Lord Cherwell), who was backed up by a small staff, as a sort of personal think-tank, providing analysis and advice to the prime minister, challenging Whitehall inertia and chasing up on decisions. Churchill was always seeking and using a variety of advice and views, was always determined to make up his own mind, but seldom refused to listen, and was always prepared to weigh a good argument from whatever source it came.

His experiment with another organisational reform – the ministerial 'overlords', or supervising ministers, he appointed when he returned to power in 1951 - was less successful and abandoned after only a year or two. But Churchill had identified a genuine problem – that of coordinating and giving coherence and direction to the policies of different parts of government, and tackling the centrifugal forces of 'departmentalism' - that has bedevilled British governments of all parties, even if his solution (similar to what some other PMs have also tried from time to time) did not work out (Theakston 2004: 202-207).

Churchill had of course tremendous political experience, gathered over a long career as a professional politician. He had spent 38 years as an MP before becoming prime minister (only one other British PM has had a longer parliamentary apprenticeship before moving into Number 10). He fought over his whole career 21 elections, giving him deep practical experience of what he called democracy's 'rough and slatternly foundations' (Theakston 2004: 113). He served for 20 years in various ministerial posts before becoming PM. And he had much experience of the ups and downs and twists and turns of fortune of political life. He handled the problems of balancing the different parties, and some wayward and conflicting personalities, in his wartime coalition government with care and skill. But Churchill, over his career, was arguably a better minister or better in government than he was as a political operator. Perhaps Churchill was sometimes too straightforward, too transparent and readable, to be a good Machiavelli. He could be a poor judge of people and situations. He could misread the public mood – as in the abdication crisis in 1936 and again in 1945, when his aggressive election campaigning against the Labour Party struck the wrong note and rebounded against him. The cartoonist David Low once said that Churchill was 'not naturally a good politician, but [was] astute from experience' – a perceptive remark (Benson 2015).

Churchill's limitations during his second premiership in the 1950s were obvious, at least to 'insiders' at the time (Hennessy 2001). By then in his late-70s, reluctant to deal with his paper-work, slow in transacting ordinary routine business, rambling in Cabinet meetings, and often ignorant or hazy about the details of policy (particularly economic policy), he struck one minister as 'turn[ing] avidly to minor problems . . . because he cannot grasp - or at any rate sees no way out of - the big ones' (Catterall 2003: 162). After his serious stroke in 1953 that almost killed him (and was covered up at the time in a way inconceivable in a later era), he was increasingly ineffective, unfit for office and 'carried' by his closest aides and advisers. He should probably have resigned two or three years before he actually did so in 1955.

But at his best, during the war years, he had ranged energetically between geo-politics and grand strategy at one end of the spectrum and administrative details at the other. His staggering capacity for hard work and his capacity to absorb, analyse and act on mountains of material was an immense asset. With his constant probing and prodding, he kept others (ministers, generals, officials) up to the mark (Gilbert 2004). 'His mind worked through a process of rapid intuition nourished by a fertile imagination', commented Paul Addison (2005: 247). His was not a calm, calculating approach: 'his decisions are never founded on exact knowledge, nor even on careful or prolonged consideration of the pros and cons', wrote a political colleague. 'He seeks instinctively for the large and preferably novel idea'. Impulsive, intuitive and amazingly fertile in ideas, he needed ministers, officials and advisers around him to argue him out of the bad or impractical ones and to take the good ones forward (Addison 2005: 122-23). 'Winston produces 100 ideas a day, of which only six are any good', said President Roosevelt. Similarly, Lloyd George once told Attlee: 'there's Winston, he has half a dozen solutions to it and one of them is right, but the trouble is he does not know which it is' (Theakston 2004: 195). But another top Conservative, Harold Macmillan, working with him after the war and in the 1950s, felt that on economic questions in particular he was 'uncreative and unimaginative, in marked contrast to his contributions on wider issues'. He was open to the proposals of his colleagues but 'was not [himself] capable or desirous of initiating new concepts of financial, monetary or economic policy' (Theakston 2012: 18). In truth he had always had little knowledge of or feel for economic policy and financial management, and left them to his Chancellor of the Exchequer and other ministers.

In personal terms, Churchill was mercurial and experienced great mood swings: according to one aide, 'either on the crest of the wave or in the trough, either highly laudatory or bitterly condemnatory; either in an angelic temper or a hell of a rage' (Ghaemi 2011: 60). 'His moods alternated', wrote a minister, 'and there was no attempt at concealment; at times he was benign, at others bleak and morose; he could be gentle or ferocious, wise or irresponsible, cautious or incorrigible, sombre or frivolous, wonderfully generous or woundingly unfair' (Theakston 2012: 18). This helped to make him a difficult boss and colleague to work with. His wife warned him during the war of his 'rough, sarcastic and overbearing manner' towards colleagues and officials (Roberts 2018: 567). He was a sentimentalist and openly exhibited his feelings: 'I blub an awful lot', he once admitted (Roberts 2018: 971). Frenetic activity was a way of holding off his so-called 'black dog'; and this factor may have made him reluctant to give up office in the 1950s, even when he was no longer up to the job and his ministers were increasingly frustrated and desperate for him to retire. But views of Churchill as a sort of alcohol-soaked manic-depressive are a caricature (Moran 1968; Attenborough 2014). Churchill could be selfish, egocentric, moody, and unpredictable to deal with – he was not calm and stable - but despite his flaws and limitations in terms of emotional intelligence there was not the sort of dark side to his leadership as seen with those political and historical figures who seem to have been consumed by grudges, hatreds and inner demons. He was a man of exceptional personal courage and did not shrink from making difficult political decisions (shown, for instance, in his order to attack and destroy the French fleet, not then an enemy, in July 1940 in order to prevent it from falling into German hands). But while he could be ruthless, there was also a tremendous humanity (he was a warmer and more genuine human being than, say, FDR or Stalin), magnanimity and unswerving moral decency.

Context

Churchill made a huge personal difference in 1940, at a backs-to-the-wall moment in history, by rallying the nation to continue the war even though it was not easy then to see how defeat could be avoided, let alone victory some day secured. If Lord Halifax – or perhaps someone else – had become prime minister, rather than Churchill, it is possible that some sort of peace settlement with Germany would have been negotiated, and the War Cabinet secretly discussed this option. But Churchill strongly rejected the idea, understanding that Hitler's promises and any sort of agreement with him would be worthless, and believing that Britain and the values it stood for would be finished if it tamely threw in the towel.

For a year after June 1940 Britain faced a Nazi-dominated Europe alone though with the threat of immediate invasion fading as the Battle of Britain was won. But Churchill knew that the war could not be won without allies. He worked hard at cultivating US President Roosevelt and securing American assistance in the shape of military equipment and supplies that came under the Lend-Lease agreement (though Britain ended up paying heavily for this lifeline). But it was not until the Japanese attack on Pearl Harbor in December 1941 that the US finally came into the war. Earlier, in June 1941 when Germany had invaded Russia, Churchill - hitherto a consistent opponent of

25

communism - pledged assistance and aid in the common fight against Nazism. 'If Hitler invaded Hell,' he said, 'I would at least make a favourable reference to the Devil' in the House of Commons (Addison 2005: 187).

Throughout the war years Churchill put a tremendous effort into the top-level diplomacy of the 'Grand Alliance'. He was the first globe-trotting prime minister, undertaking numerous – often pretty uncomfortable and hazardous – journeys by air and sea to see things on the spot, make assessments and take decisions, and to negotiate, parley and plan with the other allied leaders and heads of state. He invented the term 'summits' to describe these meetings. He travelled altogether some 150,000 miles (to North America, North Africa and the Middle East, Russia, and elsewhere) at some cost to his health: he was 65 years old when he became prime minister in 1940, worked punishing hours, and had a heart attack and a near-fatal bout of pneumonia during the war. Relations between the 'Big Three' – Roosevelt, Stalin and Churchill – were in reality often tense and uneasy, they frequently clashed over strategy and the conduct of the war, and ultimately they had divergent national interests and long-term aims. As the war went on Churchill grew increasingly aware that America – whose leadership was hostile to what it saw as British 'colonialism' - was the dominant partner in the 'special relationship'. And he had few illusions about Stalin, becoming gravely concerned about the dominant position the 'Russian Bear' would be left in after the war in Eastern and Central Europe and the Balkans. But the war exposed and exacerbated the great inequalities in national and international power - Britain, Churchill came to realise with dismay, was increasingly almost in the position of a spectator as the big decisions were made elsewhere.

For a long time the war brought little but one grim disaster after another and the tide started to turn only at the end of 1942 and in 1943 – after the battle of Stalingrad on the Russian front, and with El Alamein and Anglo-American landings in French North Africa. Churchill was a great champion of a Mediterranean strategy – attacking the enemy's 'soft underbelly', as he told Stalin – leading to the invasion of Sicily after the

German/Italian forces had been expelled from North Africa, and then to the invasion of Italy itself in 1943. The Americans saw this as a sideshow, however, and gave priority to the cross-channel invasion of France – something Stalin, too, was always pressing insistently for. Churchill had great doubts and fears about whether this could succeed, and fought to delay it for as long as he could, operation 'Overlord' finally taking place in June 1944. American military preponderance meant that Churchill's influence over allied strategy continued to decline after 'D-Day' and in the last, hard-fought, year of the war. He got nowhere, for instance, when he urged Roosevelt and General Eisenhower to speed up the advance of British and US forces in order to capture Berlin before the Russians could get to it.

Churchill personally had amazingly high polling ratings during the war, with 80 per cent satisfaction ratings for his performance as prime minister. But while Churchill the war leader may have been popular, the British people did not think he would be the right man to deal with the problems of peacetime. One survey in 1944 found 62 per cent of the public were against him becoming the post-war premier. He seemed out of sympathy with or disengaged from plans for welfare reform and reconstruction that were being talked about and drawn up. Churchill himself admitted, 'I have no message' (Moran 1968: 205). The public mood had undoubtedly swung to the left. Wartime opinion polls showed big leads for the Labour Party over the Conservatives. Churchill did not help matters with a poor campaign in 1945, but in a wider sense the big Labour landslide was a verdict on the Conservatives' record in the 1930s – the wasted years of the slump and of appeasement.

Back in Number 10 in 1951 with a small majority, Churchill had no great policy ideas of his own on the domestic policy front during his peacetime premiership, but thought the country needed a period of quiet, steady administration rather than further upheaval and reform. Rationing was ended, house-building was prioritised, the government showed it was anxious to get on with – rather than to take on – the trade unions, there was no attempt to undo the big nationalisations of the Attlee government (with the exception of the steel industry and road haulage), and care was taken to show the welfare state was safe in Tory hands. Churchill presided benignly over a middle-of-the-road government. Economic circumstances improved from 1952, with growing living standards, low unemployment and inflation, and growing international trade, though some later critics, with the benefit of hindsight, argued that a tougher free-market and modernising stance should have been adopted and that Britain started to lose ground in this period compared to its economic rivals. But at the time, the government seemed competent, moderate and relatively successful (Seldon 1981).

Churchill's primary personal interests and his great ambitions for his second premiership lay in foreign affairs. He wanted to revive and strengthen the wartime 'special relationship' with the USA, and launched a one-man campaign for a high-level summit meeting with the Americans and the Russians to try to defuse Cold War tensions. He often clashed with the Foreign Office and his Foreign Secretary and designated successor, Anthony Eden. Britain was still a great power, Churchill believed, and the government decided in 1954 to build the hydrogen bomb. But Churchill saw his last great role as being that of international peacemaker and he felt deeply the need to do all he could to avert the danger of a nuclear holocaust. The Americans were personally welcoming, and Churchill visited Truman and then Eisenhower in the White House. But the cold-eyed view in Washington DC was that Churchill was trying to re-live the glory days of the Second World War 'Big Three' and that his outlook and plans took no account of the new realities of power. Half American as he was, Churchill over-sentimentalised the Anglo-American relationship and over-estimated the influence he and Britain could have on US policymakers. The Russians rebuffed him, too, and in the end nothing came of his plans.

Conclusion

Churchill was a protean and iconic figure who holds an almost mythological place in modern British history. He was a unique, multi-talented, brilliant - but also flawed - individual. Different book titles hint at the range of verdicts possible on his career and status, including: *Churchill: A Study in Greatness* (Best 2001), or *Churchill: Walking With Destiny* (Roberts 2018), or T*he Greatest Briton* (Harvardi 2009) - but also *Churchill: The End of Glory* (Charmley 1993) and *Churchill: A Study in Failure 1900-1939* (Rhodes James 1970). There is a definite Churchill cult in some quarters and plenty of hagiographical studies, but on the other side are those raising big questions about the competence of his leadership, the true level of his popularity, his achievements and legacy.

Churchill topped a BBC 2002 poll to find the '100 Greatest Britons', attracting over 400,000 out of the more than one million votes cast. His heroic status as a wartime leader, together with the continued centrality of the Second World War in Britain's historical and cultural self-understanding, explains his hold on the public mind. He was a dominant figure and the indispensable war leader. But of course rather than 'winning' the Second World War, it is more accurate to say that Churchill's real contribution was to keep Britain in the war, inspire the nation and avoid defeat in the dark days of 1940; winning the war and defeating Germany and Japan took the military might and power of Russia and the USA. While Britain was on the winning side at the end, it was virtually bankrupted in the process. And if the great and aged war-leader was far from 'ga-ga', as it is sometimes suggested, during his peacetime administration in the early 1950s, he was certainly past his best, struggling with failing powers, and clung on to office too long – but that did not derail or undermine what was in the end the moderately successful first-term of what became 13 continuous years of Conservative government between 1951 and 1964.

Churchill always had a powerful sense of history, saw and imagined himself in history, and wrote lots of best-selling old-fashioned history, narratives of kings and battles and high command. In some ways Churchill was acting out his 'Great Man' theory of history throughout his political career. Historically, he casts a bigger shadow than any other British prime minister.

References

Addison, P. (1993). *Churchill on the Home Front 1900-1955.* London: Pimlico.

Addison, P. (2005). *Churchill: the unexpected hero.* Oxford: Oxford University Press.

Attenborough, W. (2014). *Churchill and the 'Black Dog' of Depression.* London: Palgrave Macmillan.

Ball, S. (2001). 'Churchill and the Conservative party', *Transactions of the Royal Historical Society*, Sixth Series, XI: 307-330.

Benson, T. (2015). 'Sir David Low on Sir Winston Churchill', The Political Cartoon Society, [https://www.original-political-cartoon.com/cartoon-history/low- churchill/]

Best, G. (2001). *Churchill: A Study in Greatness.* London: Penguin.

Catterall, P. (ed) (2003). *The Macmillan Diaries: The Cabinet Years 1950-57.* London: Macmillan.

Charmley. J. (1993). *Churchill: The End of Glory.* London: Hodder and Stoughton.

Cohen, E. (2002). *Supreme Command: soldiers, statesmen and l eadership in wartime.* New York: The Free Press.

Colville, J. (1981). *The Churchillians.* London: Weidenfeld & Nicolson.

Ghaemi, N. (2011). *A First-Rate Madness.* London; Penguin.

Gilbert, M. (2004). *Winston Churchill's War Leadership.* New York: Vintage Books.

Harvardi, J. (2009). *The Greatest Briton: essays on Winston Churchill's life and political philosophy.* London: Shepheard-Walwyn.

Hennessy, P. (2001). 'Churchill and the Premiership', *Transactions of the Royal Historical Society*, Sixth Series, XI: 295-306.

Moran, C. (1968). *Winston Churchill: The Struggle for Survival 1940-1965.* London: Sphere Books.

Rhodes James, R. (1970). *Churchill: A Study in Failure 1900-1939.* London: Weidenfeld & Nicolson.

Robbins, K. (1992). *Churchill.* London: Longman.

Roberts, A. (2018). *Churchill: Walking with Destiny.* New York: Viking.

Seldon, A. (1981). *Churchill's Indian Summer: the Conservative Government 1951-55.* London: Hodder and Stoughton.

Theakston, K. (2004). *Winston Churchill and the British Constitution.* London: Politico's.

Theakston, K. (2012). 'Winston Churchill, 1945-51', in T. Heppell (ed), *Leaders of the Opposition: from Churchill to Cameron.* London: Palgrave Macmillan.

Theakston, K. (2015). 'The oratory of Winston Churchill', in R. Hayton and A. Crines (eds), *Conservative Orators from Baldwin to Cameron.* Manchester: Manchester University Press.

Wheeler-Bennett, J. (ed) (1968). *Action This Day: Working with Churchill.* London: Macmillan.

Chapter 3
Clement Attlee (1945-51)

Clement Attlee was leader of the Labour Party for fully 20 years, from 1935 to 1955 - a tenure not matched by any other leader of a major political party in twentieth century Britain - and he was wartime deputy prime minister for five years, and prime minister for six years. His 1945-51 government has gone down as one of the great reforming administrations of British history (Morgan 1984; Hennessy 1992). Attlee himself, though, was long misunderstood and under-estimated: sharing the political stage with Churchill and with a bevy of Labour Party 'big beasts', he seemed overshadowed by more flamboyant, glamorous and substantial figures. On some accounts he seemed almost the reverse of a leader - a 'modest little man with much to be modest about' (Howell 2006: 134). But he led his party to a landslide election victory and his government pushed through a huge and lasting programme of reform. Attlee is these days rightly seen as one of Britain's greatest prime ministers. His leadership was more subtle, skilful and effective than that of many of his successors, and compared to some of them he stands out as one of the more highly-motivated and ethical prime ministers.

Party Leadership
It would be wrong to depict Attlee as almost falling into the leadership by accident, but certainly luck, timing and circumstances were important factors in him securing and then holding on to the leadership for so long. Attlee's route to the leadership of his party was not through being a heavyweight senior Cabinet minister, a long-term heir apparent or a charismatic insurgent challenger. Elected an MP in 1922 (the first Oxford graduate on the Labour benches), he had two short stints (in 1924 and 1930-31) as a minister in Ramsay MacDonald's minority Labour governments. But there were no real signs of leadership potential, and he seemed the sort of steady, reliable, competent and fairly anonymous figure that any government needs to fill its junior and middle ranks.

What created his chance was the Labour wipe-out in the 1931 general election, when MacDonald split from the party to form the National government with the Tories and some Liberals, and Labour was reduced to just 52 MPs. Attlee narrowly hung on to his seat in London's East End by 551 votes and - one of only three ex-ministers to survive the cull - was made deputy leader of the party. Under the elderly and ineffective George Lansbury, he became the workhorse of the Labour opposition frontbench, stepping in as acting/caretaker leader when Lansbury resigned just before the 1935 general election. More senior, experienced and well-known party figures then came back into parliament, and a formal leadership vote was held in which Attlee saw off the challenges of Arthur Greenwood and Herbert Morrison. His rivals and detractors (not for the last time) under-estimated him and his ambition, toughness and determination. Attlee did not have a political or factional base of his own in the party but his rivals' flaws and his own ability to avoid making enemies, to appeal to and be trusted by different groups across left and right and in the trade unions, and to locate and loyally articulate the majority view or work out a consensus in the party all made him a less-surprising choice than it is sometimes portrayed. Moreover, Attlee's appeal was also that he seemed worthy, honest, self-effacing and low-key - offering the party the very opposite to the vanity, egotism and highly-personalised leadership of the despised MacDonald. Attlee would be the efficient servant, not the master, of the party.

All the same, Attlee's leadership seemed hesitant and somewhat provisional until the outbreak of the Second World War. The policy running in the Labour opposition in the late 1930s was made by other powerful figures in the party. If peace had held, Labour would probably have lost the general election due by 1940 and Attlee would likely have been ousted. But Labour's experience in the all-party Churchill coalition 1940-45 was crucial in the development of his leadership reputation, stature and skills. In executive office, Attlee grew as a leader (Crowcroft 2011). He admired Churchill (but not uncritically) and they mostly worked well together. As the country's first-ever deputy prime minister he sat alongside Churchill in the small

War Cabinet and on the Defence Committee, and also effectively took charge of 'home front' matters and domestic issues, operating through what was called the Lord President's Committee. Although other ministers and Labour politicians were more publicly visible, Attlee's abilities as an organiser, coordinator and facilitator of government business, and as an effective committee chairman (including of the Cabinet when Churchill was away) working to make things happen, were increasingly recognised and appreciated by insiders.

Like most other politicians and contemporary commentators, Attlee did not expect Labour to win the 1945 general election. It could not be said that he personally 'won' the election for Labour, but he campaigned in a steady and quietly reassuring manner. In a landslide result, Labour ended up with 393 seats, giving them a parliamentary majority of 146, the party's vote going up by almost 10 per cent (on the 1935 result) to 48 per cent, a lead of 8.4 per cent over the shattered Tories (reduced to 210 seats). Just as the electorate had seemingly made Attlee prime minister, his long-time rival Herbert Morrison tried to organise a parliamentary caucus vote to challenge him and seize the leadership himself, but was brushed aside when Attlee, with the support and encouragement of the powerful Ernest Bevin, went directly to the Palace to see the King and take up office. Bevin protected Attlee again two years later when, in 1947, Morrison, Stafford Cripps and Hugh Dalton plotted to push him out. Their rivalries cancelled each other out, however: Morrison wanted the top job for himself not Bevin; Bevin hated Morrison; Cripps was coolly bought off by Attlee with a Cabinet promotion. The 'little man' survived as the figure who divided the party least, because there was never a single obvious successor that opponents could agree upon, but also because of his own qualities and character and approach as a leader.

Compared to other periods of Labour government, for most of the Attlee government the party was broadly united and relations with the unions were stable and supportive (Crowcroft and Theakston 2013). This was mostly for broad political and structural reasons rather than down to Attlee's personal input (arguably, Morrison - in parliament - and Bevin - with the unions

- played more crucial roles here). On the whole, the Parliamentary Labour Party presented few problems in terms of party management. A Liaison Committee worked well as a bridge between ministers and MPs, standing orders were suspended, and seventeen specialist policy groups were set up to keep backbenchers busy (though this experiment was not a success in the case of the foreign affairs group, which clashed with Bevin). There was some dissent and periodic rebellions by varying groups of MPs - mostly on foreign policy and defence issues – but no sustained and organised internal opposition endangering the government's majority or significant parliamentary revolt, even from the 'Keep Left' group. Later, the wafer-thin majority after 1950 actually assisted party management as backbench critics felt constrained to toe the party line in the face of increased Conservative pressure, though tensions were building up on the left after Bevan's resignation during the government's final months in 1951. In contrast to the damage they caused to the later Wilson and Callaghan governments, relations between the government, the party and the unions were also generally good and close in this period, based on a tight alliance between the key union bosses (who were at this time on the right of the party) and the parliamentary leadership, and on a broad sense of union satisfaction with the achievements and record of the government. The union block vote was put firmly behind the leadership at the party conference, a body that gave Attlee's government little real trouble (again in contrast to the later situation with Wilson and Callaghan).

Ideology and Aims

For all that historians and commentators often talk of the 'Attlee consensus' or the 'Attlee settlement' as a sort of shorthand term for the mixed-economy welfare state politics that dominated post-war Britain (Burridge 1985: 2), Attlee himself actually contributed little or nothing to shaping party ideology, ideas and policy thinking. In his conception, a leader and prime minister was not meant to be an active policy contributor, strongly pushing his own views, but instead someone who spoke for the agreed or majority party position or, if necessary, arbitrated between the competing policies and proposals of departmental ministers.

'Labour's agenda was Attlee's agenda', as Brookshire (1995: 76) put it. He was always the loyal party man, aiming to ensure the party's programme was implemented. Unlike a Thatcher or a Blair, Attlee would never attempt to drag or push his party in a different ideological direction. As a leader, says Burridge (1985: 316), 'he derived his strength from the representativeness of his opinions, not from their originality.' He basically believed in 'mainstream Labour Party socialism' (Brookshire 1995: 6), including Clause IV and public ownership (in a mixed economy) as part of Labour's creed - but, revealingly, when his successor, Hugh Gaitskell, battled to remove that commitment from the party's constitution, Attlee thought he was mistaken and that Labour's 'passion for over-definition' should always be resisted (Harris 1982: 543). He was an immensely practical man - interested in practical solutions to practical problems, and in party unity, not in arguments over political philosophy or abstractions.

If Attlee was 'hard to pin down to any precise ideological position' (Pearce 1997: 72) that was because he was more a man of ideals than ideas. As John Bew's (2016) biography has shown, Attlee's socialism was rooted more in a strong ethical and emotional commitment to building a new world and new notions of citizenship, fellowship and society, and in a moral critique of capitalism, inequality and poverty - all of which he had developed while living and working as a social worker and political activist amid the squalor of the East End of London before and after the First World War - rather than in economic doctrines or theories (about which he knew little). Instinctively, he was always himself more left-of-centre in Labour Party terms than perhaps any other Labour prime minister we have had. Behind the exterior personal reserve and blandness, he held strong opinions and had a firm sense of right and wrong. He was in some ways a 'conviction politician' with a clear sense of purpose in the sense of being a radical social reformer, passionately determined to achieve definite social improvements. On another level, he was also a late-Victorian of the upper-middle classes who had fought bravely as an officer in the First World War and took notions of duty, service and responsibility seriously, and was not embarrassed to be a strong patriot with small-'c' conservative views on traditional institutions (such as the monarchy, the civil service, the army, the public schools) and very conventional personal social values. It probably helped Labour at this time, that it had a leader who could come across as a reassuring and respectable suburban figure when the country faced huge challenges and the government was making great changes (Pearce 1997: 130).

Attlee was not afraid of the 's' word and did not shy away from describing himself and his party as socialist. But it is striking that Labour's 1945 manifesto, *Let Us Face the Future*, used the term socialist or socialism only three times - compared to four times that the term progressive or progressives was used - appealing, in Attlee-ite fashion, to all who looked for 'constructive change', and reminding voters that Labour was 'practical-minded' and that change was needed to tackle real social and economic problems but also so that Britain could 'keep her place as a Great Power.' Emphasising full employment, public ownership, planning, housing, education, health and social security, Labour fought the election on the promise of a better life and 'winning the peace'. In some ways, it was the culmination of half a century of Labour campaigning but, building on previous governments' social reforms, on the wartime expansion of the state's role and the postwar 'reconstruction' planning undertaken during the Churchill coalition, and on the influential ideas and proposals of Liberals like Beveridge and Keynes, it was less a complete break with the past or a socialist revolution than an acceleration of longer-term trends towards state intervention, a managed economy, collectivism and expanded welfare.

The experience of the first two or three years of the 1945 Labour government shows that a prime minister does not necessarily have to give a strong personal policy lead or himself provide ideas and a vision for a government to be radical and successful, provided that the party and the Cabinet have a sense of purpose and remain united. But the absence of the 'vision thing' and Attlee's failure and/or inability to give a lead mattered more after the initial programme had been pushed through, successive economic and political crises hit the government, and it started to lose coherence and momentum in the later 1940s. At that point, Attlee seemed to have no message for the future and had nothing to offer to the developing debate about Labour's agenda framed in terms of further socialist 'advance' or 'consolidation', and his approach of trying to find a compromise and hold the party together eventually failed as the arguments became more factionalised and personalised (particularly over 1950-51 and then afterwards in opposition).

Political style and skills

'An approach to one-man government is in my view a mistake', Attlee once said. 'The job of a prime minister is to lead and coordinate a team, not to seek to be an omnicompetent minister.' In wartime, the prime minister's position and authority was enhanced, he conceded, but in normal conditions, the principles of collective Cabinet responsibility and the PM as first among equals still held, and any sort of 'presidential' labelling of the system was wrong and misleading. Government ministers were 'not mere creatures of the prime minister' (Attlee 1960). The 'essential quality' in a prime minister was that they should be 'a good chairman able to get others to work' and get the Cabinet to take decisions. The prime minister's voice would certainly carry great weight but, he insisted, 'you can't ride rough-shod over a Cabinet unless you're something very extraordinary.' Attlee's list of the qualities required in the occupant of Number 10 sounded something like an idealised self-description and included: the absence of egocentricity, toleration, a grasp of priorities, the ability to reach quick decisions, a sense of timing, a sense of proportion, a good historical background, the ability to keep 'a hand on the pulse' while letting ministers get on with their jobs, and the 'architectonic sense' (seeing the whole building not only the bricks) (Williams 1961: 83-84; Harris 1982: 591). It wasn't really 'intellectual power' that was needed, he maintained - being prime minister was about judgement not cleverness. And it is not surprising that the uncharismatic Attlee thought that a 'charming personality' might help but was not absolutely necessary in a prime minister.

Attlee once noted that the prime minister was expected to be 'the figurehead of the government vis-a-vis the nation' (Harris 1982: 590) and needed to be 'a good House of Commons man and not afraid of publicity' (Times 1957). But in practice he had a mixed record on that front. Attlee has often been portrayed as a poor communicator, with references to his innate shyness, to 'Clem the Clam', his monosyllabic responses to interviewers, and his distrust of showmanship. There was, it was said, 'nothing which his voice and delivery could not make uninspiring' (Burridge 1985: 2). He said he hated the idea of politicians being turned by the new emerging medium of television into 'entertainers' (Cockerell 1988: 27). As one biographer puts it, 'he squirmed in the limelight' (Bew 2016: xv). 'He underplayed every big occasion', commented a veteran political correspondent of the period (Margach 1978: 87). He had no time for image-mongering, public relations and presentation. 'I have none of the qualities which create publicity', he once said (Nicolson 1966: 163). He paid hardly any attention to the media, describing himself as 'allergic to the press' (Pearce 1997: 157-8).

Low-key, lacking glamour and presence, a dull speaker, laconic, and bad at self-dramatisation, Attlee would never be able to 'out-Churchill' Churchill in those terms, as it were. Hennessy (2000: 170) is right to describe his approach to the media as, even in his own era and context, almost pre-modern: he was certainly a less skilful and canny communicator than Stanley Baldwin had been back in the 1920s and 1930s, and there was none of the tough media management and manipulation that Neville Chamberlain had run from his Number 10. However, Attlee cannot be completely written off. He came across as calm and reasoned, and reasonable, in radio broadcasts at general election-time, finding the words and arguments to counter Churchill and the Tories. He could be very effective in the House of Commons, with his terse, sometimes stinging, replies to parliamentary questions and his calm command of the facts in debate, more than able to hold his own and even see off

Churchill's bluster and bombast. But all the same, a rather passive attitude to the media was self-defeating in the face of the sustained press attacks, bias and hostility the government faced (it also cannot have helped popularise the work of the government that Whitehall's publicity and information staff were cut by three-quarters) (Fielding 1991: 115). Attlee's unwillingness and/or inability to aggressively 'sell' his government's policies and achievements, and to 'educate' the public about Labour's programme and the situation and challenges the county faced, allowed Labour's critics and political opponents to make more of the running and to some extent contributed to its defeat in 1951.

In contest to his communication weaknesses and failures, Attlee's real strengths as prime minister were in administration and in running and managing government (Harris 1982: 401-418). Before becoming prime minister, in fact, Attlee had thought a great deal about the working of the Cabinet system and Whitehall, and had some radical ideas about the need for a smaller policy- and strategy-focussed Cabinet and the need for coordinating ministers overseeing broad functions of government (Brookshire 1981); he had also learned a lot during his five years as Churchill's wartime deputy prime minister. As it turned out, his first Cabinet had 20 ministers rather than the ten or so he had envisaged as the ideal, later cutting the number to 16 or 17. And in practice much of the coordination and policy-making in government was channelled through an elaborate interlocking system of Cabinet committees. Over the six years of the Labour government there was a total of 148 standing committees and 313 ad hoc (counting ministerial and official groups) - prompting some complaints, however, that the proliferation perhaps did as much for 'indecision and overload all round' as for effectiveness and decisiveness in government (Hennessy 2000: 164).

Attlee's approach has been described as the 'chairmanship' or 'facilitator' model of leadership (Thomas-Symonds 2010). He usually ran the Cabinet in an orderly and brisk way, moving things on, sticking to his brief, getting agreement round the table and decisions taken in a timely way.

But as one civil service observer noted, 'he rarely produced any constructive ideas of his own or seemed to give a powerful lead. His chairmanship was only a negative success. He was like a schoolmaster who kept order very well but did not really teach you very much' (Mallaby 1965: 58). Others describe him as playing the role not so much of team captain than of referee or umpire. He 'doodled when he ought to have led', one ministerial critic (Herbert Morrison) complained (Bew 2016: 394). But this probably downplays the extent to which he could exert influence through control of the agenda of government, orchestration of the committee system, and managing the discussion to make sure he could extract the views of those he wanted when he needed them (Burridge 1985: 187). And on occasion he could and did play a strong personal role, intervening and controlling matters himself, as seen in the decisive role he played in directing and driving through policy on independence for India, and in the decision (kept secret from most ministers and from parliament) to develop a British nuclear weapons programme.

It is easy to underestimate the political skills of someone like Attlee, who was able to get a talented team of top ministers with strong rivalries and discordant opinions to work together constructively. Probably only someone with his personality and style could have got the likes of Herbert Morrison (domestic affairs supremo as Lord President of the Council), Ernie Bevin (Foreign Secretary), Hugh Dalton (Attlee's first Chancellor of the Exchequer), Stafford Cripps (President of the Board of Trade, then Attlee's second Chancellor), and Nye Bevan (Minister of Health) to, as it were, stay inside the tent together and achieve so much (Radice 2008). Attlee largely left ministers to get on with their jobs and did not interfere. He has a reputation as a 'good butcher', unceremoniously despatching under-performing and dud ministers ('you're not up to the job'), but this can be exaggerated - some (such as Manny Shinwell, for example) were kept on or brought back even after big failures and demonstrable incompetence (Pearce 1997: 122). And some of his appointments and reshuffles did not work out well (such as Morrison's move to become Foreign Secretary in 1951; and the way in which Bevan was left feeling dangerously frustrated by

Hugh Gaitskell being promoted ahead of him to become Chancellor in 1950, and then being passed over for the Foreign Office). The only minister he was personally close to was Bevin - the two of them largely kept in step and ran foreign policy together on the basis of a strong and trusting partnership in this period of the emerging Cold War, with growing superpower tensions and the creation of NATO and the western alliance. Much of the basic architecture of postwar British foreign and defence policy was laid down by the two. Attlee also regularly privately discussed with Bevin government issues across the board. Moreover, Bevin was Attlee's most loyal colleague, strengthening his political position and watching his back when others plotted against him (Bullock 1983).

In terms of his personal approach to the job, Attlee was described by one senior Whitehall insider as 'orderly, regular, efficient and methodical to a degree that put him in a different class from any of the prime ministers who followed him' (Harris 1982: 404). His mind, it was said, 'however unadventurous, was usually open and unprejudiced; a case presented with close argument and detailed facts had a good chance of winning on its merits' (Beckett 2000: 251). He worked through paper rather than through listening to people, and notoriously taciturn, he was not good at thinking out loud or exchanging embryonic views. His patience, stability, self-control and self-effacement helped him to manage the personality clashes and political infighting in his party and Cabinet. He was once called a 'desiccated calculating machine' (Harris 1982: 522), appearing remote, self-contained, brusque, impersonal and unemotional. His shyness was certainly impenetrable, but beneath it Attlee had plenty of intellectual self-confidence and self-belief, and could be cunning, ruthless and tough. He was a loner and it was one of Attlee's great strengths, as Gaitskell once wrote in his diary, 'that he did not mind whether people liked him' (Williams 1983: 422).

All the same, there were some clear limitations and leadership failures. Attlee, says Kenneth O. Morgan (1987: 143), 'was at his best piloting the party quietly and efficiently along a predestined and well-charted course, as in 1945-7. . . But he could not take control when complex events were throwing the government off course, when the winds of change gave way to a hurricane.' Being 'tone deaf', as Harold Wilson put it, on economic and financial issues did not help (Wilson 1977: 297). Attlee seemed completely adrift and out of his depth, unable to give any sort of lead, during the damaging politico-economic crises of 1947 (the fuel crisis and then the convertibility crisis), 1949 (devaluation of the pound) and 1950-51 (the arguments over the burden of the excessive rearmaments programme following the outbreak of the Korean war). It was not surprising that ministerial unhappiness with his performance led to moves against him in 1947. Then, his handling of the confrontation between Gaitskell and Bevan over the 1951 budget and proposals for health service charges was pretty disastrous. Although hospitalised with health problems, he could and should have done more to try to find a compromise, patch things up, defuse tensions, and head off the ministerial resignations (of Bevan and two other ministers) that rocked the government and widened splits in the party at a time when a general election could not be far off.

Context
For its first two years or so after 1945 the Labour government was 'triumphant and seemed unshakeable', as one of its Conservative opponents put it (Crowcroft and Theakston 2013: 62). It had a parliamentary majority of 146, pushed strongly ahead with its programme, and the Opposition were shell-shocked and ineffective. Landmark reforms – to the welfare system, health, public ownership, and more – were implemented. But from 1947 onwards the government started to run into difficulties and its reputation for competence took a battering as it struggled with economic crises and other problems. The government never recovered its sense of direction. There were Conservative opinion poll leads for most of the period from the second half of 1947 through to January 1950 and Tory advances at Labour's expense in local government elections, but, remarkably, no Labour seats were lost in parliamentary by-

43

elections to the Conservatives (though there were often large swings against them). However the general context of 'austerity' and the media and party-political criticisms of bureaucracy, nationalisation, government mismanagement, red tape, queues, shortages and rationing sapped Labour's popularity. Added to this by the late-1940s, and very obviously in 1950-51, Labour seemed to have run out of steam, displayed few new policy ideas, its key leaders were ageing and physically exhausted, and factional splits were emerging. Even so, its electoral support remained strong to the end, and particularly in its working-class heartlands.

Attlee's economic inheritance in 1945 was horrendous. The cost of the Second World War had left the country on its knees, depriving Britain of around a quarter of its wealth and leaving it dependent on US support through the lend-lease programme. No sooner elected, and in the face of what Keynes called a 'financial Dunkirk', the government needed to negotiate a huge US loan to stave off financial and balance of payments disaster. The economic statistics, however, then tell a story of painful economic reconstruction and recovery under Labour. The Attlee government saw increased industrial production, growth in exports, and - in contrast to the aftermath of the First World War and the interwar experience - full employment (unemployment below 2 per cent). It was a creditable performance but ultimately a political price was paid - in part because of the way in which consumer spending was held down and living standards were squeezed in a climate of 'austerity' for the sake of exports and investment, and in part because of the destabilising economic crises that punctuated the life of the government.

Labour's appeal to the public in the 1950 and 1951 elections was lacking in ambition, freshness and clarity. In both election campaigns Attlee largely opted to fight on the record of his government, combining this with suggestions that the Conservatives could not be trusted with the welfare state and the economy. But the 1950 election saw Labour's majority in the Commons collapse to just six as Labour lost 78 seats while the Conservatives gained 88 seats. The party's overall share of the vote (46.1 per cent) remained three per cent higher than that of the Conservatives (43.5), but the proportion of non-manual workers voting Labour declined from 55 per cent to 47 per cent – a clear warning of the dissatisfaction with austerity and that Labour was losing the wide base of support that had swept it into office in 1945.

The second Attlee government (1950-51) certainly had few legislative achievements to its name and Attlee discovered no new sense of purpose for his administration. But in the short-term it was able to carry on, winning votes in parliament despite Conservative harassing tactics, remaining popular in the polls, and presiding in the first half of 1950 over an improving economic situation (with the balance of payments moving into surplus, the announcement that Britain would make no further calls on Marshall Aid, production and exports strong, and 'points' rationing and petrol rationing ending). 'It looks as though those bastards can stay in as long as they like', Churchill even complained at one stage (Morgan 1984: 412). It was 'an entirely unforeseen external development' (Jefferys 1993: 25) – the outbreak of the Korean War in June 1950 – that, we can see with hindsight, marked the beginning of the end for the Attlee government, the massive rearmament programme it triggered placing serious strains on both the Labour party and the national finances.

Though he had high personal approval ratings and was an undoubted electoral asset, it must be said that Attlee himself has to bear some responsibility for the government's problems and defeat. Indeed Martin Pugh, in his history of the Labour Party, calls Attlee an 'inadequate' party leader (as opposed to his achievements in government as a PM) whose misjudgements in relation to party interests meant he 'threw it away' (Pugh 2010: x). One factor here is the way the redrawing of constituency boundaries in 1948, taking seats from Labour's urban strongholds and rebalancing them to more suburban areas, helped the Conservatives. If the 1950 election had been fought on the old boundaries, it has been suggested that Labour could have ended up with a comfortable majority of about 60 - the party probably then able to hold on to office longer than it actually did. In the 1960s, a later Labour government strategically - or cynically - delayed a disadvantageous seat redistribution, but that was not Attlee's style.

Then, to adapt Oscar Wilde, to mistime one general election may be regarded as a misfortune; to mistime two looks like carelessness. Certainly, the February 1950 election has been described as 'astonishingly ill-timed' (Marquand 2008: 146) and Attlee, as prime minister, must carry the ultimate responsibility for that, though there had been a number of Cabinet discussions and ministerial exchanges about the next election from mid-1949 onwards with some pressing for an early election and others wanting to hold on. A crucial influence was Stafford Cripps, who refused (with threats of resignation) to produce a pre-election budget - the mixture of the chancellor's moralism, personal strain, poor political judgement and fears for sterling, leaving the prime minister with no choice but to go to the polls at a rather unpropitious time. Polls in May 1950, after petrol had been de-rationed, suggest that if the election had been held later Labour may have won with a majority of 40 or 50 seats in the House of Commons, a secure enough platform for the government to carry on longer than it did in fact do so.

Attlee can also be faulted for the poor timing of the October 1951 general election. The prime minister's innate conservatism and sense of propriety led him to conclude that the political uncertainty in the country had to be resolved before the king set off on a planned Commonwealth tour of six months' duration. (In the event, illness prevented the king from going on his tour and he died in February 1952.) Other ministers backed an autumn election but Morrison and Gaitskell were not confident about the prospects of defeating the Conservatives again and both advised soldiering on into 1952 in the hope that something would turn up. But Attlee made the decision not to do so and called the election even though the state of the economy and the opinion polls (with the Conservatives enjoying an 11 per cent lead in September 1951) were not favourable. If Attlee had held on, instead of appealing to the country in the trough of the crisis, he (rather than the Churchill government) may have reaped the benefit of the subsequent economic recovery and rising prosperity of the early 1950s, with Labour enjoying a longer period in office than the six years it managed. In the event, the quirks of the electoral system meant Labour polled more votes than the Conservatives (13.9 million or 48.8 per cent, compared to 13.7 million or 48 per cent) but ended up with fewer MPs (295 to 321, resulting in a Conservative majority of 17), the collapse of the Liberal vote (and fewer Liberal candidates) also helping tilt crucial seats away from Labour.

Conclusion

There was no call from within the party for Attlee to quit after the 1951 election defeat. But it might have been a good moment to step down (as he later admitted) as he was 68 years old, exhausted after 11 gruelling years in government, and had been hospitalised twice while prime minister, in 1948 and 1951, suffering from duodenal ulcers. The four years, until December 1955, in which he continued to lead Labour in Opposition were not a happy or successful period for him or for the party (Theakston 2010). Outstanding in government, Attlee underwhelmed (as in the 1930s) back in opposition. Out of office - in a pattern repeated so often over the decades - internal Labour Party politics became exceptionally bitter and factionalised, policy and ideological arguments intensified, and it became more difficult to paper over the cracks, hold the party together and broker compromises. Attlee just seemed to be hanging on rather than making any positive contribution in the role. He led the party into a fifth general election, Labour going down to defeat again in 1955. Determined to block his long-time rival Herbert Morrison, he once seemed to have been inclined towards the left-wing Aneurin Bevan as his successor but thought that he had thrown away his chance of the leadership by being too undisciplined and too much of a rebel, and the right-wing Hugh Gaitskell (who he was not particularly close to or keen on) won decisively and then proceeded to lead the party in a very un-Attlee fashion.

Attlee now regularly comes in at number one position in surveys of academic experts rating and ranking the leadership and performance of modern British prime ministers. But in his own lifetime he was often under-estimated and written-off by journalists and other politicians as a mediocrity. His *Times* obituary in 1967 called him a 'successful if not a great prime minister.' 'A very significant prime minister . . . who did great things often by keeping out of the way, . . . perhaps . . . not a great prime minister' was the historian A.J.P. Taylor's judgment at that time. And a 1970s verdict was that 'if not one of the very greatest prime ministers, Clement Attlee was, at the least, a very good prime minister. He was less the cause of events than the means by which great events came to pass.' But his reputation rose further as historical researchers from the 1980s onwards began to look in depth at the record of his government and at his role in keeping it going, practising a collective model of leadership (Theakston 2013: 236).

In the 1980s, as Thatcherism swept all before it, his government was seen to rank with hers as one of the two ground-breaking and transformational administrations, bookending the years of the postwar consensus and making fundamental and long-lasting differences to politics, the economy and society. In Labour Party mythology, too, Attlee's government came to be seen in 'lost golden age' terms. By 1982 Attlee's biographer Kenneth Harris was calling him 'a great prime minister' (Harris 1982: 567). Immediately there followed the qualification that he was only great 'seen in the context of his time and events . . . In another context, the assessment might have been different' (Harris 1982: 569). But that comment can perhaps be understood by reference to something one of Attlee's ministers, Hugh Gaitskell, wrote in his diary in 1950, predicting that history would record Attlee as 'among the most successful British prime ministers' because 'the qualities needed for success in peacetime are by no means the ones normally associated with greatness' (Williams 1983: 189).

Post-Blair, Attlee was hailed as a model of non-celebrity leadership who was 'authentic' and achieved great things through facilitating the effective management of government business, puncturing the 'myth of the strong leader', but who could not have survived in the modern media-dominated political culture (Thomas-Symonds 2010; Brown 2014). More recently, over the last decade or so, Attlee has also perhaps been hailed more for his ethical and values-driven leadership, his seriousness, and his commitment to driving through social progress and reform even in an age of economic challenge and austerity (Bew 2016; Jackson 2018). In different political periods and situations, in other words, commentators and politicians seem to be able to find in Attlee's career and experience supposed lessons and examples that both reflect and fit contemporary needs and purposes and arguments. There may be a danger in all this that, in the focus on his strengths and achievements, his flaws, limitations and failures are unduly neglected. What Attlee got wrong may be as important as what he got right. But certainly no one now writes him off as the ineffectual 'little mouse' (Bew 2016: 199) that one Labour critic thought the party was getting back in 1935.

References

Attlee, C. (1960). 'Premier and his Team: Advantages Over Presidential System', *Daily Telegraph*, 9 August.

Beckett, F. (2000). *Clem Attlee: A Biography*. London: Politico's.

Bew, J. (2016). *Citizen Clem: A Biography of Attlee*. London: riverrun.

Brookshire, J. (1981). 'Clement Attlee and Cabinet Reform 1930-1945', *Historical Journal*, 24 (1): 175-188.

Brookshire, J. (1995). *Clement Attlee*. Manchester: Manchester University Press.

Brown, A. (2014). *The Myth of the Strong Leader*. London: The Bodley Head.

Bullock, A. (1983). *Ernest Bevin: Foreign Secretary 1945-1951*. London: Heinemann.

Burridge, T. (1985). *Clement Attlee*. London: Jonathan Cape.

Cockerell, M. (1988). *Live from Number 10: the inside story of prime ministers and television*. London: Faber & Faber.

Crowcroft, R. (2011). *Attlee's War: World War II and the Making of a Labour Leader*. London: I.B. Tauris.

Crowcroft, R. and Theakston, K. (2013). 'The Fall of the Attlee Government, 1951', in T. Heppell and K. Theakston (eds).

How Labour Governments Fall. London: Palgrave Macmillan.

Fielding, S. (1991). '"Don't know and don't care": popular political attitudes in Labour's Britain, 1945-51.' In N. Tiratsoo (ed). *The Attlee Years.* London: Pinter.

Harris, K. (1982). *Attlee.* London: Weidenfeld & Nicolson.

Hennessy, P. (1992). *Never Again: Britain 1945-1951.* London: Jonathan Cape.

Hennessy, P. (2000). *The Prime Minister: The Office and Its Holders Since 1945.* London: Allen Lane.

Howell, D. (2006). *Attlee.* London: Haus Publishing.

Jackson, B. (2018). 'Citizen and Subject: Clement Attlee's Socialism', *History Workshop Journal,* (86) Autumn: 291-298.

Jefferys, K. (1993). *The Labour Party Since 1945.* London: Macmillan.

Mallaby, G. (1965). *From My Level.* London: Hutchinson.

Margach, J. (1978). *The Abuse of Power: The War between Downing Street and the Media.* London: W.H. Allen.

Marquand, D. (2008). *Britain Since 1918: The Strange Career of British Democracy.* London: Weidenfeld & Nicolson.

Morgan, K. (1984). *Labour in Power 1945-1951.* Oxford: Oxford University Press.

Morgan, K. (1987). *Labour People: Leaders and Lieutenants: Hardie to Kinnock.* Oxford: Oxford University Press.

Nicolson, N. (ed). (1966). *Harold Nicolson Diaries and Letters 1930-1962.* London: Collins.

Pearce, R. (1997). *Attlee.* London: Longman.

Pugh, M. (2010). *Speak for Britain! A New History of the Labour Party.* London: Bodley Head.

Radice, G. (2008). *The Tortoise and the Hares: Attlee, Bevin, Cripps, Dalton, Morrison.* London: Politico's.

Theakston, K. (2010). *After Number 10: Former Prime Ministers in British Politics.* London: Palgrave Macmillan.

Theakston, K. (2013). 'Evaluating Prime-Ministerial Performance: The British Experience', in P. Strangio et al (eds). *Understanding Prime-Ministerial Performance:*

Comparative Perspectives. Oxford: Oxford University Press.

Thomas-Symonds, N. (2010). *Attlee: A Life in Politics.* London: I.B. Tauris.

Times. (1957). 'Lord Attlee on Art of Being Prime Minister.' *The Times*, 15 June.

Williams, F. (1961). *A Prime Minister Remembers: The War and Post-war Memoirs of the Rt Hon Earl Attlee.* London: Heinemann.

Williams, P. (ed) (1983). *The Diary of Hugh Gaitskell.* London: Jonathan Cape.

Wilson, H. (1977). *A Prime Minister on Prime Ministers.* London: Michael Joseph and   Weidenfeld & Nicolson

Chapter 4
Anthony Eden (1955-57)

Anthony Eden was the future once. For the best part of two decades - from the mid-1930s into the 1950s - he was widely seen as the country's 'next prime minister'. Glamorous, elegant, cultivated, moderate, popular, and a figure with an international reputation before he was 40, he was for many the embodiment of hope and idealism in the 'low, dishonest decade' of the 1930s and remained immensely popular with the public through the Second World War and beyond. The contrast between expectations and the disappointing and, in the end, disastrous reality of his premiership, as character collided with events, is stark. Occupying Number 10 for less than two years, Eden soon became the past as the Conservatives, under his successor, Harold Macmillan, ruthlessly moved on and rebuilt.

Party Leadership

With a brave Great War record, Eden had been first elected to parliament in 1923. He soon became a rising star and the golden boy of interwar British politics. In 1935 he became, aged just 38, the youngest Foreign Secretary for over a century. He was tipped as the likely peacetime Conservative leader after Neville Chamberlain, who had become prime minister in 1937 aged 68 and was not expected to have a long tenure. But he clashed with Chamberlain, resigning over disagreements on policy towards Mussolini, and perhaps gaining more of a reputation as an opponent of appeasement than he really deserved. Re-entering government on the outbreak of the Second World War, he then soon became the designated heir apparent and crown prince to Winston Churchill. But, as the years of waiting for Churchill to go dragged on, Eden was more the ageing, bitter and impatient dauphin when he finally succeeded to the premiership in April 1955.

The problem was, though poll evidence suggested he was more of an electoral asset for the Conservatives than Churchill, that Eden would never play Brutus and plot, conspire or act decisively to push Churchill out. He was also stymied by the bad luck of his own life-threatening illness coinciding with Churchill's stroke in 1953 that might otherwise have provided the opportunity for him to take the reins. Perhaps Eden was, in a sense, kept waiting too long. He became frustrated, anxious, tense, brittle and possibly stale and past his best. And other insiders' doubts about him multiplied (including on Churchill's part) - that he was perhaps more 'image' than substance, that he was too concerned with popularity, that he was not tough enough or had the wrong sort of character and temperament for the top job, that he would actually turn out to be a poor prime minister.

In policy and governance terms, Eden's long apprenticeship probably did him more harm than good as a preparation for Number 10. Through three stints at the Foreign Office (1935-38, 1940-45 and 1951-55), he proved himself an exceptionally skilful diplomatic technician, international negotiator and manager of British foreign policy. But his knowledge of and his feel for domestic affairs was much more limited. He had never led a department pushing significant legislation through parliament, for instance. 'I do not really feel confident in myself as No. 1 at home . . . and I do not know enough of economics', he had privately admitted during the war (Dutton 1997: 253). Having to carry in practice much of the day-to-day burden of opposition leadership under the frequently-absent Churchill in the late-1940s did not really compensate much for that deficiency, and Eden refused offers of a move to take charge of domestic policy when back in government after 1951, fearing it might somehow delay or even endanger the succession. Not surprisingly, many wondered if he actually had the breadth of experience to be a successful prime minister.

In party management terms, it was also a weakness in Eden's position that he did not really have a strong parliamentary base to sustain his leadership through thick and thin. He was never a strong 'House of Commons man' in the sense of feeling at home in Westminster's bars and corridors, networking, gossiping and cultivating alliances and supporters among MPs. He had in fact few close political friends, followers or cronies. 'When he looked at the Conservative benches', according to biographer Robert Rhodes James, 'he saw in the main the faces of complete strangers.' The majority of Conservative MPs hardly knew him, except from afar. 'From the beginning, he was an aloof and distant prime minister' (Rhodes James 1986: 406). At the end of it all, the fact that Harold Macmillan was very much a 'House of Commons man', artfully attentive to Conservative MPs, made him a much more dangerous colleague and rival.

Ideology and Aims

After only a few months in office, the Eden government gave the impression of being 'leaderless and without ideas', as Ian Gilmour put it: headed by someone who 'had known for a long time that he was going to succeed Churchill, yet . . . did not seem to have given any thought to what he would do when the great day came' (Gilmour and Garnett 1997: 102). Eden had long been an unideological, pragmatic, middle-ground figure, with little interest in wider political and economic ideas. He was never going to play the role of a great reforming leader with a strong policy agenda of his own.

Clarissa Eden, his wife, once reported him as saying, 'I'm not really a Conservative. I'm an old-fashioned Liberal.' He 'never felt at ease with the True Blues', she commented (Haste 2007: 121). His First World War experiences had engendered what David Dutton (1997: 248) called 'an ill-focussed but by no means insincere desire to improve the lot of ordinary British people, with whom his time in the trenches had given him a lifelong empathy.' In the early phase of his political career, he had identified with the consensual Conservatism of Stanley Baldwin. Noel Skelton's notion of a 'property-owning democracy' was another strong and life-long influence, though Eden never really got beyond the level of cliche, generalisation and even the political equivalents of motherhood and apple pie in spelling out what that slogan might mean in concrete policy terms (Dutton 1997: 276). Different biographers have claimed him for the cause of 'enlightened Conservatism' (Thorpe 2003: 81) and 'humane, liberal and progressive Conservatism' (Rhodes James 1986: xi). Certainly, Conservative right-wingers always distrusted him, and in return he had no time for them and their politics or for unbridled free market ideas. In fact, he often appeared to dislike the Tory Party itself and particularly during the Second World War seemed to hanker after some sort of centrist realignment, thinking that his natural political constituency and appeal was to non-party 'middle opinion' (Dutton 1997: 251).

Eden had, according to David Carlton (1981: 217), a 'large share of responsibility for pushing the Conservative party towards acceptance of the post-war consensus' and a broadly social democratic/'welfareist' policy framework. In fact, the hard policy grind to that end after 1945 was primarily the work of R.A. Butler and the Conservative Research Department, but Eden backed the rethink and the 'new Conservatism'. He largely went along with the prevailing climate of ideas, and his importance lay less in the formulation of specific policies than in the way in which, as Dutton (1997: 276) put it, 'he symbolised better than anyone else did or could that the Conservatives had become a forward-looking party capable of responding to the social and economic aspirations of the mass electorate.' Against that background, the criticism of 'missed opportunities' by later commentators, looking at the way in which his government backed off from immigration controls or from forcing tougher industrial relations legislation on the trade unions, exaggerates the scope for radical changes in the context of that time, in terms of what was practical politics, the framing of those issues and the sense of feasible options in Whitehall, Westminster and the wider society. Eden opted to 'mark time', as it has been argued (Carlton 1981: 375), unwilling to risk his 'liberal' and moderate reputation in domestic politics by pushing forward with controversial schemes (Lamb 1987).

Eden was also a man of his times, in line with the then-mainstream political, public and 'establishment' opinion, in his views on Europe, being sceptical about European integration and opposed to supranationalism and the pooling of sovereignty in a federal Europe. In that context, it would have been astonishing had his government wholeheartedly accepted, rather than dismissing, the invitation to join in with the moves on the continent, with the Messina Conference of 1955, towards the formation of the Common Market. That was simply not within the boundaries of political possibility in mid-1950s British politics; only later was it seen as Britain 'missing the bus'. Eden's view of Britain as a world power with a global role, his strong commitment to the Empire/Commonwealth and his Atlanticism were also the conventional wisdom of the time. Where he did perhaps think differently from other elite policymakers was in his belief that Britain could, and sometimes should, act with a measure of independence from the United States - something that boomeranged badly on him in the Suez crisis.

Political style and skills

In a book on the leading political orators among senior Conservative politicians from the 1920s to the 2010s (Hayton and Crines 2015), there is no chapter on Eden - understandably so, because he was a workmanlike but not a distinguished speechmaker. What he could do, says David Dutton (1997: 264), was give expression to 'what the average person was thinking quite competently.' 'Eden never makes a really remarkable speech, since he never says anything memorable. But he never makes a bad speech', was Harold Macmillan's rather catty view. 'If he never says anything very striking, he is never guilty of a "gaffe" or even of an indiscretion' (Catterall 2003: 53, 491). A contemporary study of the 1955 election campaign similarly concluded that Eden 'said nothing memorable but said it very well' (Butler 1955: 75). If his style was undramatic, reasonable, simple and clear it also tended to the banal and platitudinous. But he was, as Frank Longford (1984: 87) noted, 'a platform draw. He seldom, if ever, disappointed his . . . audiences, though he never possessed . . . any particular gift of phrase. Churchill is supposed to have said that one of his speeches contained every cliche in the language except, "Please adjust your clothing on leaving the toilet."'

From Eden's time onwards, television was becoming an inescapable part of a prime minister's political world (Cockerell 1988), and he was 'one of the first politicians to recognise the potential power of the medium as well as to have the confidence to put himself at the mercy of the cameras' (Shaw 2009: 102). He took naturally to TV, in fact, came across well on it, and was, says David Dutton (1997: 478) 'the first prime minister to use the ministerial broadcast as a weapon of political debate.'

In terms of political media management and public relations strategy, however, Eden's approach and record were less good. Although he had been a professional politician for 30 years before entering Number 10, he had apparently 'never heard of spins or deliberate leaks' and did not really 'understand the demands of a modern press' (Haste 2007: 221). He has been described by one commentator (Shaw 2009: 95) as 'a complete amateur in the realm of press manipulation'. Deciding to hold regular private meetings with the editor of *The Times*, as he did, was never likely to be enough to develop a firm press base or wide backing. Worse still, Eden was fantastically preoccupied with, and over-sensitive to, media criticism. A strong press secretary might have compensated for some of this but Eden's choice of the journalist William Clark for the job did not really work out - necessary relations of confidence and close working did not seem to be established, and Clark eventually resigned during the Suez crisis.

Eden was not a good prime-ministerial 'butcher'. The new prime minister failed at the start to stamp his own identity on the government, through carrying out a major reshuffle to make it clearly an Eden government rather than almost a continuity-Churchill government. 'Anthony never built a Cabinet in his own mould', one of his ministers later commented: 'he inherited one, and then tinkered with it' (Rhodes James 1986: 405). Only one minister from Churchill's last Cabinet was sacked when Eden first took over, and there was little new blood brought in to the wider ministerial team. He kept the Chancellor of the Exchequer, R.A. Butler, in place, despite feeling it was time he was moved, and made the mistake of appointing the strong-willed Harold Macmillan to the Foreign Office (something he soon regretted, as they clashed on policy), backing away from giving that post to his political ally and friend Lord Salisbury. Nor was there a major shake-up after the election victory. And when Eden did finally make some more significant changes, in December 1955, the reshuffle did not get a good press and actually served to aggravate divisions, tensions and rivalries at the top of the government. In the key moves, an unhappy Butler was shunted across to become Lord Privy Seal and Leader of the House of Commons, and was replaced at the Treasury by a reluctant Macmillan. Eden got the more compliant Foreign Secretary he wanted in the shape of Selwyn Lloyd, so that he could effectively run foreign policy himself, but at the cost of having as his new Chancellor a powerful and ambitious figure, with ideas of his own, and with whom he was soon at loggerheads over economic policy and decisions. Eden's chances of leading a successful government were certainly not helped by having a Cabinet that was 'neither loyal nor united', as historian Richard Lamb (1987: 14) noted.

To make matters worse, Eden's methods of working often put his ministers' backs up. In contrast to the rambling Cabinets of Churchill's final years, Eden chaired meetings in an effective and businesslike way. But - in part a matter of temperament, and in part his lack of confidence and experience on domestic policy - he turned out to be poor at delegating to and trusting his ministers. Attlee shrewdly noted that he had no experience of 'running a team' (Thorpe 2003: 461), and ministers were soon afflicted and exasperated by what one of them called Eden's 'chronic restlessness' (Carlton 1988: 376) and his interference in their day-to-day departmental business (something he had always himself resented when working under Chamberlain and Churchill), accompanied by 'a mass of telephoning' and constant fussing and meddling over small as well as large issues (Catterall 2003: 513, 583).

As a decision-maker, Eden's 'mental processes . . . seemed heavily dependent on intuition and quickness of perception.' 'His approach to problems often strikes one as instinctive rather than based on long, intellectual process', thought one adviser. Not a man of ideas or great imagination he was, however, a workaholic and had a huge appetite for detail - perhaps too much so, sometimes being criticised for not being able to 'see the wood for the trees'. Some advisers felt that he was not open to unpalatable advice or alternative ideas unless he had asked for them, tending to make his own decision and then consult others, without revealing what he had decided (Dutton 1997: 463-66).

In character terms, Eden ultimately stands out as someone not emotionally well-equipped for the highest office. The outside world saw the urbane and charming exterior; insiders saw that he was vain, highly-strung, volatile, over-sensitive to criticism, lacking self-confidence, bad-tempered and petulant, easily upset and annoyed, prone to jealousy and a great fusser. A prima donna who lacked the necessary inner toughness, there were doubts about his character, temperament and ability to do the job before he became prime minister, and they continued when he was in Number 10, even before he failed the ultimate test of the Suez crisis.

Context
Eden's decision to plump for an early general election paid off. Announcing the election (to be held on 26 May 1955) only nine days after assuming the topmost office (on 5 April) carried the risk of entering the record books as the shortest-serving prime minister ever. But the circumstances favoured the Conservatives. Their record on full employment and the welfare state since 1951 had been reassuring; the years of rationing and austerity had been ended; living standards were improving. The Labour Opposition was dogged by factionalism and ideological infighting, and its leader, Attlee, was now 72 and visibly running out of steam. Just to make sure, however, Butler introduced a tax-cutting electioneering budget in early May, even though there were serious concerns inside Whitehall about the likely deteriorating economic outlook later in the year (which had persuaded Eden not to hold on for six months before going to the polls). Eden himself campaigned well and made a good impression, particularly on television, speaking directly to the voters in the first-ever prime-ministerial solo TV live broadcast (Cockerell 1988: 36). Compared to 1951, the Conservative vote share increased by 1.7 per cent to 49.7 per cent (the highest percentage share attained by any party in the postwar era), while Labour's fell 2.4 percent to 46.4 per cent, and the

Conservatives' majority in parliament went up from 17 to 59 seats. The Conservatives' vote total had actually fallen by half a million votes, compared to 1951, to 13.2 million, but Labour's total fell even more, its 12.4 million total being 1.5 million down. The Conservatives had been privately fearing electoral defeat if Churchill had stayed on, but the government had actually become the first in 90 years to increase its majority at a general election.

The gloss quickly wore off, however, and Eden's political honeymoon was a short one. His personal popularity rating in opinion polls fell from a 73 per cent approval rating in April 1955 to 50 per cent by February 1956 and 41 per cent by April 1956. By-election results registered swings against the Conservatives and reduced majorities. There was muttering, unhappiness and misgivings, and a growing feeling that perhaps the choice of Eden had been a mistake, in the Conservative party. The government, and the prime minister personally, came under sustained hostile press criticism for lack of grip, direction and purpose, with headlines like 'Eden is a flop' and 'Eden must go', and a wounding Daily Telegraph attack at the beginning of 1956 demanding the 'smack of firm government' (Thorpe 2003: 459). When stories circulated that he may be about to resign, instead of ignoring the matter he overreacted and unwisely rushed out a statement denying the rumours. Adding to the sense of a prime minister and government on the defensive, the election of Hugh Gaitskell to head the Labour Party in December 1955 revitalised the Opposition's leadership, and from that time until the end of Eden's premiership Labour led the Conservatives in the opinion polls for all but one month (November 1956, when the Tories had a small lead).

Nor did the economy seem properly under control. Over 1955 the balance of payments deteriorated, the pound came under pressure, there were growing concerns about inflation, and an atmosphere of economic crisis built up. A politically-damaging emergency budget to deal with the over-heating economy had to be introduced by Butler in October 1955 that imposed expenditure cuts and increased indirect taxes (taking back about two-thirds of the tax cuts made in the pre-election

60

give-away budget). Economic problems continued through the first half of 1956 while Eden and his new Chancellor, Macmillan, had strong and frequent arguments (with the Chancellor threatening resignation at one stage) over the abolition of subsidies on bread and milk prices and about tax and spending decisions in the budget. Macmillan, on the basis of Treasury advice, warned the prime minister in April 1956 of the economic dangers that were looming and the threats to the pound, saying the crisis would come between August and November that year - a prediction that came true but in a context and for reasons that could not have been anticipated at that time.

Had Eden's government been visibly more competent and successful over its first year, and had the prime minister felt in a stronger political position, then perhaps the decisions taken over the Suez affair may have been different, and with a different outcome. But when Britain and France responded to the Egyptian President Nasser's nationalisation in July 1956 of the company running the Suez Canal by colluding with Israel and mounting military action in an abortive attempt to seize control of the canal and topple Nasser, the political consequences were disastrous. Eden needed a big success and had become, as Keith Kyle (2003: 68) noted, 'obsessive about not appearing to dither'. He needed to strengthen his image, unite the party behind his leadership, assert himself and decisively refute criticisms of weakness and drift. Instead, he ended-up pressing the self-destruct button on his premiership.

There is no doubt that there were many failures of leadership and judgement on Eden's part during the crisis. These included over-personalising the conflict with Nasser: 'it is either him or us, don't forget that', Eden warned one adviser (Kyle 2003: 96). There was over-reliance on misleading historical analogies and so-called 'historical lessons' (going back to the 1930s dictators). Eden (and other ministers) fatally misread American and international opinion - particularly the views of President Eisenhower on the use of force - believing that Britain could act militarily without US support. Throughout, Eden and other ministers in his inner circle were also 'running in blinkers', as one senior official put it (Hennessy 2000: 235), by keeping most of Whitehall in the dark at crucial points, cutting out potentially awkward advice and advisers, and with the PM selectively reading and 'cherry-picking' intelligence reports to fit his own preconceptions. Reviewing Eden's conduct of the Suez crisis, and particularly his management of collective Cabinet government processes in a 'limited war', the importance of avoiding 'tunnel vision', the handling of the international diplomacy of the conflict, and the need to account to and carry the support of parliament and the public, Peter Hennessy (2000: 237) concluded that he provided 'an object lesson in how not to do it.'

The Suez crisis became a hugely divisive and intensely controversial episode in British politics. Initially supportive, Labour leader Gaitskell switched to opposing the use of force without United Nations sanction and bitterly attacked Eden. There were strong public divisions but opinion moved in favour of Eden: before the intervention the public had opposed military action by 44 per cent to 37 per cent, but in a 'rally round the flag' effect at the height of the crisis in November 1956 Eden's approval rating was 52 per cent (8 per cent ahead of Gaitskell's), and actually rose to 56 per cent the following month. There were splits on the Conservative side, with some MPs unhappy about military intervention but the majority - and a vocal group of right-wingers in particular, who opposed compromise - favouring tough action. There were also some influential doubters and waverers in the Cabinet, who were mostly sidelined or brushed aside through Eden's use of an inner group (the Egypt Committee acting as a sort of War Cabinet), though the full Cabinet did sign up to the use of force in the last resort, if negotiations failed (Brady 1997). Eden took crucial decisions into his own hands in the final run-up to hostilities, involving only a few other trusted aides and ministers, including in agreeing the pact with France and Israel. The Cabinet was told about those secret talks, though it is not clear in what sort of detail (and Eden later denied allegations of collusion in parliament). Some critics claim Eden misled the Cabinet about what was going on but Hennessy's (2000: 223) conclusion that 'if ministers remained deceived about collusion, it involved a high degree of self-deception' is a sound one.

As an attempt at regime change in Cairo, the Suez adventure failed in a humiliating way, but as a way of ousting the British prime minister it was a tremendous success. Nasser was left in possession of the canal, and his position and prestige strengthened. It was not just that the military action was called off almost as soon as it began under massive pressure from the United States, including on the economic front - panicking the Chancellor Macmillan, who had been one of the strongest supporters of military intervention, into suddenly flipping round, in the face of a run on the pound and threats to oil supplies, to demanding an immediate halt to the invasion. Eisenhower and the US government seem thenceforth to have regarded Eden as irretrievably politically damaged goods. Cracks were appearing but the Conservative party, though deeply unhappy, more or less held together, helped by the strenuous work of Eden's chief whip Edward Heath to steady the ship, and only a couple of junior ministers resigned. Domestically, it was the collapse of Eden's health that really forced the issue - or at least accelerated the ending of his premiership - with some senior figures 'on manoeuvres', to use a common shorthand, in the last couple of months of 1956.

Eden had faced some health issues earlier in his career, and he had been seriously ill, and had almost died, in 1953 when a gallstones operation went wrong and his bile duct was accidentally cut. He had needed emergency surgery and a long convalescence but, although experiencing occasional fevers and chills in the interim, believed that he was in good enough health to become prime minister in 1955. However, the strains of the Suez crisis, compounded by a recurrence of illness and the effects of the drugs used to treat him, made a crack-up almost inevitable, and in late-November 1956 he needed to be whisked off to Jamaica for three weeks to recuperate. Butler and Macmillan - rivals for the succession - stepped into the vacuum to run the government, and Eden's colleagues did not always keep the absent premier fully informed as the broken pieces of British policy were picked up and key decisions were taken.

David Owen, a former Foreign Secretary and himself a medic, believes that a fully fit and well Eden would not have made the mistakes of judgement and decision-making he did in 1956 (Owen 2008: 109-140). That may be difficult to absolutely prove one way or the other, but the mistakes and miscalculations of Suez cannot in any case be fully explained in these terms - Suez was not a one-man war and there is no evidence of Eden's Cabinet colleagues being afflicted by decision-altering illnesses. Whatever the case, Eden's political position had been fatally undermined in his party and the Cabinet, and power was draining away from him, even before his doctors insisted in the New Year that if he did not immediately resign he would soon collapse again and would endanger and shorten his life.

Conclusion

Eden resigned as prime minister on 9 January 1957, his premiership and reputation wrecked by the Suez fiasco. He lived for another twenty years, wrote three fat volumes of self-defending memoirs, was very prickly about Suez and his reputation, and was given a peerage, but was pretty firmly marginalised - he had no chance of a political comeback or of having an influential elder statesmen role.

Even leaving aside Suez (which obviously is not possible), a tenure of twenty-one months is, as Roy Jenkins (1988: 78) once commented, too short a period in which to establish a positive prime-ministerial reputation. Eden won a general election but had little apparent idea of what he wanted substantively to do in office, and he seemed to be floundering and running through his political capital from a surprisingly early stage. The top job exposed his limitations and weaknesses, and even before the failure of Suez and the breakdown of his health, the odds were stacking up against him being able to continue long in office or achieve much. As Philip Norton (2020: 386) has commented, 'Suez was the culmination of poor leadership rather than an exceptional instance of it.'

To quote Roy Jenkins (1988: 237) again, Eden's premiership was a 'tragic epilogue' to a 'long period of distinguished waiting'. His 'chief and insoluble problem was that he was not Winston Churchill', as Ian Gilmour neatly put it: whoever succeeded the historic national hero would always have faced an immensely difficult task in terms of measuring up against their predecessor and coming out from under his shadow (Gilmour and Garnett 1997: 91). It might have been better for Eden's reputation if he had turned out to feature in the books about the 'prime ministers we never had' (Richards 2021) or the 'might-have-beens' of British politics rather than having to be ranked in the actual prime-ministerial league tables. *Omnium consensu capax imperii, nisi imperasset*, Tacitus wrote about one of the less-illustrious Roman emperors - 'had he never been emperor, no one would have doubted his ability to rule.' It would be a good verdict, too, on the failed premiership of Anthony Eden.

References

Aster, S. (1976). *Anthony Eden.* London: Weidenfeld & Nicolson.

Brady, C. (1997). 'The Cabinet system and management of the Suez Crisis', *Contemporary British History*, 11 (2): 65-93.

Butler, D. (1955). *The British General Election of 1955.* London: Macmillan.

Carlton, D. (1981). *Anthony Eden.* London: Allen Lane.

Catterall, P. (ed) (2003). *The Macmillan Diaries: the Cabinet Years 1950-1957*, London: Macmillan.

Cockerell, M. (1988). *Live from Number 10: the inside story of prime ministers and television.* London: Faber & Faber.

Dutton, D. (1997). *Anthony Eden: A Life and Reputation.* London: Arnold.

Gilmour, I. and Garnett, M. (1997). *Whatever Happened to the Tories: The Conservative Party Since 1945.* London: Fourth Estate.

Haste, C. (ed) (2007). *Clarissa Eden: A Memoir: From Churchill to Eden.* London: Weidenfeld & Nicolson.

Hayton, R. and Crines, A. (eds) (2015), *Conservative Orators from Baldwin to Cameron.* Manchester: Manchester University Press.

Hennessy, P. (2000). *The Prime Minister: The Office and Its Holders Since 1945.* London: Allen Lane.

Jefferys, K. (1997). *Retreat From New Jerusalem: British Politics 1951-64.* London: Macmillan.

Jenkins, R. (1988). *Gallery of 20th Century Portraits.* London: David & Charles.

Kyle, K. (2003). *Suez: Britain's End of Empire in the Middle East.* London: I.B. Tauris.

Lamb, R. (1987). *The Failure of the Eden Government.* London: Sedgwick and Jackson.

Longford, F. (1984). *Eleven at Number 10.* London: Harrap.

Norton, P. (2020). 'Sir Anthony Eden', in I. Dale (ed), *The Prime Ministers.* London: Hodder and Stoughton.

Owen, D. (2008). *In Sickness and In Power: Illness in heads of government during the last 100 years.* London: Methuen.

Rhodes James, R. (1986). *Anthony Eden.* London: Weidenfeld & Nicolson.

Richards, S. (2021). *The Prime Ministers We Never Had.* London: Atlantic Books.

Shaw, T. (2009). *Eden, Suez and the Mass Media.* London: I.B. Tauris.

Thorpe, D. R. (2003). *Eden.* London: Chatto & Windus

Chapter 5
Harold Macmillan (1957-63)

Harold Macmillan, who was Conservative prime minister for six years and nine months, from 10 January 1957 until 18 October 1963, has long intrigued and puzzled historians and biographers, as indeed he often did contemporary political observers and commentators. 'A study in ambiguity' was the subtitle of the first serious book on his life and career (Sampson 1967), published in 1967; a parliamentary reporter who had watched him in action on a daily basis wrote about 'the masks of Macmillan' and the enigma of his multi-faceted personality (Shrapnel 1978: 25-38). He seemed a supremely stylish and commanding figure on the political stage (attracting the 'Supermac' label), starting his premiership with his party's fortunes almost at rock bottom after Suez but going on to win a stunning general election victory, and with a strong grip on power. Yet his government came to an end amidst some turmoil and disarray, and his legacy and achievements remain contested. As the last prime minister to have been born in the reign of Queen Victoria and the last to have fought in the trenches of the First World War, and with the traditional upper class markers of an Etonian education and marriage to a Duke's daughter, he seemed at one level a throwback to an earlier age. But at the same time, he was one of the few prime ministers who had significant business experience (with the family publishing firm) before taking up ministerial office, and he was in many ways very modern, and indeed radical, in his economic and political thinking and approach, and a thoroughly professional, ambitious and relentless politician (Horne 1988 and 1989; Thorpe 2010; Turner 1994; Ball 2004; Williams 2009).

Party Leadership
Politics is 'not a flat race', Winston Churchill once told Macmillan; 'it's a steeplechase' - a description that certainly applies to the gruelling, long-haul routes, with many obstacles to overcome,

that both of them took to Number 10 (Catterall 2003: 413). Both had often been written off and seen as political failures at different points in their careers, and had needed exceptional amounts of ambition, willpower and luck to keep in the race and make it to the top. For his part, Macmillan was a 'later starter', first becoming an MP in 1924, aged just 30, but then having to wait until 1940 - when Churchill became prime minister - to get his first toe-hold on the ministerial ladder as a lowly parliamentary secretary. Later, and unusually for those who become prime minister, he was over 60 before he was finally appointed in 1955 to one of the 'great offices of state' as Foreign Secretary (Jenkins 1988: 126).

In the 1930s Macmillan had been in a political and personal dead-end - a marginalised and frustrated rebel, at odds with his own party on the big issues of the day (unemployment, the economy, appeasement), widely seen as a bore and a maverick, and deeply unhappy in his private life (cuckolded by a fellow Tory MP, his marriage tragically became something of a sham, though public appearances were kept up and they found a form of companionship). At crucial points Churchill gave his protege two assignments that could have amounted to little, or in which Macmillan could have underperformed and failed, but he took the most of the opportunities to show what he was capable of. First, during the war as Minister-Resident in the Mediterranean theatre 1942-45, he showed great diplomatic skill in liaising with the Americans, dealing with the French, and in handling strategic-political issues in North Africa, Italy and Greece. Later, as Minister of Housing 1951-54, he displayed great skills in showmanship and executive push in achieving the Tories' manifesto pledge to build 300,000 house a year. Even so, in an opinion poll in 1954 less than two per cent named him as a possible prime minister (Horne 1988: 340). Swift moves through and short stints in the Ministry of Defence, the Foreign Office and at the Treasury over the 1954-56 period left little in the way of a record of reputation-enhancing major policy achievements.

'When you get a chance, take it', Macmillan once explained (Horne 1988: 454). Suez gave him his chance. At the top of the mid-1950s Tory party, there were strong tensions and jealousies between Eden, Butler and Macmillan. But with Eden three years younger than him, and Butler eight years younger and more senior in terms of experience and status, Macmillan's chances of the succession, under normal conditions if Eden's premiership lasted a full term, were probably not high. The failure of the Suez adventure, however, upended political normality. Eden's leadership was politically discredited and his health destroyed. Butler's vacillations, hesitations, and coded indiscretions about Suez, together with having to bear the odium of leading the government (with Eden away ill) through the climb down after the controversial military intervention and its aftermath, made him seem 'wet', weak and apologetic in the eyes of Conservative backbenchers. In this situation what Macmillan had - which Butler lacked - was the killer instinct.

Some writers (Evans and Taylor 1996: 105) have used the language of 'coup' and conspiracy to imply that Macmillan had egged on Eden over Suez, backing strong action but then pulling the plug on it all by putting the fear of God into the Cabinet by exaggerating the financial pressures Britain faced, in the hope that would somehow force him out of Number 10. The label 'first in and first out' over Suez could truthfully be stuck on Macmillan (Horne 1988: 441), but this Machiavellian reading of motives and events is not very convincing (Sampson 1967: 123; Thorpe 2010: 356, 363-66). However, there is little doubt that, in the crucial period in late 1956 when Eden's premiership was falling apart, Macmillan was willing and able to cultivate younger members of the Cabinet, exploit his American connections and links with key US government figures, and project an image of confidence, decisiveness and resolution to shell-shocked and anxious Conservative MPs to, first, 'give the stricken prime minister a helping hand into political oblivion' (Charmley 2008: 169) and, second, to ruthlessly undermine and elbow aside Butler, whom many in the press and the political world viewed as the natural successor to Eden. When Eden resigned in January 1957 (and he was not asked to give formal advice to the Queen as to his successor), a sort of private roll call of Cabinet ministers was organised (Thorpe 2010: 361-62) which revealed that only one backed Butler, and the chief whip and the chairman of the

1922 Committee reported that backbenchers also favoured Macmillan, as did Churchill when he was asked by the Palace for his views.

As leader, Macmillan left the details of party organisation and management to successive Party Chairmen and chief whips (Edward Heath being particularly close to him, and influential and effective in that role 1957-59). Unlike Eden, he knew the importance of time and effort spent in talking to and cultivating backbench supporters in parliament. There was some unhappiness on the backbenches (and in the wider party), that particularly made itself felt in regard to the policy direction on the European Common Market and on decolonisation. While the Tory right had supported him at the start of his premiership, they did not, on these grounds, at the end. Usually able to play off rival ministers against each other, Macmillan sometimes suspected (actually rather unlikely) plots against his leadership of the party - when Thorneycroft resigned as chancellor in 1958, and later when he purported to fear that Butler might play Disraeli to his Peel over the Common Market. But for the most part his grip on the party and on the leadership seemed strong until the last year or two. Then, the government's accumulating troubles and particularly the mishandling of large-scale Cabinet changes (1962) and of the Profumo affair (1963) called into question the ageing and battered prime minister's judgement, popularity and value as an electoral asset to the party. Backbench disaffection spread, with 27 MPs abstaining and a much-reduced majority in a vital vote on the Profumo scandal, and with a growing sense in the media, in political circles and among Tory MPs and ministers that Macmillan's days were numbered. All the same, it is worth noting that Macmillan was not in the end overthrown by critics and opponents in his party but pulled down the curtain on his leadership himself, on health grounds.

Ideology and Aims

In the 1930s, Macmillan had seemed 'on the extreme left of Conservatism' (Ramsden 1998: 360), setting out in a sort of personal manifesto, his book *The Middle Way* (1938), his belief in greater state intervention, Keynesian economics, nationalisation of the coal mines, a national investment board, a minimum wage, public works schemes, and economic planning in conjunction with trade unions and employers' organisations as partners with government in decision-making. He attacked the failures of 'casino capitalism,' and argued for a 'levelling-up' approach to raise living standards and tackle regional inequalities (Horne 1988: 105, 107). Much of this chimed with policy-thinking and ideas that he pushed years later during his premiership. As he told his chancellor of the exchequer in 1961, he favoured 'more direction' and intervention in the economy rather than 'the laissez-faire tradition' (Turner 1994: 244). But the originality or revolutionary nature of these ideas should not be overstated. Macmillan was espousing much of the orthodox, centre-ground economic conventional wisdom of the 1930s onwards in terms that Conservatives could support and defend (Turner 1994: 36). Planning was seen as an alternative to socialism, preserving freedom and democracy, and promoting stability and prosperity, by balancing both state and private enterprise.

It has been claimed - including by no less a person than Clement Attlee - that Macmillan came close to 'crossing the floor' and joining the Labour Party in the 1930s. Attlee even described him as 'by far the most radical man' he had known in politics and mused that if he had switched then Macmillan, rather than him, would have become Labour prime minister (Margach 1978: 116). Macmillan actually resigned the Conservative whip for nearly a year in 1936-37 and advocated a new centre party government (saying it would have to be 'left centre rather than right centre') (Thorpe 2010: 125). He was also close to Lloyd George, attracted by his radicalism and dynamism. But he stuck with the Conservatives - 'I have to remember that I am a very rich man!', he once explained to a Labour friend (Clarke 1991: 216). In opposition after 1945, he floated the idea of changing the name of the Tory party to New Democratic Party and urged an alliance with the Liberals - these ideas came to nothing but he welcomed the change of image and policy stance associated with the Industrial Charter as the Conservatives came to terms with the mixed-economy and the welfare state. It is striking how both Macmillan and Butler, who played key roles in remaking the Tory party after 1945 and in its electoral and governing successes in the 1950s, were divided less on policy grounds as liberal and progressive Conservatives, than in terms of a much more personal political rivalry.

Macmillan was 'the most un-conservative Conservative of all time', was the judgement of veteran political correspondent James Margach (1978: 116). 'One of the most radical prime ministers of the [twentieth] century', and 'certainly more radical than any of its Labour ones', was the verdict of historian and former MP David Marquand (2008: 187). Macmillan himself admitted he was not 'a very good Tory' (Horne 1988: xi) or a 'very orthodox Tory' (Horne 1989: 38), once defined Toryism as 'a form of paternal Socialism' (Thorpe 2010: 86) and considered that 'the great thing is to keep the Tory Party on modern and progressive lines' (Thorpe 2010: 447). The Conservatives, he thought, should always 'occupy the middle ground' (Horne 1989: 138). His aim, he once recalled, was to run the government 'as a centre party. I was not prepared to run it on an extreme right-wing basis' (Horne 1989: 37).

Critics in the 1930s labelled him 'a dangerous Pink' (Horne 1988: 109), and later Thatcherites attacked him as a 'neo-socialist', but he could actually be located in a recognisable Conservative tradition, described variously as 'Disraelian' or 'Tory radicalism' or 'Tory democracy', concerned with the 'condition of the people' and with British security and influence in the world, combining paternalistic conservatism with a liberal approach, and building a cross-class alliance as the basis for electoral success. At the same time, other observers view Macmillan's politics in terms of the Whig, not the Tory, tradition in British political history. As Enoch Powell (1987) put it, 'he had no use for the conservative loyalties and affections: they interfered too much with the Whig's true vocation of directing trends in events and riding them skilfully so as to preserve the privileges, property and interests of his class.' This involved rejecting a doctrinaire approach, seeking balance and stability, and accommodation and adaptation in the face of changing circumstances - or, as Macmillan himself once explained, what was needed in the 'conduct of affairs' was 'constancy of purpose with flexibility of exercise' (Jefferys 1997: 64).

Political style and skills

Macmillan was one of the most accomplished political operators to have occupied Number 10. We know that in his free time he was reading studies of Machiavelli during the Suez crisis and before he seized the premiership (Davenport-Hines 1992: 262), but in some ways he did not need to. He had 'formidable personal political skills' (Williams 2009: 472) and was 'the supreme tactician' (Jefferys 1997: 62). Combining polished urbanity, wit, cunning and ruthlessness, he was a master of 'the oblique approach' (Davenport-Hines 1992: 252) or operating by stealth or indirection to outflank opposition and skilfully manoeuvre through his policies, whether on Europe or decolonisation or anything else. He was guileful, even cynical, in handling his party and parliament, and patient, determined and subtle in managing his Cabinet. One biographer describes his methods: 'evasive, postponing confrontation, blurring issues and professing support to those [he was] moving against' (Davenport-Hines 1992: 278).

A prime minister who made time to think and read widely, and stand back from the day-to-day pressures, Macmillan could also take a broad, sweeping, strategic and historically-informed view of politics. He was one of the more intellectual British prime ministers, comparable to Arthur Balfour or Gordon Brown in that respect, but with the difference that he had a flair for publicity and knew how to adopt a populist style to win a general election (Thorpe 2010: 42). Behind the stylish facade of the nonchalant patrician quoting Trollope or Thucydides, Macmillan was, as one contemporary commentator noted, 'adept at the rough stuff, given half a chance' (Shrapnel 1978: 31).

None of this came easy, however, but seemed to carry a heavy emotional price. Macmillan was a complex personality, hidden by different 'masks' that were put on or taken off as the situation or audience required: 'the fierce tribal leader, the unworldly scholar, city man, clubman, soldier' (Shrapnel 1978:

28) or alternatively 'the last Edwardian at Number 10' (Hutchinson 1980). Another description is of his 'aristocratic pantomime' (Davenport-Hines 1992: 295). He had, it has been suggested, an exceptional personal and political talent for concealment and for acting a part (Davenport-Hines 1992: 273). The crafty, cynical, devious, ruthless and opportunistic professional politician was well camouflaged. He may have projected an image of worldliness, coolness and confidence - 'unflappability' - but underneath there was at times considerable self-doubt, anxiety and uncertainty, someone who was a lonely man, who lived on his nerves and was vulnerable to depression, sometimes struggling with the stresses of office (Davenport-Hines 1992).

Macmillan was, according to James Margach (1978: 115), a 'brilliant communicator' and a 'sophisticated performer'. Perhaps it would be better to say that he made himself one - taking political presentation seriously, working hard and taking advice to develop his skills, and constantly having to overcome nerves and a shyness that could make him sick before big parliamentary or public appearances. At his peak he could dominate the House of Commons - 'one of the most effective parliamentarians of the age', as Richard Thorpe (2010: 538) puts it - being particularly 'formidable at question time and dealing with interruptions' (Shrapnel 1978: 31-2). He regularly outclassed and got the better of Hugh Gaitskell as Leader of the Opposition in their parliamentary contests, but was more equally matched and faced tougher battles when Harold Wilson took over as Labour leader. Outside of parliament, although he was 'always wary lest public relations became a substitute for policy' (Thorpe 2010: 442), the Macmillan era saw some distinctly 'modern' political PR techniques being used - the 'photo opportunity', for instance, with the prime minister sporting a big white fur hat on a trip for talks in Moscow, and more organised political marketing with a professional advertising company being hired to boost the Tory campaign in the run up to the 1959 general election. Between the general elections of 1955 and 1959 the proportion of the population with television sets nearly doubled (to reach three-quarters of all homes) and Macmillan quickly grasped the significance and potential of this development. He certainly hated and feared what he called 'the modern torture chamber' (Ramsden 1998: 359) of the TV studio but nevertheless mastered the requirements of broadcasts, interviews and image projection on the small screen, coming across as 'urbane, witty, eloquent, moving' (Blake 1980). Macmillan was, says Michael Cockerell (1988: 52), 'highly skilled as a television performer and extremely adept at presenting the cameras with favourable images of himself and his government.' 'Macmillan was well aware', noted biographer Anthony Sampson 1967: 157), 'as Baldwin had been with the wireless thirty years before, that the new medium gave him a unique chance to by-pass the press Lords and project himself - and nobody else - to the nation.'

In running the government, Macmillan - like Edward Heath, afterwards - seemed almost happier working with civil servants as his closest policy advisers, aides and confidants rather than more party-political figures. He gathered his civil service private secretaries plus the Cabinet Secretary round him like virtually a private 'court' or a Number 10 'family'. He has been described as 'a master of acquiring ideas' and 'receptive to the suggestions of others' (Davenport-Hines 1992: 289), keeping his small private office staff fully 'in the picture' of all that was going on, and encouraging them to give their views: 'he liked to throw out ideas and provoke ideas' (Horne 1989: 161). Macmillan trusted Norman Brook, the Secretary to the Cabinet and Head of the Civil Service up to the end of 1962, implicitly and relied greatly on him for advice and support across the board, including on handling the Cabinet, international issues (Brook travelled with him on overseas trips), security and intelligence matters, and even ministerial reshuffles, appointments and dismissals (Seldon and Meakin 2016: 126-138). John Wyndham was brought in as an unpaid personal aide in the private office, handling more of the work on the party political side. (A rich, aristocratic landowner, he had worked with Macmillan during the war.) But it is striking how unusually influential officials like Freddie Bishop, Tim Bligh and Philip de Zulueta were in the private secretary role under Macmillan, and how personally identified with him they became - to a degree that some commentators describe them as playing 'important roles in deciding government policy', and as consulted and used by the prime minister 'often in preference to the ministers responsible and their departments' (Lamb 1995: 1). A minister in fact once complained of 'government by private secretary' (Aldous and Lee 1996: 150). Macmillan also looked to use his own private source of economic advice, feeding in suggestions and ideas he picked up from the strongly-Keynesian Oxford economist Roy Harrod, to provoke and irritate the Treasury.

Macmillan's approach to government attracted the 'presidential' tag at the time and subsequently. Some observers talk of his 'full control' of government (Lamb 1995: 1), but that is a slightly misleading description. 'Cabinets were run tightly', as Peter Hennessy (2000: 255) put it; 'he was very much in charge.' He imposed his authority on the government in a way that Eden had never managed to, and he certainly 'dominated his Cabinet from the start', as Robert Blake (1997: 280) noted. 'He knew what he wanted but he was a believer in delegation and he did not bother his colleagues with detailed supervision. They were expected to get on with the job.' Very deliberately, he did not constantly interfere and fuss as Eden had done, but projected an image of calm authority. Maintaining a 'strong central control over government strategy' (Thorpe 2010: 376), however, and knowing from long experience how to operate the levers of power, he nevertheless mainly looked to keep a tight personal grip on foreign policy and economic policy.

Forming his government, Macmillan denied 'Rab' Butler the job of Foreign Secretary he craved and instead he was made Home Secretary (and also, until 1961 Lord Privy Seal and Leader of the House of Commons), before becoming Deputy Prime Minister and First Secretary of State in 1962. Butler stayed amazingly loyal to Macmillan (who remained wary of him), carved out an influential role supervising home affairs policy, and often acted as a general ministerial trouble-shooter. Keeping on the compliant Selwyn Lloyd as Foreign Secretary (until 1960) signalled that Macmillan intended to drive foreign policy from Number 10. Meanwhile, Macmillan got through chancellors of the exchequer faster than Henry VIII got through wives - four in seven years. He clashed with his first, Peter Thorneycroft, who resigned in January 1958 after losing a Cabinet battle over public spending cuts and economic priorities (Macmillan purported to shrug this off as 'little local difficulties') (Horne 1989: 74). Heathcoat Amory (1958-60) was very much the prime minister's lieutenant, while Selwyn Lloyd (1960-62) disappointed him by not in the end delivering the sort of positive policy he wanted to see at the Treasury, his final chancellor, Reginald Maudling (1962-64) being more in tune with his economically expansionist instincts. Lloyd's dismissal was a central plank of the 'Night of the Long Knives' purge in 1962, when Macmillan also fired six other Cabinet ministers - a third of the Cabinet. At one level this refreshed the government and brought in some new talent, but the way it was done and the political and press reaction it sparked were disastrous. Macmillan seemed to have lost his nerve, panicked, misjudged the situation and acted brutally. He was left looking politically weaker, rather than stronger, than before; his personal popularity ratings took a big hit; and it was a watershed moment in his premiership, sparking a sense of a prime minister losing control and with his authority on the slide.

Context

'Events, dear boy, events', Macmillan is supposed to have said when asked what was the greatest challenge for a statesman. The quote may actually be apocryphal but an argument can be made that, as prime minister, Macmillan successfully rode and exploited 'events' up to 1959-60 but from around 1961 onwards there were growing signs of him and his government being more at their mercy (Lamb 1995; Jefferys 1997).

The Conservatives' 1959 general election victory was a personal triumph for Macmillan. The Conservatives were 5 per cent behind Labour in the polls when he took over in January 1957, and at times over that year and also into 1958 Labour had a double-digit poll lead, but the Tories edged back ahead in August 1958 and polled more strongly still after the 1959 tax-cutting budget. Election-day in October 1959 saw the

Conservatives win a third successive victory, increasing their overall majority to 100 seats and winning one and a half million votes more than the Labour Party (49.4 per cent voted Conservative, with Labour on 43.8 per cent). Central to the result was the economic 'feel-good' factor provided at that point by the combination of full employment, stable prices, growth, and a strong balance of payments - although the government could not always keep all those balls in the air at the same time over its tenure of office. 'Life's Better Under the Conservatives. Don't Let Labour Ruin It', was the Conservatives' resonant advertising slogan for the election (Thorpe 2010: 442). 'Most of our people have never had it so good', as Macmillan himself had put it in a speech the year before (although this remark is often taken out of context and was more a warning against taking increased prosperity for granted, and of the dangers of inflation, rather than simply boastful boosterism) (Horne 1989: 64-5). In a memorable contemporary magazine cartoon, the election-winning prime minister was depicted sitting surrounded by a television set, a washing machine, a fridge and a car, saying 'Well, gentlemen, I think we all fought a good fight. . . ' (Ramsden 1998: 368).

Treasury officials in this period apparently kept a tally of the number of times Macmillan (as chancellor and then prime minister) mentioned in any one week Stockton-on-Tees, his old constituency in the North-East (up to 1945), devastated by unemployment and the slump between the wars. Macmillan consistently pressed for economically expansionary policies against Treasury caution and orthodoxy, urging one of his chancellors (in 1963) to go 'for the big stuff . . . expand or die' (Thorpe 2010: 546). A more cynical view, as put by Harold Wilson, is that as prime minister, 'he never lost control of the Treasury, which he saw as the means of creating a favourable financial system for winning elections.' Macmillan 'played the [trade] cycle', argued Wilson, timing give-away budgets or reflationary policies (in 1958-59 and 1962-63 periods) for their electoral impact (Wilson 1977: 315). The problem was, as critics said, that Tory policy involved 'either too little too late or too much too late' (Turner 1994: 249), the different measures and the turning on and off of the budgetary taps in response to various crises exacerbating the 'stop-go' swings of the economic cycle rather than promoting a stable growth path. In the last year or two of his premiership, with the 'Modernisation of Britain' initiative, he tried to focus on longer-term structural and productive aspects of economic organisation, and on new tripartite and dirigiste planning machinery (how to 'boom without busting', as he put it), but there was relatively little in the way of concrete results to show from that by the time he left office.

On the foreign policy front, Macmillan's first priority had been to move speedily on from Suez, repair relations with the White House and rebuild the 'special relationship'. He put a lot of effort into his personal relationships with Eisenhower and then Kennedy, winning from them the important prize of access to US missiles and sharing of nuclear technology to maintain Britain's nuclear deterrent capability. Macmillan sometimes talked in terms of Britain being like the Greeks in the Roman (American) empire but perhaps that was a necessary self-deception that exaggerated the closeness of the relationship and the extent of British importance to and influence with the US.

Macmillan liked to think in long-term and strategic terms about the political, economic and defence issues facing Britain and the West (commissioning big Whitehall reviews such as the 'Future Policy' exercise in 1959, and writing personal big 'think pieces' like 'The Grand Design' in 1961, to put the problems and decisions in a broader framework). He realistically recognised (ahead of many in his party) that Britain had no future as a colonial power, the run down of Britain's colonial commitments in Africa gathering pace during his premiership as he famously talked about the 'wind of change' in that continent (Thorpe 2010: 457). The counterpart to this was a European 'tilt' but, constrained by a divided party, an uncertain public, and Commonwealth connections, Macmillan had to move slowly (perhaps too slowly) and carefully towards negotiations to see if Britain could join the Common Market, which foundered on de Gaulle's suspicion and resentment of the US-UK axis. The French veto in January 1963 brought the centrepiece of Macmillan's overall strategy - linking together modernisation on the home/ economic front, a new international role, and a new Conservative approach and appeal after a dozen years in power and with an election on the horizon - crashing down.

The government's troubles had in fact been mounting over 1961 and 1962 with unpopular deflationary economic measures, including a 'pay pause' and tax increases, to tackle inflation, pressure on the pound and balance of payments problems; an increasingly hostile and critical press; Labour moving ahead in the opinion polls; evidence of a Liberal revival also taking votes off the Conservatives; and Tory set backs and defeats in key by-elections. Labour leader Hugh Gaitskell managed to beat back challenges to his leadership, and started to look more commanding and like a prime-minister-in-waiting. When he suddenly died in January 1963, Harold Wilson became Leader of the Opposition and projected a dynamic, 'modern' and 'classless' image that contrasted strongly to an apparently fading prime minister. This chimed with a wider shift in popular culture and social attitudes (expressed in part through the so-called 'satirical boom') critical of 'establishment' values and institutions, and leaving the prime minister, in his late-sixties, looking out of date and old fashioned. On top of all this, the government started to seem accident-prone, with a damaging series of spy scandals culminating in the extraordinary and squalid sex-and-security saga of the Profumo affair in 1963, when the War Minister had to resign. The government's authority was rocked to its foundations, Conservative MPs were shaken, unhappy and worried about the electoral fallout, and it was the beginning of the end for Macmillan, who had handled the issue badly, and came across as tired, uncertain and out-of-touch.

Conclusion

In the end, Macmillan's exit was a rather messy one. He dithered over the summer and early autumn of 1963, wondering whether he should resign before the next general election or not, and changing his mind a number of times. But then sudden illness, and the need for an emergency prostate operation, forced the issue and he decided to quit. It has sometimes been suggested that he thought (wrongly) he had cancer and might die, but his doctors had reassured him and did not advise him to resign. Indecisive and wavering about resignation, it is more probable that he seized on a medical bolt from the blue to provide and rationalise a more-or-less dignified exit, rather than being forced or harried out.

Having been ruthless in his acquisition of the premiership, Macmillan was ruthless in his departure. He unscrupulously manoeuvred and 'fixed' party procedures - and in effect 'bounced' the Queen - to arrange the succession to Lord Home (Alec Douglas-Home) and to block his old rival, Rab Butler (though he later purported to regret this after Home lost the 1964 general election).

Macmillan left parliament in 1964, going back to the family publishing company, writing multiple and lengthy volumes of memoirs the reading of which was described by Enoch Powell as 'akin to chewing cardboard' (Davenport-Hines 1992: 333), and enjoying himself as Chancellor of Oxford university. From time to time he entertained fantasy ideas of a come-back in a coalition government of national unity to deal with the crises facing the country. He had always despised the House of Lords ('the morgue', he called it) but finally in 1984, aged 90, accepted a peerage and strutted the political stage for the last time, making some witty, memorable and mischievous attacks on Mrs Thatcher's philosophy and policies, and the direction in which she was taking the country. He died in 1986.

Macmillan's significance and legacy remain disputed. To Peter Hennessy (2000: 531-2), he falls into the 'promise unfulfilled' category, aiming to be a 'system-mover' and a moderniser of the economy and British society, reversing relative economic decline, but someone who identified the problems rather than overcoming them. He has been more often viewed favourably on the political centre-left than on the right. David Marquand (2008: xii), for instance, described him as 'the nearest thing to a great prime minister in the post-war years' while Roy Jenkins (1988: 127) put him, as a peace-time head of government, in a group (though not at the top) with Asquith,

Baldwin and Attlee in that category, rating him as one of the 'more significant' prime ministers of the twentieth century.

On the Conservative side, there is a sense in which Edward Heath (whom Macmillan did not particularly rate as a leader and prime minister) carried forward his approach and strategy, finally taking the country into the EEC, intervening heavily in the economy, and trying to pursue a form of 'corporatist' planning through agreements with unions and business and an incomes policy. But Heath's failure opened the way to a very different form of Conservative politics and a different approach to public spending, inflation, the state and markets, and post-1979 Macmillan tended to be seen on the right of the political spectrum as out-of-date, semi-socialist and someone wh had been a bad prime minister, sharing responsibility for creating the problems Thatcher was sorting out. Later, David Cameron, when in opposition, let it be known that he kept a photograph of Macmillan in his office, suggesting he was one of his political heroes and perhaps trying to signal that he, too, could be a 'One Nation' election-winner, though the austerity economics that marked his time as prime minister together with the mishandling of the European issue, resulting in Brexit, arguably took the country in the opposite direction to that which Macmillan had worked towards.

References

Aldous, R and Lee, S. (1996). "Staying in the Game": Harold Macmillan and Britain's World Role', in R. Aldous and S. Lee (eds). *Harold Macmillan and Britain's World Role.* London: Macmillan.

Ball, S. (2004). *The Guardsmen: Harold Macmillan, Three Friends and the World They Made.* London: HarperCollins.

Blake, R. (1980). 'Grand Old Man'. *London Review of Books.* 2 (8), 1 May.

Blake, R. (1997). *The Conservative Party from Peel to Major.* London: Heinemann.

Catterall, P. (2003). *The Macmillan Diaries: The Cabinet Years 1950-1957.* London: Macmillan.

Charmley, J. (2008). *A History of Conservative Politics since 1830.* London: Palgrave Macmillan.

Clarke, P. (1991). *A Question of Leadership.* London: Hamish Hamilton.

Cockerell, M. (1988). *Live from Number 10: the inside story of prime ministers and television.* London: Faber & Faber.

Davenport-Hines, R. (1992). *The Macmillans.* London: Heinemann.

Evans, B. and Taylor, A. (1996). *From Salisbury to Major: continuity and change in Conservative Politics.* Manchester: Manchester University Press.

Hennessy, P. (2000). *The Prime Minister: The Office and Its Holders Since 1945.* London: Allen Lane.

Horne, A. (1988). *Macmillan 1894-1956* London: Macmillan.

Horne, A. (1989). *Macmillan 1957-1986.* London: Macmillan.

Hutchinson, G. (1980). *The Last Edwardian at No.10: An Impression of Harold Macmillan.* London: Quartet Books.

Jefferys, K. (1997). *Retreat From New Jerusalem: British Politics 1951-64.* London: Macmillan.

Jenkins, R. (1988). *Gallery of Twentieth Century Portraits.* London: David & Charles.

Lamb, R. (1995). *The Macmillan Years 1957-1963: The Emerging Truth.* London: John Murray.

Margach, J. (1978). *The Abuse of Power: The War between Downing Street and the Media.* London: W.H. Allen.

Marquand, D. (2008). *Britain Since 1918: The Strange Career of British Democracy.* London: Weidenfeld & Nicolson.

Powell, E. (1987). 'Macmillan: The Case Against', *The Spectator,* 10 January: 15-16.

Ramsden, J. (1998). *An Appetite for Power: A. History of the Conservative Party Since 1830.* London: HarperCollins.

Sampson, A. (1967). *Macmillan: A Study in Ambiguity.* London: Penguin.

Seldon, A. and Meakin, J. (2016). *The Cabinet Office 1916-2016.* London: Biteback.

Shrapnel, N. (1978). *The Performers.* London: Constable.

Theakston, K. (2010). *After Number 10: Former Prime Ministers in British Politics.* London: Palgrave Macmillan.

Thorpe, D.R. (2010). *Supermac: The Life of Harold Macmillan.* London: Chatto & Windus.

Turner, J. (1994). *Macmillan.* London: Longman.

Williams, C. (2009). *Harold Macmillan.* London: Weidenfeld & Nicolson.

Wilson, H. (1977). *A Prime Minister on Prime Ministers.* London: Michael Joseph and   Weidenfeld & Nicolson.

Chapter 6
Alec Douglas-Home (1963-64)

Alec Douglas-Home was Conservative prime minister for just under a year, from 19 October 1963 to 16 October 1964 - in some ways, an interim prime minister heading an interim government. To critics, he seemed an anachronistic one-off in the context of the second half of the 20th century - representing 'the very end of the thin purple line', as David Cannadine (1992: 667) put it in his account of the 'decline and fall of the British aristocracy'. He was modest, decent, amiable and often caricatured as a tweedy aristocratic amateur. But his political career spanned over 40 years and he should not be underestimated as one of the 'great survivors' of British politics. He was, for all his charm and courtesy, a shrewd and tough political operator – 'iron painted to look like wood', as Harold Macmillan said of him (Thorpe 1996: 8).

Party Leadership
There is a sense in which Douglas-Home's rivals for the premiership in 1963 did not see him coming until it was too late. For much of his political career he had seemed an unassuming but quietly competent second- or third-rank figure, little-known to the wider public (Dickie 1964). He was first elected to parliament in 1931 in his late-twenties, later serving as parliamentary private secretary to prime minister Neville Chamberlain (whom he admired and served loyally to the bitter end, though escaping being damaged by association with appeasement and the 'men of Munich'). He lost his seat in 1945 and was out of the Commons until 1950 but the following year, on the death of his father, had to move across to the House of Lords as the 14th Earl of Home, and it was from that base that he moved up the ladder as minister of state at the Scottish Office 1951-55 before entering the Cabinet as Commonwealth Relations Secretary under Eden, continuing in that job under Macmillan while also becoming Leader of the House of Lords. His

appointment as Foreign Secretary in 1960 was briefly controversial, Labour and the press fussing about the first peer in the role for twenty years as a democratic affront, but he proved himself skilful and effective in that post, working well with the prime minister and with his Foreign Office deputy in the Commons (who was also a Cabinet minister), Edward Heath, who carried special responsibility for European issues. But in his late-fifties, as a hereditary peer, this must have seemed about as far as Home's political career could take him.

The circumstances in which Home became prime minister in a short, intense period in the autumn of 1963 would make a good political drama - a play or film by the likes of James Graham, Howard Brenton or Peter Morgan, exploring the interplay of politics, duty and ambition, and opportunity, motive and character, across various 'public' (front-stage) and 'private' (back-stage) scenes. The background to the drama was the decay of the Macmillan regime, with the prime minister battered by events and his reputation starting to crumble, shilly-shallying about whether and when to stand down, before suddenly falling ill and, from his hospital bed, ruthlessly manipulating the situation to manage the succession. There was, inevitably, in the era when Conservative leaders still 'emerged' rather than being elected, and there were no fixed selection rules, a complex behind-the-scenes process of 'high politics' manoeuvre, intrigue and poker-play. This was later controversially and publicly - and damagingly for Douglas-Home and the image of party unity - bitterly condemned as a secretive and cynical Old-Etonian 'magic circle' fix by Tory politician Iain Macleod, who had found himself on the losing side of the succession struggle (Macleod 1964). Meanwhile, Labour leader Harold Wilson spoke witheringly of 'the machinery of aristocratic cabal' (Young 1970: 169). But there were also elements of public political theatre because of the way in which the Conservative party conference at Blackpool took on something of the character of an American nominating convention (though the party mass membership did not of course have a vote at that time). Various leadership rivals - R.A. Butler, Lord Hailsham (Quintin Hogg), Reginald Maudling - found their prospects affected by 'dud' speeches or mis-firing campaigning antics, while the part of 'reluctant candidate' could have been specially written for Alec Home (see: Thorpe 1996: 270-315; Dutton 2006: 44-60; Gilmour and Garnett 1997: 186-203).

Home was lucky in the timing of the contest. The recent passage of the Peerage Act gave him and also Hailsham a window of opportunity in which they could renounce their hereditary peerages and become able to stand for election to the House of Commons. His chances were helped also because there was no single obvious alternative to Macmillan and no overwhelmingly strong swell of support behind other possible contenders. As Macmillan himself noted at one point: 'the party in the country wants Hogg; the parliamentary party wants Maudling or Butler; the Cabinet wants Butler' (Catterall 2011: 607). The outgoing prime minister seems at one point to have favoured Hailsham, and then switched to backing Home, but was consistent throughout in his aim of blocking Butler. Moreover, for all his seniority, status and long experience, a sizeable group of right-wing Tory MPs hated Butler and wouldn't have him as leader on any terms.

Macmillan cunningly devised a procedure for taking 'soundings' of opinion among Conservative ministers, MPs, peers and the party grass roots that showed that what is important in any election or selection is not just who is voting or expressing a view, but how the question or questions are framed, and who is counting the votes or weighing the answers. There is a strong suspicion that Macmillan and the party managers and grandees working with and for him knew the answer(s) they wanted, and acted accordingly. Asking the 'selectorate' for first and second preferences, and also for negative opinions - who they were definitely opposed to - together with some 'creative accountancy' in adding up the figures, helped skew the whole exercise in favour of Home as the 'unity' candidate or the compromise figure everyone could supposedly rally round.

Home was popular with the Tory rank and file mass membership. His ministerial colleagues liked and respected him (or mostly so - Macleod being a notable enemy). Though probably not scheming for power from the start, he was not so self-effacing or unconfident as to turn down his chance of the premiership when it came to him, and he acted with some calculation, steel and determination during the succession crisis. He may have been a surprising choice as prime minister but he was not really an unwilling one. He could could have been stymied if Butler, Hailsham and Maudling had united in refusing to serve under him, but they caved in (though Enoch Powell and Iain Macleod would not join his government).

Home's appointment as prime minister was met with widespread public and media surprise and shock, even incredulity. The Conservatives seemed to be admitting that they could not find a prime minister from their 363 MPs in the House of Commons. The Labour Opposition were relieved at the selection of someone they thought would be easily beatable. Constitutionally, the clock was being turned back more than 60 years by the first prime-ministerial appointment from the House of Lords since the time of the Marquess of Salisbury, who left Number 10 in 1902 (the year before Home was born). Home also won a place as a footnote in constitutional history as the first PM to have disclaimed a peerage and as one who was not actually a member of either House of Parliament during the fortnight between his renunciation of his hereditary titles and his return to the Commons following victory at a by-election (fortunately for him, a seat in Scotland, which he could be parachuted into, had become vacant a few months earlier).

Ideology and aims

Douglas-Home was a very traditional Tory and not an ideological politician or a 'conviction leader' like Thatcher later (who was a lowly junior minister in his government), nor an imaginative and innovative figure like his predecessor Macmillan. He 'thought practically rather than philosophically', being 'a man of principle rather than principles' and not a politician who 'bubbled with new ideas and fresh initiatives', according to one biographer (Young 1970: 84, 194, 271). Earlier in his career he had been drawn into the circle of Noel Skelton, but it was Eden who was most associated with the 'property owning democracy' theme of Skelton's vision of 'constructive conservatism'.

Although Douglas-Home could be seen as somewhat to the right of centre compared to Macmillan (and later Heath) - indeed with leanings towards 'a form of right-wing aristocratic paternalism', according to one commentator (Dutton 2006: 70) - he was far from being a reactionary or blimpish figure. Douglas Hurd (2004) summed up Douglas-Home's style of conservatism well: 'He distrusted abstract philosophising, whether of left or right. He had no rigid devotion to the free market or to any other economic or social creed . . . He [believed] that Conservatives should use their traditional skills not to avert change but to guide it.' It was a rather traditional and defensive stance: looking for a 'reasonable compromise', trying to solve practical problems and 'doing the right thing at the right time', rather than dying in the ditch or making a radical ideological lurch.

In any case the situation Douglas-Home faced allowed little scope for anything like a major policy or ideological overhaul or change of direction. 'All our policies had been put into place and . . . there was nothing to do', he once explained to Peter Hennessy (2000: 289). One factor here was that by the early 1960s, as David Dutton (2006: 69) puts it, the Conservative party 'was firmly entrenched in the centre ground of the post-war consensus, its policies . . . more interventionist, corporatist indeed, than ever before or since. Douglas-Home as prime minister did nothing to change this.' Moreover, coming in to Number 10 after his party had already been in power for twelve years and with the clock ticking down to a general election, he had no time or opportunity to develop a programme of his own and little option but to continue with Macmillan's 'modernising' agenda, though the 'grouse-moor image' that critics and opponents hung around his neck, and his own professed ignorance of economics (fatally confessing a year before he became PM that he had to work out economic problems with the aid of matchsticks), made it hard for him to be a convincing spokesman for that sort of political project (Thorpe 1996: 257).

Political style and skills

Douglas-Home turned out to be a rather better prime minister than many expected or predicted at the time, or have judged since, but he was much more effective in terms of the 'inner face' of government and administration than in relation to the 'outer face' and the more public tasks of political leadership. Though he recognised (Home 1976: 192) that key to Macmillan's political success was his 'absolute mastery of every parliamentary occasion' and his gifts as a 'showman', Douglas-Home not only failed to measure up in those terms but actually recoiled from the more performative aspects of the job and at marketing himself. While it is true to say that he and Attlee were the least media-conscious post-war prime ministers (Hennessy 2000: 282), that was perhaps more damaging for Douglas-Home because, as he only belatedly understood himself, by the 1960s television had become one of the main channels of communication with the public and - whatever he himself wryly noted as the drawback of his un-telegenic, gaunt and cadaverous appearance - it was self-defeating to shrink from being 'an actor on the screen' and to distrust the arts of image-building and projection (Home 1976: 203). In his first television broadcast as prime minister he played to his character by promising 'no stunts . . . just plain straight talking' (Thorpe 1996: 320-21) but, in a year inevitably dominated by the looming general election, that approach undoubtedly handed the advantage to Labour leader Harold Wilson, a master of political presentation, communication and theatrics.

Though he could perform well enough in front of an audience of the party faithful or when speaking on his specialist subject of foreign policy, Douglas-Home was more used to, and better suited to, the calmer atmosphere of the House of Lords rather than the partisan rough and tumble of the Commons, and the confident and fluent Wilson regularly trounced him in their gladiatorial jousts at question time. He staged a busy programme of speaking tours around the country to make himself better known to the public but, as even a sympathetic biographer admitted, he was 'no crowd-swayer' and 'had no gift for raising an audience's temperature' (Young 1970: 186). Douglas-Home did become rather more sure-footed in the parliamentary arena as time went on, but during the heat of the 1964 election campaign his gaffe in referring in a TV interview to old-age pensions as 'donations' (Thorpe 1996: 366) and his inability to deal with heckling and disruption during his platform speeches further underlined his presentational weaknesses relative to Wilson in what was widely seen at the time as a very 'presidential' contest (Howard and West 1965).

In contrast, once the famous black door of Number 10 was closed, Douglas-Home had a surer touch in terms of running the government and dealing with the prime minister's daily business. Rather like Attlee, Douglas-Home was something of a model chief as far as the top civil servants were concerned: he was on top of the paperwork in his red boxes and was calm (much more 'unflappable' in fact than Macmillan), clear and decisive in decision-making. He chaired cabinet meetings briskly and effectively, and cut back and reorganised some of the cabinet committee sprawl that had developed under Macmillan. If he had had more time in Number 10 he would have liked to have gone further in reforming the procedures and machinery of government (Home 1976: 202). It was revealing that Burke Trend, the Cabinet Secretary 1963-73, thought him the best of the four prime ministers he served as an orderly manager of cabinet government - though, of course, he had hugely less impact as a policy initiator than the other three, and not just because of his short tenure.

In fact Douglas-Home himself thought that a prime minister should devolve decision-making and largely leave ministers to get on with their jobs. He had, as David Dutton (2006: 72) says, 'no desire to keep every aspect of government policy within his personal control.' In any case, the weakness of his political position - a legacy of the 1963 leadership struggle - meant that Douglas-Home 'needed his cabinet colleagues more than they needed him', as historian Kevin Jefferys (1997: 186) put it. Of all the mid-term post-war prime-ministerial successions, Douglas-Home's stands out for involving no dismissals from the old cabinet by the new PM (though, of course, two outgoing ministers refused to serve, as noted earlier). There were a couple of new cabinet ministers appointed and Selwyn Lloyd - dismissed by Macmillan in 1962 - was brought back, but otherwise there was no brutal shake-up on the scale seen under Theresa May and Boris Johnson, to pick much later examples, and fewer changes even than Macmillan had made on assuming power back in 1957. Given how important it was for Douglas-Home to hold the party together, it was not surprising that the old faces around the cabinet table largely remained in place. Among the senior ministers, Maudling continued as Chancellor of the Exchequer, while Butler became Foreign Secretary and Heath assumed a new powerful role heading up trade, industry and regional development.

With all his experience and expertise in foreign affairs, it was not surprising that this was the one area of policy in which Douglas-Home was active and closely involved. (Holt 2014). His ambitions for Number 10 thwarted yet again, Butler was disheartened and a somewhat fading presence in the government; Home in effect acted as his own Foreign Secretary as well as prime minister. Though always perfectly courteous towards Butler, and aware that he had needed his leadership rival's acquiescence to become PM, Douglas-Home was, however, unsentimentally planning to replace his Foreign Secretary had he won re-election in 1964. Foreign powers were well aware of the uncertain prospects of Douglas-Home's administration and the possibility of a change in government in London. Lyndon Johnson, who became US president in November 1963, quickly decided that Douglas-Home was simply a stop-gap, anticipating Wilson would soon be in power. In contrast to the close personal relations that Macmillan had forged with Eisenhower and Kennedy, Douglas-Home and Johnson did not seem to hit it off, and there were UK/US policy disagreements over trade with Cuba and on some other issues.

When it came to economic and domestic policy, Douglas-Home was a much less credible leadership figure. Macmillan before him, and Wilson, Heath and most other premiers after him were deeply and continually involved in economic policy-making. In contrast, Douglas-Home largely left matters to his Chancellor of the Exchequer, Reginald Maudling, whose 'dash for growth' was in full swing though with increasing signs through 1964 of 'overheating' and strains in the economy, and particularly inflationary pressures and a rapidly deteriorating balance of payments situation and risks to the pound. 'There are two problems in my life', Douglas-Home once reportedly said. 'The political ones are insoluble, and the economic ones are incomprehensible' (Keegan and Pennant-Rae 1979: 80). The real problem in 1963-4 was the interaction of the two dimensions, in that he had little option but to continue with an economic strategy he had inherited that risked the Conservatives' reputation for economic competence, while hoping that the election finishing-line would be crossed before the bubbling crisis got out of control and hard decisions   and counter-measures would be needed.

The government's main domestic policy achievement - the abolition of Resale Price Maintenance (RPM), the system allowing price-fixing by producers of goods - also highlighted Douglas-Home's dependence on his ministers. If it had been left to himself, he would not have originated this contentious measure, but the relevant minister, the tough-minded Edward Heath, wanted to show his modernising mettle and boost his own reputation. Small shopkeepers - the bedrock of many local Tory constituency parties - were outraged, but Heath bulldozed it through, overcoming strong Cabinet opposition with prime-ministerial backing, after threatening to resign, and in the teeth of the biggest parliamentary revolt by unhappy Conservative MPs since the overthrow of Neville Chamberlain in 1940. It could be claimed the RPM initiative showed the government had not run out of ideas, but it was arguably politically mistimed and, while the electoral impact is hard to definitively pin down, looking back, Douglas-Home himself thought it might have helped lose the party a few crucial seats in what was in the end a very tight race.

Context

From the start, the odds were stacked against Douglas-Home. He was in effect fighting a rearguard action. He inherited a divided and demoralised party and a tired government running out of steam, simply hanging on, and facing what looked like being an electoral rout (Conservative Central Office estimated the party would have lost an election by 100 seats in November 1963). The Conservatives seemed old-fashioned and out-of-date, and after 13 years in power the 'time for a change' mood was hard to resist in the face of a revived and dynamic Labour Opposition and shifts in the wider climate of opinion in the early-1960s hostile to Conservative and 'Establishment' values and traditions, many of which Douglas-Home himself seemed to embody.

Douglas-Home's personal poll ratings were always well behind Wilson's, and he trailed behind the Labour leader in the polls with a bigger gap than that between the Conservatives as a party and the Labour party. But his decision to hang on and wait almost to the very last date possible for a general election paid off as the polls narrowed over 1964 and Labour's lead shrank. The October 1964 general election turned out to be much more of a close-run thing than many had expected at the start of Douglas-Home's premiership. Labour squeaked into office with only a small majority of four seats. Labour's 12.2 million votes total was actually down by 11,000 compared to 1959 (its vote share of 44.1 per cent only up by 0.3 per cent); crucial to the outcome were a Liberal revival (nearly doubling their vote tally to 3 million, albeit winning only three more seats) and an overall drop in the Conservative vote of over 1.7 million votes (a fall of 6 per cent). A few hundred extra Conservative votes in a small number of key marginals could have changed the final result. As it was, Douglas-Home had done much better than expected - most Conservatives had expected a bigger defeat, his achievement being, in a sense, to postpone or help hold that off until the next time around, in 1966.

Conclusion

Harold Wilson thought the Conservatives would have won the 1964 general election if Butler, not Douglas-Home, had been the Tory leader. Indeed, Douglas-Home himself, came to think it might have been better if Butler had been picked in 1963 since anyone else was going to be seen as an 'unnatural' successor.

Macmillan, too, came to believe that the premiership was a job too far for Douglas-Home who, he thought, 'did his best - with courage and dignity. But he could not impress himself on Parlt. [sic] or people enough for a PM.' Looking back, Macmillan thought Home 'didn't have enough fire in his belly', and that it would after all have been better if Butler had got the leadership because he would have won in 1964 (Clark 1998: 329; Dutton 2006: 110).

In the real political world of 1964-65, as opposed to the alternative 'what ifs' universe, Douglas-Home continued as Tory leader for nine months after his general election defeat. But, no match for Wilson, he was soon being described by Labour Cabinet minister Richard Crossman as 'totally ineffective as Leader of the Opposition' and as 'our asset' (Theakston 2010: 170). His heart was not really in it and ultimately he was not willing to fight hard to keep the position.

Addressing the problems of democracy and legitimacy that had surrounded his own emergence as party leader, Douglas-Home oversaw the introduction of new procedures in February 1965 by which future leaders would be elected by Tory MPs. (Ten years later, he chaired a party committee that introduced rules also allowing a leader to be challenged and removed.) If he had immediately put himself up for election he would have very likely won the ballot, in the absence at that stage of a clear successor, and perhaps bought more time for his leadership. However, discontent built up within the party, with calls for more robust leadership and suggestions of a covert campaign to force him out involving Heath's supporters and allies, if not Heath himself. As rumours, plotting and press speculation continued, Douglas-Home declared in June 1965 that he would be carrying on but then Wilson's announcement that there would be no general election that year made him more vulnerable still by giving time for any new leader to settle in before facing the voters. After that, Douglas-Home's position collapsed pretty quickly. Criticism in the Tory press increased and the Conservatives (and Douglas-Home personally, compared to Wilson) fell further behind in the opinion polls. He decided to stand down while he could do so with dignity rather than be forced out in a putsch, announcing his resignation as party leader on 22 July 1965, and Edward Heath then became the first elected Conservative leader.

After 1965 Douglas-Home went on to provide a model of dignified, loyal and supportive behaviour towards all his successors as Conservative leader (when their turn to quit the leadership came, not all of them were willing or able to be so magnanimous and follow his example). Somewhat like Arthur Balfour earlier in the 20th century, Douglas-Home's time as prime minister was a short and unsuccessful interlude in a longer ministerial and political career, which in his case continued with a constructive post-leadership role and front-bench posts for another decade, including a second stint as Foreign Secretary in Edward Heath's government 1970-74. In all, fourteen former prime ministers in British history have staged come backs and served in the governments of later administrations and under other PMs, but Douglas-Home is the only example of this pattern after 1945 and none of his successors in Number 10 have (to date) gone back into government (Theakston 2010). He finally retired from full-time front-bench politics in 1974 and returned to the House of Lords with a life peerage, continuing into his final years to be a respected, even somewhat revered, Tory elder statesman figure.

Douglas-Home is too easily written-off as an outmoded, amateurish, P.G. Wodehouse-type figure, out-of-date and out of his depth. Tony Benn rightly viewed him as 'a much underestimated figure . . . very competent and hard-working', shrewdly commenting that 'that's why the Tories picked him, they wanted a straight man after a fixer' (Thorpe 1996: 375). On the other hand, there is much force in Ian Gilmour's conclusion that in 'choosing him the Conservative party was pleasing itself rather than protecting its future' (Gilmour and Garnett 1997: 202). He may have been the natural 'compromise leader' in 1963 but he had clear limitations for a party needing to fight an imminent general election in a difficult climate of opinion and seeking to promote a 'modernising' agenda. But if he was something of a stopgap, the eventual outcome of the 1964 general election also showed he was no pushover (Clarke 1996:

293). And he deserves high marks for his decency, probity and honesty (clearly being in a different moral league to, for instance, someone like Boris Johnson), and his performance as a steadying figure and as a traditional-style chairman of the Cabinet should not be disparaged. As a very short-tenure 'suffix' prime minister (at the end of a long period of Tory rule) and something of a 'punctuation mark' between the Macmillan and Wilson eras (Dutton 2006: 109), his prime-ministerial legacy is inevitably a meagre one. However, the controversy over his selection and the changes then made to democratise the Conservatives' leadership rules were significant for the party itself and opened the way for individuals with very different background to Douglas-Home's to follow him into (and ultimately be removed from) the party leadership. There would be no more 1963-style 'fixes', chicanery and (allegedly) 'reluctant peers' at least.

References
Cannadine, D. (1992). *The Decline and Fall of the British Aristocracy*. London: Picador.
Catterall, P. (ed) (2011). *The Macmillan Diaries Vol. II: Prime Minister and After 1957-1966*. London: Macmillan.
Clark, A. (1998). *The Tories*. London: Weidenfeld & Nicolson.
Clarke, P. (1996). *Hope and Glory: Britain 1900-1990*. London: Allen Lane Penguin Press.
Dickie, J. (1964). *The Uncommon Commoner*. London: Pall Mall Press.
Dutton, D. (2006). *Douglas-Home*. London: Haus Publishing.
Gilmour, I. and Garnett, M. (1997). *Whatever Happened to the Tories: The Conservative Party Since 1945*. London: Fourth Estate.
Hennessy, P. (2000). *The Prime Minister: The Office and Its Holders Since 1945*. London: Allen Lane.
Holt, A. (2014). *The Foreign Policy of the Douglas-Home Government*. London: Palgrave.
Home, Lord (1976). *The Way the Wind Blows*. London: Collins.

Howard, A. and West, R. (1965). *The Making of the Prime Minister*. London: Jonathan Cape.

Hurd, D. (2004). 'Home, Alexander Frederick [Alec] Douglas-, fourteenth earl of Home and Baron Home of the Hirsel (1903–1995)', in *Oxford Dictionary of National Biography*, [https://doi.org/10.1093/ref:odnb/60455]

Jefferys, K. (1997). *Retreat From New Jerusalem: British Politics 1951-64*. London: Macmillan.

Keegan, W. And Pennant-Rae, R. (1979). *Who Runs the Economy?* London: Maurice Temple Smith.

Macleod, I. (1964). 'The Tory Leadership', *The Spectator*, 17 January.

Theakston, K. (2010). *After Number 10: Former Prime Ministers in British Politics*. London: Palgrave Macmillan

Thorpe, D.R. (1996). *Alec Douglas-Home*. London: Sinclair-Stevenson.

Young, K. (1970). *Sir Alec Douglas-Home*. London: Dent.

Chapter 7
Harold Wilson (1964-70 and 1974-76)

A North-of-England lower-middle-class grammar school and Oxford university meritocrat, Harold Wilson succeeded three Old Etonian 'Establishment' figures in Downing Street, ending 13 years of Conservative rule, becoming in 1964 the youngest PM of the century up until that point (aged 48), and establishing himself as a dominating figure in British politics from the early 1960s to the mid-1970s (Pimlott 1992; Ziegler 1993). However, Wilson's record of personal policy achievements was in practice rather limited. While initially coming across as a dynamic, reforming and modernising figure of apparent radical promise, he ended up in his last term of office having little to offer beyond a sort of Baldwinesque quiet life, hoping something would turn up. He is often written off as a sort of shabby and unprincipled manager of economic decline and a practitioner of political expediency and gimmickry, a master of political deception. For Wilson, says historian Robert Saunders (2018: 63), 'ambiguity was a political art form. No prime minister of the modern era so baffled and bewildered his contemporaries, or found such a happy home in the fog of political warfare.' Yet Wilson won more general elections than any other prime minister in the twentieth century (four out of the five he fought as Labour Party leader - albeit only one of his victories with a decent parliamentary majority). He is now the only PM in over 60 years to have returned to power after losing an election and enduring a stint in Opposition, winning re-election after only one term in opposition. And Labour was in government for 8 of his 13 years as party leader (1964-70 and 1974-76). After his October 1974 victory, Labour did not win another general election for 23 years. He deserves credit at least for his role in establishing and maintaining Labour as a competitive and credible party of government in his years at the top, something not all his predecessors and successors as party leader were able to do (Thomas-Symonds 2022).

Party Leadership

Wilson did not have a background in the Labour Party as a political activist, or in the trade unions, starting out as an academic researcher and wartime Whitehall official before becoming an MP in 1945 and the youngest Cabinet minister (aged just 31) for over a century, in 1947. He was at the beginning of his career a rather colourless technocratic figure but acquired a reputation as being somewhat on the left when he resigned from Attlee's Cabinet in 1951, along with Aneurin Bevan, in a big argument over health spending and the economic costs of the rearmament programme driven by the Korean War. But he rather dodged and weaved his way through Labour's factional divisions and ideological battles in the 1950s, often disappointing the left while being mistrusted by the right, and sometimes appearing a wily opportunist and a careerist, devious and disloyal – though his political skills were recognised by all. Wilson in fact always remained something of a political loner, with only a small coterie of close personal supporters.

His chance for the leadership came with the sudden death of Hugh Gaitskell early in 1963, Wilson essentially hoovering up support from the centre and the left, while the votes of the Labour right were split between George Brown and James Callaghan (Heppell 2010). He was a devastatingly brilliant and energetic Leader of the Opposition 1963-64 but all the same only squeaked into power in October 1964 with a knife-edge majority of four, timing things well to go on and win a much bigger majority of 97 in the March 1966 general election.

Party unity was always Wilson's first aim. Labour's divisions had seemed deep and almost unhealable under his predecessor. But for Wilson any amount of fudging, trimming or deviousness was justified if it served the overriding end of keeping the party together, bridging political differences, avoiding difficulties, splits or resignations – and helping to keep Labour electable. He always carefully balanced left and right and other political divisions and factors in his government appointments and reshuffles, though the most important departments generally went to centre-right figures. Wilson was not the sort of leader ever able or willing ruthlessly to 'take on' his party and confront its vested interests or sacred cows, as seen, for example, in 1969 when the proposals to reform the trade unions and industrial relations set out in Barbara Castle's *In Place of Strife* were defeated by the combined forces of the trade unions, Labour MPs and opposition from within the Cabinet; Wilson supported the reforms but ultimately would not fight to the death for them.

In the 1970s Labour's internal ideological and factional divisions – on left/right issues and over Europe – became still more intense and fractious. Bernard Donoughue (2005: 11) saw from up close, as one of his advisers, how Wilson 'exhibited consummate skills in holding together a fissiparous party which was increasingly just a loose coalition of different and often conflicting interests and beliefs . . . it was . . . a remarkable feat of party management.' Wilson himself said graphically he had to 'wade through shit' to hold Labour together on the Common Market issue (Healey 1989: 360). 'I'm at my best in a messy middle-of-the-road muddle', Wilson remarked in the middle of one political row in 1975 (Benn 1990: 305). But the gulf between the prime minister and the increasingly left-dominated party machine, Labour headquarters, the party conference, and the NEC – and the left at the parliamentary and Cabinet level - became wider and wider in those years. Perhaps, it has been argued, his concern with trying to preserve Labour Party unity only delayed rather than averted the all-out conflict between Bennite left-wingers and Labour's social democrats manifested in the SDP split and the fierce infighting of the 1980s. Wilson tried to manage rather than confront head on Labour's internal tensions and divisions, and resolve the issue of what sort of party it was or should be, and what it stood for. It was probably the only thing he could realistically do at the time, but it brought him little thanks then or later.

Ideology and Aims
Wilson's politics were more about positioning and manoeuvre than about ideology and doctrine (which he tended to dismiss as 'theology'). When he became leader he brilliantly used a vague

rhetoric of modernisation and reform of supposedly out-dated and inefficient institutions and practices, opportunistically latching on to fashionable 1960s reformist ideas. Talking about science, technology and socialism, and about planning and purposive government, he captured the contemporary public mood, wrong-footing the supposedly old-fashioned and out-of-touch Tories and bypassing Labour's bitter internal arguments over nationalization, nuclear disarmament and the meaning of socialism, providing a platform both wings of the party could buy into and also a broad and modern public appeal (Pimlott 1992: 302-305). All this is sometimes dismissed as a shallow commitment, but Wilson was in fact consistently committed over his whole political career to a mixed economy, with a role for an interventionist, planning and modernising state. In practice, he aimed to head a moderate government pursuing moderate policies of progress and gradualist reform within the prevailing system.

A master political tactician, not a strategist, Wilson practised a short-term, pragmatic 'keep-the-show-on-the-road' style of politics. 'A week is a long time in politics' he once revealingly quipped (Thomas-Symonds 2022: 198). Political manipulation was second nature to him – he was someone, it was said, who 'thought four moves ahead' in the political chess game. Richard Crossman (1976: 159) described him as 'an opportunist, always moving in zig-zags, darting with no sense of direction but making the best of each position he adopts.' His political agility and skills were seen to best effect when he had a knife-edge majority in 1964-66 and (maybe more cynically) later when finessing the Common Market issue in the 1970s. The drawback with that approach was also noted by Crossman, who almost as soon as he entered the Cabinet in 1964, was complaining that 'what we lacked was any comprehensive, thoroughly thought-out Government strategy. The policies are being thrown together' (Crossman 1975: 39). Wilson's main aim was 'to stay in office', Crossman (1976: 160) felt: 'That's the real thing and for that he will use any trick or gimmick.' In practice Wilson's political methods often involved postponing hard choices, playing for time and strategic sequencing of decisions.

At its best, this could mean lowering the political temperature or anaesthetising dissent and opposition. More negatively it could mean trying to evade important but insoluble questions – a belief that 'a problem shelved is a problem solved' (Ziegler 1993: 432, 435) – something that only stored up trouble for later.

Political Style and Skills

Wilson was indisputably one of the most effective public communicators among recent prime ministers. It has been said that he deliberately acquired a sense of humour, and he certainly transformed himself from being a dull and boring speaker as a young MP and rising minister, into one who, at his best, was devastatingly sharp, lucid and witty and a brilliant parliamentary debater. In his time, he was also the best television communicator in politics, a complete professional who mastered all the tricks of the media and took great pains, in his early years as PM at least, to cultivate the press (though relations with the media turned very sour and conflictual after a while). He also carefully cultivated his image – the Northern background and accent, the pipe and raincoat, the unpretentious personal tastes – a partial smokescreen for the brilliant Oxford academic and Whitehall planner, and a supremely ambitious and highly-professional politician.

Wilson was an innovator in Downing Street, saying in 1964 that he wanted Number 10 to become a 'powerhouse'. That overstated things, but he did look to go beyond traditional civil service sources of support and advice for the PM. He created the Political Office in 1964 and the Number 10 Policy Unit in 1974, and there was also in the 1970s the extension and institutionalisation of the appointment of ministerial special advisers. These all became enduring features of the Downing Street machinery and were retained in one form or another by successor governments, albeit Wilson's SPADS and Number 10 aides being in smaller numbers than under later PMs. Bernard Donoughue (2003: 106), his head of policy in the 1970s, noticed how Wilson's two chief advisers, Joe Haines (his press secretary from the late-60s) and Marcia Williams (his long-time personal and political secretary, who linked him with the party and with

103

the trade unions) were both 'fiercely independent and very ready to express firm disagreement with Harold Wilson ... Both said to Wilson exactly what they thought and believed, however critical. Wilson in turn was almost masochistic in inviting contradiction and in accepting dissent from those who worked for him.' But there was a sometimes dubious atmosphere of plotting, intrigue and leaking around his Number 10, the downside of his reliance on a 'kitchen cabinet', as it was called, being the way in which his cronies, hangers-on and aides often fed his paranoia and suspicions of political conspiracies.

Always at home in Whitehall (with his experience as a wartime temporary civil servant), Wilson worked well with civil servants and regarded them highly, rejecting left-wing allegations of bureaucratic sabotage and political bias (Theakston 1992). In turn, officials widely respected him as an efficient, industrious, rational and personally easy-going political master. Wilson as prime minister in the 1960s was very close to Sir Burke Trend, the powerful and discreet Cabinet Secretary and an indispensable and trusted adviser and confidant. He was ever aware of the presentational advantages of reorganisation and redesign in government institutions, constantly rejigging the pattern and the titles of Whitehall departments throughout his premierships in the 1960s and 1970s. However his constant tinkering with the departmental architecture and machinery of Whitehall showed little evidence of strategic purpose or design, often being prompted by presentational, political or 'divide-and-rule' motives (Peter Hennessy (2000: 310) calls him 'the untidiest of all the postwar premiers in administrative terms').

Wilson is said by Hennessy (2000: 180-1) to have had 'a career-long animus against the Treasury' and a desire to check its power and cut it down to size, and his personal economic adviser Thomas Balogh absolutely hated that department and what it stood for. The Department of Economic Affairs (DEA) was created in 1964 with the hope that it would be a champion of industrial modernisation, economic growth and planning, and a rival to the Treasury. Incidentally, it also had the political advantage of setting his two rivals for the leadership – George Brown (at DEA) and James Callaghan (as Chancellor) – at each other's throats. But this attempt at introducing 'creative tension' into Whitehall (together with the creation of a Ministry of Technology to spearhead industrial modernisation) failed to break the Treasury's predominance over economic policy. The division of functions between the two departments was ill thought out, ministerial leadership of the DEA was volatile and unstable, and – crucially - the Labour government's decision to give priority to the defence of the pound and the exchange rate and the balance of payments ensured that the Treasury would inevitably emerge victorious in the inter-departmental struggles (Theakston and Connelly 2018: 127-135).

In the first few years Wilson was a dominant prime minister: interventionist and leading from the front, helped by the fact that few ministers in his 1964 government had any prior ministerial experience. But the 'big beasts' soon started to assert themselves, and ministers like George Brown, James Callaghan, Roy Jenkins, Denis Healey, Barbara Castle and Tony Crosland carried real weight and could not be ignored or overridden. Wilson probably reshuffled his ministers too frequently, trying to stop any single rival becoming a clear 'crown prince' and also keeping too many second-rate placemen in the Cabinet to bolster his own position. However, he generally showed remarkable skill in handling his Cabinet: 'knowing when to press and when to ease off, when to defer a decision, when to take a vote and when to sum up in a way patently at variance with the drift of the discussion . . . [or] to allow the argument to drift on interminably until he got his way through the confusion and frustration of his opponents' (Ziegler 1993: 189). As Robert Saunders (2018: 63) puts it: 'In Wilson's capable hands, tedium and obscurity became potent tools of party management. He excelled at asphyxiating contentious topics, delivering "rambling résumés" in Cabinet that left colleagues too bored and exhausted to fight. Ministers could be astonished at what slipped past their defences while minds were wandering. As Barbara Castle confided to her diary, "when Harold reduces everything to boring, and almost bored, low key, I reach for my critical faculties."' His techniques were not heroic but they worked - the problem was that these skills were not harnessed to a strong policy vision.

Later, he was far from being a dominant – or even active – PM in his 1974-76 government, being by that time exhausted and increasingly disengaged – a fading figure, who seemed at times to have lost interest, and who was carried by the Number 10 and Whitehall machine. On returning to office he had said he would run things differently from his earlier tenure in the 1960s, playing the role of a football sweeper, but by the end his role was more hands-off and his inputs to government business and policy-making were more limited even that that image would imply. Callaghan (at the Foreign Office), Healey (at the Treasury) and Michael Foot (Employment Secretary) had great ministerial and political clout in those years.

Wilson's mind was, at his peak, razor-sharp, fast and described as being of 'Rolls Royce' calibre. 'But he was not an intellectual in the conventional sense, with little interest in theories, concepts or high-flown ideas' (Donoghue 2005: 12). To his critics he was too clever by half. The manipulation of political power and solving definable problems were what fascinated him, not abstractions (Ziegler 1993: 42). He liked 'verbal advice and a lot of gossip', jumping from topic to topic and welcoming advisers popping in and out for quick discussions (Donoughue 1987: 12-13). In his second term (1974-76), however, there was visibly less energy and spark. 'The trouble is when the old problems reappear I reach for the old solution', he confessed. A Number 10 official compared him to a player of Space Invaders: 'he would take the first blip to cross the screen whether it was important or not' (Hennessy 2000: 357).

In personal terms, Wilson was actually quite thin-skinned, wanted to be liked and was eager for approval. The emotional balance sheet is mixed in his case: some of his qualities helped him succeed as a leader while others limited his achievements. On the positive side he was someone who took trouble over personal relations, being unassuming, unpretentious, kindly, amiable and considerate to people, even if not truly warm or knowable. 'The outer ring of his personality was permeable', as Shirley Williams (2009: 200) observed, 'but the inner ring was impenetrable.' He was equable, calm and kept his head and his cool in a crisis. He had an 'india-rubber self-confidence' and resilience, and could bounce back, putting things behind him. More problematic was the way in which he shied away from confrontations (disliking having to say 'no' to people or having to sack them) and his insecurities and bouts of paranoia and suspicion about plots and real or imagined enemies. There was also his strange dependence on Marcia Williams, whose extraordinary tantrums drained him of energy in 1974-76 and weakened his capacity for governing (Donoghue 2005). To the extent that realism is a virtue in leaders, the way in which Wilson's optimism could tilt over into Walter Mitty-like self-delusion was another problem.

Context
'Breach of Promise' is the title of one book about Wilson's 1964-70 government (Ponting 1989). 'The worst of governments' is the title of another analysis of Labour's record after 1974 and his second stint in Number 10 (Seldon and Hickson 2004: 316). The critical narrative of broken promises, ditched manifesto pledges, disillusionment and 'failure' in the Wilson years is familiar and fairly easily put together, but often overdone (Coopey et al 1993; Dorey 2006; Crines and Hickson 2016). He did not lead great reforming governments; staying afloat and survival were more the order of the day. Not least the reason for this was that on both occasions when Wilson entered Number 10 – in 1964 and again in 1974 – he inherited massive economic crises. He certainly made serious policy errors of his own in handling these problems but the extent to which so much was beyond his control has to be acknowledged.

The battle between 1964 and 1967 to deal with the balance of payments crisis and avoid devaluation of the pound entailed the sacrifice of Labour's much-trumpeted plans for economic growth (which reached only half of the ambitious 4 per cent annual target), rounds of painful public spending cuts and deflation, a squeeze on wages, and clashes with the unions. But politically, Wilson felt that there was no alternative, with what was initially a tiny majority and the expectation of another election round the corner, and to avoid Labour being damned as the party of devaluation (as in 1931 and 1949). When it finally and inevitably came, it was a huge defeat and a humiliation for Wilson personally and destroyed Labour's claims to economic policy competence (Bale 1999).

There were plenty of other headaches in the 1960s, with Wilson expending a lot of political time and capital on the fruitless search for a solution to the Rhodesia problem; Cabinet battles over ending the UK's expensive and unsustainable 'East of Suez' role; and trying to maintain the 'special relationship' while fending off pressure from US President Johnson for British troops to support the Americans in a war in Vietnam that was very unpopular in Britain (Dyson 2007). The damaging failure of attempted union reforms to deal with the problem of rising strikes has been noted earlier. A hostile media, Labour's dismal record in the opinion polls and a run of by-election defeats intensified the sense of being politically beleaguered. On the positive side were the whole series of reforms that did much to modernise and liberalise British law, society and culture in the late 1960s, albeit Wilson himself (something of a social conservative) being not greatly involved or personally associated with them. Although Labour's poll position and the economic indicators had recovered somewhat by 1970, it is in retrospect easy to understand – given the government's overall record since 1964 and the depths of its mid-term unpopularity – why Labour lost the general election of that year, though it came as a surprise at the time (Dorey 2013).

Wilson again took over as prime minister in conditions of economic crisis in 1974 – having to deal with the problem of 'stagflation' (the combination of rapidly increasing inflation, unemployment and poor economic growth), the impact of the oil price hike, a huge balance of payments deficit, and industrial unrest. The 'social contract' agreed with the unions – involving voluntary restraint in wage bargaining – barely kept the lid on things but allowed Wilson to present Labour as the party that could work with the unions, uniting rather than (like Heath and the Conservatives) dividing the nation. It is clear that he (and probably a majority of the Cabinet) was unenthusiastic about and opposed to the radical plans for more state control, nationalisation and intervention in private industry developed by the resurgent Labour left in opposition in the early 1970s and back in office, Wilson moved to neutralise and contain Tony Benn, and allowed the Whitehall machine and the Treasury to rewrite and water down the plans. After a period of drift, action came in 1975 with cuts to public spending plans, the introduction of cash limits that further squeezed government spending, an incomes policy and the shift in priorities from reducing unemployment to containing and cutting inflation – all demonstrating the government's recognition of the economic realities it faced. By the time Wilson left office in 1976 inflation was falling, the balance of payments was improving and public expenditure being brought under control.

Politically, Wilson was in a tight corner, heading a minority government from March 1974 and winning only a tiny Commons majority of three in the October 1974 general election. His major achievement in this term of office was navigating his way through the European Common Market issue minefield through skilful political management and timing. Wilson was personally at best only lukewarm or agnostic about Europe, always harbouring a strong commitment to the Commonwealth but understanding the economic case for EEC membership. His own application to join had been vetoed by the French in 1967, but then after 1970 the logic of opposition politics and the current of opinion in the Labour Party had driven him to come out against the terms Heath had negotiated rather than the principle of membership. In practice, Wilson did not want to pull out of the EEC but wanted to keep his party united and in power. His balancing act was designed to keep pro- and anti-marketeers on board and put back the day of reckoning. Back in government, he cleverly engineered a fairly cosmetic 'renegotiation' of those terms and then called a referendum in 1975, allowing ministers to argue their pro or anti cases in public, keeping the party uneasily together and resulting in an overwhelming 'yes' vote – his last great political 'fix' (Saunders 2018).

Conclusion

Wilson was the first prime minister for nearly 40 years (since Baldwin) – and there has arguably not been once since – to retire voluntarily and at a time of his own choosing – not rejected by the electorate, forced out by party pressure or a Cabinet coup, or pole-axed by illness (though there may be some qualifications in relation to the last point). Secure in the post, he was in 1976, as his policy adviser Bernard Donoughue (2003: 178) points out, 'unchallenged as leader of his Government and his party.' His announcement in March 1974 that he would resign the premiership, and stay just long enough for the Labour Party to elect a new leader, was greeted with shocked disbelief.

Retiring early had been Wilson's intention for quite some time. Had he won re-election in 1970, at the end of his first period in Number 10, he would probably not have stayed as prime minister for a full term but gone after two or three years. But having lost to Heath he wanted to get back into power first and so endured a miserable and embattled period of Opposition 1970-74. But from the time he became prime minister again in 1974, he had a settled intention to remain no more than two years. The Queen, his Downing Street 'Kitchen Cabinet' advisers, and a number of senior ministers were all told what to expect or dropped hints or read the runes. Despite a couple of last minute hiccups, he stuck to his timetable and went just after his 60th birthday. Wilson had been at the top for nearly 30 years and felt that he owed it to his wife Mary – who intensely disliked political life – to get out before too long. Once he had achieved his aim of winning the 1975 Common Market referendum and keeping Britain in Europe, he became very bored and fed up with life as prime minister. He felt that he was facing the same old problems and reaching for the same old solutions, lost his zest and appetite for office, began to dread Prime Minister's Questions and to need too many brandies beforehand (and afterwards), and found the job very tiring and wearisome. He even suspected secret service plots against him – something dismissed as a fantasy at the time, but later evidence suggested there were in fact rogue elements and some right-wing malcontents in the 'secret world' trying to smear and damage him. Physically, intellectually and psychologically he was no longer up to the demands of the job by the end. He was very much winding down over his last year in Number 10, a shadow of what he had previously been, a burnt-out case. He seemed often exhausted and in poor shape, and his health was not good, his mental sharpness gone. There are suggestions Wilson may have feared that he could detect early signs of the Alzheimer's disease to which he later succumbed. If so, he deserves credit for realising that he could and should not carry on (Theakston 2010).

It was once said that British prime ministers could be divided into two categories or broad types, who often seemed to alternate in office – 'clergymen' and 'bookies'. Wilson was a 'bookie' in terms of his character, style and approach – a short-term fixer, an opportunist, a gambler, a bit of a 'cheeky chappie'. In this vein, the Tory politician Iain Macleod once said that whereas the American president John F. Kennedy had described himself as an 'idealist without illusions', Wilson was 'an illusionist without ideals' (Garnett 2015: 69). Certainly, Wilson's Conservative opponent Edward Heath and his Labour successor James Callaghan were more serious-minded 'clergymen'. But it must be said that neither type of prime minister enjoyed much success in dealing with the country's economic and political problems in the 1960s and 1970s. In the end, Wilson overall did no worse than any of the others or any of his rivals would have likely done, and in some respects he did better than Heath and Callaghan when we look at the statistics of his tenure in office and his election record. In terms of those basic measures of performance at least, he goes down as one of the great – if battered - survivors of Downing Street.

References

Bale, T. (1999). 'Dynamics of a non-decision: the "failure" to devalue the pound 1964-7', *Twentieth Century British History*. 10 (2): 192-217.

Benn, T. (1990). *Conflicts of Interest: Diaries 1977-80.* London: Arrow.

Coopey, R., Fielding, S., and Tiratsoo, N. (Eds). (1993). *The Wilson Government 1964-1970.* London: Pinter.

Crines, A. and Hickson, K. (eds) (2016): *Harold Wilson : the unprincipled prime minister? A reappraisal of Harold Wilson.* London: Biteback Publishing.

Crossman, R. (1975). *The Diaries of a Cabinet Minister: Volume One, Minister of Housing 1964-66.* London: Hamish Hamilton and Jonathan Cape.

Crossman, R. (1976). *The Diaries of a Cabinet Minister: Volume Two, Lord President of the Council and Leader of the House of Commons 1966-68.* London: Hamish Hamilton and Jonathan Cape.

Donoughue, B. (1987). *Prime Minister : the conduct of policy under Harold Wilson and   James Callaghan.* London: Jonathan Cape.

Donoughue, B. (2003). *The Heat of the Kitchen.* London: Politico's.

Donoughue, B. (2005). *Downing Street diary : with Harold Wilson in No. 10.* London: Jonathan Cape.

Dorey, P. (ed) (2006). *The Labour Governments 1964-1970.* London: Routledge.

Dorey, P. (2013) 'The Fall of the Wilson Government, 1970', in: T. Heppell and K. Theakston (eds) *How Labour governments fall: from Ramsay MacDonald to Gordon Brown.* London: Palgrave Macmillan

Dyson, S. (2007): 'Alliances, domestic politics and leader psychology: why did Britain stay out of Vietnam and go into Iraq?', *Political Psychology.* 28 (6): 647-666 .

Garnett, M. (2015). 'The oratory of Iain Macleod', in R. Hayton and A. Crines (eds), *Conservative Orators from Baldwin to Cameron.* Manchester: Manchester University Press.

Healey, D. (1989). *The Time of My Life.* London: Michael Joseph.

Hennessy, P. (2000). *The Prime Minister : the office and its holders since 1945.* London: Allen Lane.

Heppell, T. (2010): 'The Labour Party leadership election of 1963: explaining the unexpected election of Harold Wilson', *Contemporary British History*. 24 (2): 151-171.

Pimlott, B. (1992). *Harold Wilson.* London: HarperCollins.

Ponting, C. (1989). *Breach of Promise: Labour in Power 1964-70.* London: Hamish Hamilton.

Saunders, R. (2018). *Yes to Europe! The 1975 Referendum and Seventies Britain.* Cambridge: Cambridge University Press.

Seldon, A. and Hickson, K. (eds) (2004). *New Labour, Old Labour : the Wilson and Callaghan governments, 1974-79.* London; Routledge.

Theakston, K. (1992). *The Labour Party and Whitehall.* London: Routledge.

Theakston, K. (2010). *After Number 10: Former Prime Ministers in British Politics.* London: Palgrave Macmillan.

Theakston, K. and Connelly, P. (2018). *William Armstrong and British Policy Making.* London: Palgrave Macmillan.

Thomas-Symonds, N. (2022). *Harold Wilson: The Winner.* London: Weidenfeld & Nicolson.

Williams, S. (2009). *Climbing the Bookshelves.* London: Virago Press.

Ziegler, P. (1993). *Wilson: The Authorised Life.* London: Weidenfeld & Nicolson.

Chapter 8

Edward Heath (1970-74)

As an election-fighter Edward Heath compares badly with his great rivals and enemies Harold Wilson and Margaret Thatcher – Heath winning only one of the four general elections he fought as Conservative leader, Wilson winning four of the five he fought, and Thatcher winning all three she fought. And whereas Wilson enjoyed a total of eight years in Number 10, and Thatcher eleven years, Heath's premiership lasted only three years and eight months. In terms of historical impact and legacy, however, while Thatcher fundamentally reshaped British politics, there is a case for saying Heath could arguably rank above Wilson because of his achievement in taking Britain into the European Community, with all its consequences over the following half century for our economy, society and politics. But where Thatcher was a lucky politician and Wilson made his own luck, Heath was a very unlucky leader. He faced in the early 1970s some of the most daunting circumstances and challenges ever endured by a British government in peacetime. The crises sank him and his embattled government. His premiership ended in failure, frustration and electoral defeat against a background of economic crisis and industrial conflict raising the spectre of 'ungovernability' (Ball and Seldon 1996; Roe-Crines and Heppell 2021). Moreover, his own deficiencies, misjudgements and mistakes as a leader contributed to his problems and ultimate defeat. Heath cannot be described overall as a successful prime minister. But rather than just writing him off as a complete failure, it is important to try to understand why and how he failed.

Party leadership

In one sense, Heath broke the mould of Conservative leaders, coming from a relatively modest social background (his father a carpenter and then a small builder, his mother a former lady's maid) and making it to Oxford (where he was politically active) as a grammar school scholarship boy. He had a 'good war' (his experiences strongly colouring his views on European unity) and became an MP in 1950 at a time when the Conservative Party was still dominated by the upper-class products of the public schools. But in another sense he was not an 'outsider', having been fast-tracked into government and climbing the ladder as an efficient organizer and a managerial and technocratic figure. He is the only chief whip ever to have become prime minister (playing a key role in holding the Tory party together during the Suez crisis); was very much a protégé of prime minister Harold Macmillan; and was Minister of Labour before winning his laurels as the minister leading the negotiations in the first UK bid to join the EEC in the early 1960s, and then serving as a forceful and reforming Minister for Trade and Industry under Alec Douglas-Home (see: Campbell 1993; MacShane 2006; Ziegler 2010; McManus 2016). He was thus a senior and experienced 'man of government' with an executive mentality of the sort often found at or near the top in British politics.

But it is not clear that the Conservative Party ever loved (as opposed to respected) Edward Heath – or indeed that he loved it. He was the first Tory leader to be chosen – and subsequently the first to be ousted - by a contested vote of the party's MPs. When he won the leadership in 1965 nearly half the party's MPs did not want him (he got 150 votes to Reginald Maudling's 133 and Enoch Powell's 15). The party wanted someone who was not another tweedy aristocrat, and thought it needed someone to rival and take on Harold Wilson – a modern-minded, classless, meritocratic, tough and professional leader, and Heath seemed to fit the bill. But his poor performance as leader of the opposition (Garnett 2012) - regularly bested by the quicker-witted Wilson in the Commons, awkward with the media and a poor campaigner, and with low personal poll ratings - made many think they had made the wrong choice, and if Heath had not unexpectedly won the 1970 general election with a 30-seat majority and 46 per cent of the vote (a figure not equalled by any party since then) he would probably have been forced out. His remote, aloof and authoritarian style as party leader made matters worse and alienated backbenchers (Norton 2021). He had little feel for, sympathy with or understanding of the party's grassroots but they gave him a begrudging respect and more or less loyally supported him so long as he was leader. Heath practiced a top-down, disciplinary, command-and-control style of leadership which only electoral success could make tolerable. Although he had been an effective and popular chief whip in the 1950s, he seemed to despise the political arts as leader. He forged effective working relations with his Cabinet, building a loyal and united team of ministers. But he neglected his backbenchers, being frequently rude, impatient and high-handed with MPs, spurning the Commons tearoom or smoking-room skills and the canny use of patronage of a Macmillan or a Callaghan. He could just about get away with this while he was prime minister – though backbench dissent was at higher levels than under previous governments - but the knives were finally out after the two electoral defeats of 1974. A key Heath failing, then, was as a party manager – his inability to establish and maintain a strong party support base.

Ideology and Aims

Heath was broadly in the middle ground of post-war Conservatism – the 'One Nation' centrist Conservatism of Churchill, Eden, Butler and Macmillan. He set out with a broad vision of what he wanted to achieve and with a raft of detailed policy commitments planned in Opposition, but without strong underpinnings in terms of political philosophy or economic theory. He was never deeply interested in ideas, ideologies or abstractions as opposed to facts, policies and action. He was also disposed to the belief that reasonable people, reasoning and working patiently together, could find rational solutions to problems or be persuaded to act in the wider public interest. He had a technocratic, managerial, problem-solving approach to government.

Heath was never a *laissez-faire* right-wing Conservative. He was more a believer in the post-war consensus policies, seeing a role for government in economic and social policy. He wanted to rework the mixed-economy Keynesian welfare-state system, modernising the state and galvanising British industry, and taking the country into the EEC. The party platform and the abrasive language of competition, free markets, less state intervention, union controls, tax and spending cuts, more selectively targeted welfare, and the rejection of incomes policy that was to the front in the 1970 election – the so-called 'Selsdon Man' policies - did not add up to, and were not intended by Heath to mean, a fundamental ideological break (whatever the later Thatcherite mythology of betrayal) (Campbell 1993). Heath sometimes sounded like an abrasive and confrontational radical but essentially he wanted a change of course, a different style of government, a change of attitudes and, in a sense, to renew and update the status quo, and make it work better, not to overturn it entirely. 'Are you moving to the right?' he was asked in 1970. 'Just a bit', he replied, 'but we have to stay in the centre' (Whitehead 1985: 40).

Unlike Thatcher after 1979, Heath did not reject the basic institutional and conceptual framework of the postwar settlement. He would have no truck, for instance, with the ideas about privatization that a party group under Nicholas Ridley (a future Thatcherite minister) drew up in Opposition, and did not espouse monetarism or untrammelled free-market capitalism. With basically a practical and managerial cast of mind, and instinctively an interventionist, he then responded pragmatically to events and changing circumstances after 1970, overseeing some damaging policy reversals and U-turns.

He did have a 'Big Idea', which was getting into Europe. His personal determination and commitment were crucial in achieving that. And Heath was privately eloquent on his vision of the possibilities for Britain in the EEC. But he was never able to get his ideas on the subject across to the British people and win their full-hearted consent or stimulate real, deep and wide public enthusiasm. The emphasis was always put more on the instrumental economic rather than the political aspects of the European Community, and Heath rather pooh-poohed talk of the 'loss of sovereignty', though he himself was actually a strong believer in greater political integration in Europe (Young 1996; Dorey 2021). The other side of his pro-Europeanism was – in contrast to most recent prime ministers - a distinct coolness about the 'Special Relationship'. Heath was not simplistically anti-American but he had a brisk and strictly business-like approach to relations with the USA, led at that time by President Richard Nixon.

Political Style and Skills

Heath was difficult to like, though many who worked closely with him admired and respected him profoundly. 'Emotionally stunted' (Campbell 1993: 8), 'emotional austerity' (Ziegler 2010: 7) and even 'socially autistic' (MacShane 2006: 8) are terms used by various biographers in describing Heath: someone who was a loner, a solitary man, withdrawn, defensive, introverted, inhibited, prickly, aloof, awkward in social and personal relations, self-centred, and both insecure and arrogant. Yet at the same time he was almost a Renaissance Man compared to many politicians, with a serious interest in classical music and success as an international yachtsman. But his 'buttoned-up' personality (Campbell 1993: 201) seems to have affected his approach to the premiership and his conduct or style of operation in that office, being a factor in his failures of political touch and as a communicator.

His job was to govern, not to explain, Heath once said (Ziegler 2010: 234). That remark explains a lot about his mistakes and problems. He was a poor communicator and no showman. He could sometimes be effective in the Commons but was too serious-minded to be good at parliamentary knock about and point-scoring. He was wooden and uninspiring on the public platform and on television, speaking at rather than to people. He came across as a dry technocratic manager, with no feel for language or for inspirational rhetoric. He deliberately spurned public relations and image building, and kept his distance from media figures. As John Campbell (1993: 484) put it: Heath 'fatally neglected the skills of communication and presentation of government policies which are an essential part of leadership.' Ultimately, his government fell, says Campbell (1993: xix-xx), because 'he was unable to persuade the country to support what he was trying to do.'

Heath was more interested in and better at government and administration than at politics. He was rational, analytical, a

118

master of the details and the technicalities. He had an enigmatic quality and had the unnerving habit of remaining stonily silent for long periods while his advisers discussed an issue and then, once he had heard enough to make a decision, abruptly stopping the discussion. Heath's critics accused him of being too much like a civil servant and felt that he was over-influenced by senior officials. He certainly seemed to prefer to surround himself with senior mandarins, and to rely upon them for advice, rather than looking to Cabinet colleagues, party advisers or political cronies. William Armstrong, the Head of the Civil Service, became Heath's closest adviser and right-hand man, playing a sort of 'chief of staff' role. Armstrong's role and influence were such that he was dubbed 'deputy prime minister' by the media and critics (Theakston and Connelly 2018).

But although he had a high regard for the civil service as an institution, Heath was also an impatient would-be modernizer and reformer (Theakston 1996). His creation of the Central Policy Review Staff (CPRS) think-tank in 1970, with a mixed staff of civil servants and 'outsiders' and given the job of 'thinking the unthinkable' on a non-party-political basis, carrying out policy analysis, challenging departmental views and looking to the long-term, also betokens an attitude to policy advice (and perhaps an open-mindedness) not shared by Thatcher, who abolished the CPRS in 1983. Heath was fascinated by government machinery and favoured 'giant' departments, sharper policy analysis and a more strategic approach, 'hiving-off', and the importation of businessmen and business practices into Whitehall. But he perhaps exaggerated what could be achieved by reforms of the bureaucratic machine and was in office for too short a time to embed the 'new style of government' he wanted.

Heath ran his government in a business-like way. Sometimes described as authoritarian and intolerant, he was in fact very correct about the processes of Cabinet government, and – through all the upheavals and crises they faced – he ran a united, leak-free and harmonious Cabinet, with no resignations or dismissals on policy grounds, and with no plotting against the PM. It was all a very different atmosphere to the Wilson years.

On the whole he allowed his ministers full responsibility for the work of their departments (the exceptions being for the policy areas he prioritized – Europe and the economy). It was not a one-man government but he was a very dominant prime minister. Victory against all the expectations in 1970 had boosted his self-belief and sense of personal authority. He was close to Willie Whitelaw, Jim Prior and Lord Carrington, but there were no internal rivals, and few 'big beasts' or 'big hitters' in the government.

One reason for that was that Heath's government suffered a major blow with the sudden death of the Chancellor of the Exchequer, Iain Macleod, in July 1970, barely a month after taking office. His death removed the government's best political communicator, a major political heavyweight with independent views of his own, and probably the only minister capable of standing up to Heath. The government was left unbalanced as a result, allowing it to become much more centred on the prime minister. Macleod's replacement, Anthony Barber, was more of a lightweight who could and would not stand up to the PM. Moreover, Heath – who had never served in that department – appears to have distrusted the Treasury and subsequently interfered with it and overruled it far more than he would have been able to do had Macleod not died. Heath was critical of the Treasury because of its gloomy economic forecasts, and because it did not share his enthusiasm about joining Europe. The result was the prime minister, to a much greater extent than in most governments, was able to dominate and direct the main thrust of economic policy (Campbell 1993: 302-3). The mid-term economic U-turns, and the big increases in public spending, were very much driven through from Number 10, by Heath, aided and advised by William Armstrong.

Context

The circumstances - domestic and international - the Heath government came to face were extremely adverse. In a sense, it might have been wiser to batten down the hatches and try to just weather the storms, but Heath was a prime minister with a vision and in a hurry. As the problems crowded in, he came to seem a prisoner of events, not a master of them.

The government's wider support was not robust and its political space limited. Heath personally was not a popular leader – he was never an electoral asset to his party and his approval ratings as prime minister were the lowest of any postwar PM until John Major. For most of the 1970-74 period opinion polls showed a Labour lead over the Tories and voter dissatisfaction with the government's record. By-elections and opinion polls also gave evidence of the Liberal revival that proved so damaging to the Conservatives in February 1974. Much of the media was critical. Moreover, the wider climate of intellectual opinion in the early 1970s was still behind the Keynesian consensus, backing high public spending and state intervention, even as the limitations and the problems with that policy paradigm were becoming apparent – but there was no credible alternative available at that time, unlike in the Thatcher years (Kavanagh 1996).

The domestic scene – particularly industrial relations and the economy – was a battlefield. The government's Industrial Relations Act aimed to stabilize industrial relations and reduce union conflict and strikes but instead had the opposite effect, provoking a confrontation with the TUC and even more union strife and stoppages. In Opposition the Conservatives had condemned Labour's incomes policy, promising to restore free collective bargaining, but in the face of rising inflation and strikes and industrial action by the unions – and particularly after the bitter miners' strike in early 1972, which led to a state of emergency, power cuts and a three-day week – the government was driven to introduce a statutory incomes policy. Through all the confrontation, however, Heath persistently and genuinely sought agreement with the unions and with business, to try and make a 'corporate' or 'tripartite' system of economic management work. But the problem was the 'social partners' – the TUC and the unions on the one hand, the CBI representing business on the other - were unable or unwilling fully to cooperate, share responsibility and 'deliver'.

Arguments have long raged about the government's

economic policy. There was the abandonment of the original 'hands-off' policy towards industrial 'lame ducks', with the bailing out and nationalisation of Rolls Royce and the rescue of the Upper Clyde Shipbuilders. Then there was the combination of unemployment hitting one million in 1972 (for the first time in a quarter of a century) together with Heath becoming convinced of the urgent need for economic and industrial expansion prior to entering Europe and impatient with the slow response of industry - these provoking a major U-turn, leading to a huge reflation of the economy, the turning-on of the public spending taps, a credit splurge, and increased intervention in and financial assistance for industry. Was this a prime minister losing his nerve and abandoning the policies and principles he had been elected on (the later Thatcherite view)? Or one who was consistent about ends but flexible and pragmatic about means (taking this line Peter Hennessy (2000) labels Heath a 'somersaulting moderniser')?

The problem was that the floor opened up beneath the government. The international economic scene could hardly have been more difficult with the breakdown of the stable international currency and financial system put together at Bretton Woods after the war, world-wide inflation and rising commodity prices, and then the 1973-4 oil crisis, when OPEC action following the Arab-Israeli war resulted in a quadrupling in the price of oil and cutbacks in production. At home that coincided with the NUM's decision to back up a 40 per cent wage claim by beginning an overtime ban which led to a state of emergency, power cuts and a three-day week, and then another miners' strike in February 1974. The government's economic growth strategy was dealt a fatal blow and the confrontation with the miners over the incomes policy destroyed the policy and the government itself.

There were huge problems and crises on other fronts too. Throughout 1970-74, the Northern Ireland situation, for instance, took up a massive amount of the government's time and political energy. With escalating violence, Ulster was on the edge of civil war. While the internment policy was a blunder, the abolition of Stormont and the imposition of direct rule (with

Willie Whitelaw, one of Heath's ablest lieutenants, as minister) was a bold but necessary step forward. The power-sharing agreement negotiated in December 1973 was scuppered by a protestant/unionist backlash but foreshadowed the settlement ultimately achieved a quarter of a century later – the Good Friday Agreement being described as 'Sunningdale for slow learners'. One immediate consequence was the breaking of the link between the Ulster Unionists and the Conservative Party - their refusal to take the Tory whip prevented the party having the largest number of MPs after the February 1974 election.

As the battle with the miners intensified, arguments about calling an early general election raged inside the Cabinet and the Conservative Party in early 1974. Heath was reluctant, fearing an election fought against the miners might have short-term partisan advantages but damage the prospects of the sort of long-term settlement with the unions he still wanted. Other Tories wanted a showdown with the miners and pressed hard for matters to be brought to a head. Heath dithered and in the end perhaps called the election a couple of weeks too late as opinion swung against the government. 'Who governs?' was the central issue, and the electorate effectively answered, 'well, you don't'. The result of the February 1974 election was a hung parliament, with the Conservatives winning more votes than Labour (37.9 to 37.1 per cent) but fewer seats (297 to 301). Heath hung on for a few days, trying unsuccessfully to make a deal with the Liberals, before finally resigning as prime minister on 4 March when Wilson - who had privately not expected to return to power - then formed a minority Labour government.

Conclusion

After the February 1974 defeat, and still more after the October 1974 election, when Labour squeaked back in with a tiny majority while the Conservatives fell still further back, there was growing unhappiness among Tory MPs with Heath's leadership. It was obvious to virtually everyone except Heath himself that he was an electoral liability and would have to go. Had Heath resigned voluntarily, the likelihood is that one of his supporters such as Willie Whitelaw or Jim Prior would have succeeded to the Tory leadership. But his intransigence meant that they held back and the conditions were created under which demoralised and desperate backbenchers turned to an outsider like Mrs Thatcher – whom Heath himself did not take seriously - whose challenge in 1975 was expected to only to damage or dislodge him and open up the leadership contest to other more heavyweight candidates. Heath's mishandling of his exit thus opened the door to those who wanted to take the party and the country in a very different direction – one that he hated. He remained an MP and staged what was sometimes called 'the longest sulk in parliamentary history'. But his root-and-branch, highly vocal and personalised criticisms of his successor and her government, sustained through her tenure (and beyond), left him increasingly isolated in his own party and were, in a way, self-defeating, costing him any influence he may have been able to exert as an elder statesman and party grandee. He got virtually written out of Conservative Party history, at worst denounced as a traitor to the cause, at best presented as something of an embarrassing failure (Theakston 2010: 176-184).

Perhaps the best conclusion would be that Heath was, as Mark Garnett (2011: 315) aptly put it, an impressive failure. He had some remarkable qualities: he was high-minded, rational, highly- and honourably-motivated, patriotic, brave, honest, far-sighted. But he also had some crippling deficiencies and weaknesses as a political leader. Often he would not or could not do what was in his own best political interests. Perhaps a less flawed prime minister may have been able to deal more successfully with the tidal wave of problems, events and crises that battered and finally destroyed his government. But perhaps not, for Britain's experience was not unique, and around the world at that time in the 1970s other governments and leaders were also on the defensive, crumbling under huge challenges, and often ending in failure. In the end, Heath was an important, unlucky and still underrated and often misunderstood prime minister.

References

Ball, S. & Seldon, A. (eds) (1996). *The Heath Government 1970-74.* Harlow: Longman.

Campbell, J. (1993). *Edward Heath.* London: Jonathan Cape.

Dorey, P. (2021). 'Entry into the European Communities', in A. Roe-Crines and T. Heppell (eds), *Policies and Politics Under Prime Minister Edward Heath.* London: Palgrave Macmillan.

Garnett, M. (2011). 'Heath: no need to be loved', *Political Quarterly*, 82 (2): 313-316.

Garnett, M. (2012): 'Edward Heath, 1965-70 ands 1974-5', in T. Heppell (ed), *Leaders of the Opposition: From Churchill to Cameron*, London: Palgrave Macmillan.

Hennessy, P. (2000). *The Prime Minister: The Office and Its Holders Since 1945.* London: Allen Lane.

Kavanagh, D. (1996). '1970-74', in A. Seldon (ed), *How Tory Governments Fall.* London: HarperCollins.

MacShane, D. (2006). *Heath.* London: Haus Publishing.

McManus, M. (2016). *Edward Heath: A Singular Life.* London: Elliott and Thompson.

Norton, P. (2021). 'Party Management', in A. Roe-Crines and T. Heppell (eds), *Policies and Politics Under Prime Minister Edward Heath.* London: Palgrave Macmillan.

Roe-Crines, A. & Heppell, T. (eds) (2021). *Policies and Politics Under Prime Minister Edward Heath.* London: Palgrave Macmillan.

Theakston, K. (1996). 'The Heath government, Whitehall and the civil service', in S. Ball & A. Seldon (eds), *The Heath Government 1970-74.* Harlow: Longman.

Theakston, K. (2010). *After Number 10: Former Prime Ministers in British Politics.* London: Palgrave Macmillan.

Theakston, K. And Connelly, P. (2018). *William Armstrong and British Policy Making.* London: Palgrave Macmillan.

Whitehead, P. (1985). *The Writing on the Wall: Britain in the Seventies.* London: Michael Joseph.

Young, J. (1996). 'The Heath Government and British entry into the European Community', in S. Ball & A. Seldon (eds), *The Heath Government 1970-74.* Harlow: Longman.

Ziegler, P. (2010). *Edward Heath*. London: HarperPress.

Chapter 9
James Callaghan (1976-79)

In old age, James Callaghan said that he would not be surprised to be considered as the worst prime minister for more than 200 years. He felt that he must carry the can for the 'winter of discontent' - the widespread trade union strikes that paralysed and helped destroy his government – and that he should have taken 'more initiatives' when he was in Number 10. He was too harsh on himself. Historians and political scientists have actually ranked him in a far-from-disastrous 'mid-table' position when evaluating the performance of 20th century PMs. Other top politicians and insiders also often rate him highly – Denis Healey thought he was, for most of his time, the best of Britain's postwar prime ministers after Attlee. Bernard Donoughue (a Number 10 adviser) judged that Callaghan was, professionally, as a prime minister and head of government, better than many of his predecessors and successors, who may have been more successful in pursuing celebrity fame but were not his equal in terms of social values and political professionalism (Donoughue 2013).

However, Callaghan's premiership ended badly when, after losing a vote of confidence in parliament (the first government to do so for more than 50 years), he and his party went down to an emphatic defeat in the ensuing general election in 1979, one which Callaghan never expected to win. It was even, in some sense, a relief. As he later recalled: 'As a matter of fact, I didn't mind leaving. Because I'd got to the stage when I thought, "well (a) we can't win, (b) I don't know what to do next anyway." . . . I didn't want to stay on' (Theakston 2010: 190-191). But Callaghan had been in many ways an effective prime minister, combining deep roots in the Labour movement, a reassuring public image and executive ability. With his long parliamentary apprenticeship, wide experience in major offices of state, and standing in his party, he was well equipped for tasks of crisis management and political brokerage. A shrewd operator, a tough pragmatist and a skilled fixer, he has been underrated and was a successful practitioner of the politics of survival, holding his government and party together and surmounting a series of economic and political crises that could have wrecked his administration long before it finally hit the rocks in 1979 (Hickson and Miles 2020; Seldon and Hickson 2004).

Party leadership

Callaghan succeeded to the premiership at the age of 64 in April 1976 following the unexpected resignation of Harold Wilson. He is the only PM in history who had held all the 'great offices of state', having previously been Chancellor of the Exchequer (1964-67), Home Secretary (1967-70) and Foreign Secretary (1974-76). His record in these posts included some notable failures (devaluation of the pound in 1967) and successes (handling the problems of Ulster in the late-60s and renegotiating membership of the EEC in 1974-5) but he had grown in stature and reputation over his years in government, and he was clearly a tremendously experienced front-bench politician and knew all the ways of Whitehall (Morgan 1997). He was an effective communicator: a good performer in a solid, reassuring, old-fashioned way on television, on the public platform and in the House of Commons. He was Wilson's own preferred successor and was the most competent (or well-prepared), electable (in the sense of voter-friendly) and acceptable (across the party) of the six candidates who ran for the leadership, though it took three ballots of the Parliamentary Labour Party before he finally clinched it with 176 MPs votes against the 137 won by Michael Foot. The man who left secondary school at 16 had beaten Labour's Oxford glitterati to the top.

In Labour Party terms, Callaghan represented the solid, centre-right, 'labourist' loyalists, winning the leadership as a stabiliser and balancer, a consolidator and a moderate, rather than a confrontational figure (Williams 1982). His power base in the party rested on his role as a long-time champion and supporter of the trade unions. But with constituency activists, Labour's party apparatus and many of the unions lurching to the left, he faced increasingly difficult problems of party management. He forged a close and trusting relationship with Michael Foot (who became deputy leader of the Labour Party and Leader of the House of Commons) that shored up support from the left, while carefully isolating and neutralising the threat from Tony Benn. At the same time, the social democratic right was increasingly on the political and intellectual defensive within the party, and weakened by the loss of leadership figures (with the death of Tony Crosland and the departure of Roy Jenkins to become European Commission president). While Callaghan was necessarily preoccupied with trying to maintain a minimum of party unity and 'keeping the show on the road' there was a notable absence of the self-defeating Wilsonian tricks, gimmickry and ideological smoke screens.

Ideology and Aims

Callaghan had built his career as a practical, moderate and undoctrinaire Labour politician. First elected to parliament in 1945, he was a supporter of the 'Attlee settlement' - the postwar consensus policies of the mixed economy and the welfare state. On broader political, social and cultural issues, he shared the small-c conservative views of Labour's working-class base. He was close to Tony Crosland, the leading postwar social-democratic 'revisionist' intellectual (and shared his general approach), but Callaghan was always first and foremost the political operator, often giving the impression that he would prefer to allow sleeping ideological dogs to rest (Jones 1996: 84). He was, said Barbara Castle (1980: 302), 'constitutionally incapable of being stirred by great issues of principle.' He was not an 'intellectual' – and often impatient with the professional arrogance of some intellectuals - but had a powerful, practical mind and had a devastating capacity for asking the simple, central questions and to subject his advisers to precise and firm grilling.

Callaghan's immense experience was an asset to him in Number 10, but in retrospect the old pro regretted that he had not become PM when he was younger and had more energy. Moreover, Callaghan experienced the same problem of policy definition and renewal of other mid-term 'successor' prime ministers. 'I knew it would not be easy for me to leave a distinctive stamp on the new Administration', he said in his memoirs, 'for the broad outlines of the government's policy on major issues . . . had been settled before my arrival' (Callaghan 1987: 395).

Callaghan's government confirmed the change of course already started and underway under Wilson after 1975 (Ludlum 1992). Labour's period in office between 1974 and 1979 under both prime ministers thus marked a watershed in postwar British political economy - moving away to some degree from conventional Keynesian policies and deficit financing, regarding inflation rather than unemployment as the most serious problem, imposing cash limits on and big cuts in public spending, and adopting money supply targets. Callaghan had played down expectations from the start of his premiership, emphasizing the economic problems, that 'no one owes Britain a living', and that there was 'no soft option' in his first prime-ministerial television broadcast. Callaghan tried to educate his (unreceptive) party and union activists in the new economic 'facts of life' in his famous 1976 Labour conference speech warning about paying ourselves with 'confetti money' and that trying to 'spend your way out of recession' actually led to higher inflation and unemployment (Byrne et al 2020: 70-71). The motivation for this speech was, it must be said, partially tactical. He aimed to appease the money markets and win support from US and European policymakers by demonstrating British resolve, and the intended audience was as much international as domestic (Burn and Cairncross 1992: 160).

The policy shift in Callaghan's time, as in Wilson's, was more a matter of pragmatic response and adaptation rather than ideological conversion. Whatever the later charges of the left, he was no proto-Thatcherite and no monetarist. He was arguably trying to update, not completely reject, Keynesianism (Morgan 1997: 537). Callaghan himself later claimed that he was simply recognizing the limitations of a simplistic Keynesian approach in the circumstances of the time, not ruling out for all time increased public spending to reduce unemployment, though

130

emphasizing the importance of being 'prudent in economic affairs' and that 'certain monetary disciplines were essential to good economic management' (Callaghan 1987: 427). Indeed, within a short time, as the economy stabilized, the government reverted to a more orthodox neo-Keynesian position, reflating the economy to tackle unemployment and using incomes policy to limit inflation.

However, as well as questioning central tenets of the Keynesian economic management approach that no longer seemed to be working, this period also saw the crumbling of the revisionist social-democratic strategy of pursuing egalitarian and welfare goals through economic growth and high public spending, though there were some elements of social-democratic policy continuity. But Callaghan had no alternative doctrine or positive strategy to put in its place - 'remaking' the Labour Party was beyond his scope (Jones 1996). On the policy level he had no desire to reduce the size of the welfare state but, within limits, was interested in reform, though he faced internal party and union opposition to ideas about improving standards, accountability and responsiveness to citizens using or dependent on public services that he and some of his advisers contemplated.

Political Style and Skills

Callaghan's public political character as an affable, bluff and avuncular safe-pair-of- hands politician, offering a reassuring and safety-first common sense approach to everyday problems, worked to his advantage. However, behind the scenes, insiders knew that 'Sunny Jim' was an accomplished wheeler-dealer who could in practice be a bully - brusque, determined and a sometimes brutal and intimidating political operator, with a rough temper and dangerous to cross. 'He did not take prisoners' one of his Number 10 aides, David Lipsey (2012), later recalled. 'If you were hanging from a ledge by your fingers', said parliamentary sketchwriter Edward Pearce, 'he'd stamp on them.' Coming from a deprived, poverty-stricken working-class background (the orphaned son of a naval petty officer), someone who had had a tough upbringing, and who had actually worked as a trade union official as a young man, his Labour movement credentials could never be doubted (Morgan 1997). But more popular in the opinion polls than his own party and the Opposition leader (and still personally outpolling Margaret Thatcher even in April 1979), he had more of the common touch than, say, Wilson, Heath or Thatcher, and also embodied an old-fashioned patriotism and traditional law-and-order and family values and morality, which gave him a significant cross-class, 'Baldwinesque' national appeal.

His senior Downing Street policy adviser, Bernard Donoughue (1987: 88-89), once shrewdly compared prime ministerial leadership styles: 'Mr Callaghan's approach was to keep his political base wide by embracing everybody in the political debate, while himself giving a clear lead. Mrs Thatcher apparently preferred to define her political boundaries narrowly and to treat all who were unable to squeeze within them as aliens. Mr Wilson opted to leave the question of boundaries blurred and hoped that people would not make too much fuss.' Donoughue (2008: 29) was also perceptive about the 'three layers' of his boss's personality and how he compared to Wilson: 'On the surface is Simple Honest Bluff Jim. Below that is a very cunning and secretive politician. But beneath that is somebody who does believe in the simple and honest virtues.' In contrast Wilson had only two layers, claimed Donoughue: 'On top was a devious clever political manipulator. Below that was a kindly timid insecure man. But nothing beneath that' – there was just a 'void' where Callaghan had his 'root values'. Callaghan was, said Donoughue (2008: 31), 'more regular, less Byzantine and extraordinary' than Wilson.

In a technical sense, Britain was (mostly) well-governed under Callaghan, and much of his success was due to the way in which he was able to manage the practices of collective Cabinet government while giving a strong lead and imparting a coherence to decision-making as an authoritative and resolute, but not dictatorial, prime minister. Some commentators think the Callaghan years, 1976-79, saw in fact the peak and the final performance of classic, collective Cabinet government (Hennessy 2000). He was prepared to delegate to ministers and did not try to micro-manage them. He was more seriously interested in policy than Wilson had been, at least in the 1974-76 period. There was no 'kitchen cabinet', cabals or late-night gossiping and plotting with cronies, as under Wilson. (The atmosphere was helped by the fact that Callaghan's position was secure and he was under no threat from ambitious rivals or possible internal party challenges, unlike Wilson in the 1960s). Callaghan was an organized and orderly transactor of government business: direct, steady and straight dealing. He wasn't interested in media 'spin' or manipulation, his chief press secretary, Tom McCaffrey, being a professional Whitehall information officer. Bernard Donoughue, head of the Policy Unit, Tom McNally, the PM's political secretary, and two key civil servants – Ken Stowe, his principal private secretary and Sir John Hunt, the powerful Cabinet Secretary – were the key figures and aides at the centre of the machine in the Callaghan years. He used the Number 10 Policy Unit well to serve up policy ideas – 'I don't have Harold's brain for bright ideas', he once remarked, 'I need the Unit more than Harold did ... I am good at spotting the bright ideas of others and know whether they will work or not' (Donoughue 2008: 15). Callaghan was not interested in the notion of a Prime Minister's Department, though he did consider splitting the Treasury (into a finance/economics ministry and a 'Bureau of the Budget' type department) and might have done so had he won the 1979 election.

Callaghan's personal style of working was different from Wilson's. He was not informal and chatty like Wilson, but rather serious, severe, headmasterly and someone who played his cards close to his chest. He was direct and to-the-point, preferring to take colleagues and issues head-on, not shirking problems or confrontations, where Wilson tried to avoid or steer round difficulties. But 'he needed a lot of time and space', Bernard Donoughue learned: 'He did not like a crowd of advisers around him, preferring them to approach him singly, by prior arrangement and having sent a paper in advance so that he could prepare mentally .... He did not like too much sudden pressure and ... did not like "all the problems to come together"' (Donoughue 2008: 2-5). 'I like to take issues one at a time', Callaghan himself admitted. Later, this became a problem when he appeared to be rather overwhelmed by the avalanche of crises hitting the government in its final phase in 1979.

When the two are united, the prime minister/Chancellor of the Exchequer axis normally dominates British governments, and that was certainly the case with the Callaghan/Denis Healey partnership. Healey was a strong-minded and pugilistic politician but Callaghan was deeply involved and dominant in economic policy, using the top-secret 'economic seminar' to give him the information, advice and leverage he needed in this field. In the end, he would usually side with and back up Healey, though not without insisting on being consulted and brought in first and with hard testing of the arguments and proposals, but he was suspicious of the Treasury and wanted to stop any tendency for them to bounce new measures through the Cabinet. Himself a former Foreign Secretary with many international contacts, and with the relatively junior David Owen as Foreign Secretary (from 1977, after Crosland died), Callaghan was able to dominate British foreign policy-making, emerging as a major international statesman and 'summiteer'. He built close and trusting relations with Gerald Ford, Jimmy Carter, Helmut Schmidt and other world leaders, and played a major role on detente, East-West relations, and other international security and diplomatic issues. He was calm and authoritative, and had a sure touch, in handling the intelligence and security side of the prime minister's job. On domestic policy, he was a cautious and practical politician, and a consensus leader rather than a visionary or inspirational figure, but he was also, within his limits, an innovator (e.g. starting the 'great debate' on educational standards in 1976).

Context
The 1970s was a tumultuous decade in which successive Conservative and Labour governments ended in failure, frustration and electoral defeat against a background of economic crisis, social upheaval and political dislocation. The postwar consensus was breaking down; party politics became increasingly polarised; 'stagflation' and a more turbulent

international economic environment undermined the practice of and faith in Keynesian economic management; the veto power of trade unions raised the spectre of 'ungovernability'.

From the beginning of his tenure, Callaghan was constrained by daunting economic and political circumstances that meant that his premiership was largely an exercise in buying time and staving off catastrophe rather than more constructive policy achievement. The economic situation was dire, with raging inflation, high unemployment and severe pressure on sterling. But Callaghan's handling of the 1976 International Monetary Fund crisis showed his great skills in tactical political management and canny deal making. Through a marathon sequence of difficult ministerial meetings (twenty-six over two months), the prime minister patiently allowed all ministers to have their say, put forward their ideas and voice their opinions. He let the different Cabinet factions discuss the problems and the options, talk themselves out and edge towards acceptance of a £2.5 billion package of public spending cuts as the price for securing a massive IMF loan and stabilising the pound in the international markets. He had resisted IMF pressure for even more draconian cuts and avoided ministerial resignations, the break-up of the Labour Cabinet and damage to social benefits (e.g. health prescription charges) - in terms of Labour Party history, he had thus avoided a repeat of the disastrous events of 1931 and 1951. He succeeded, that is, in his primary objective of maintaining the unity of his Cabinet and keeping the Labour Party in power (Burk and Cairncross 1992; Hickson 2005).

Politically, Callaghan's government was always living on borrowed time in the sense that Labour's fragile majority in parliament disappeared almost immediately after he took over. He was not a remote presidential-type leader and took pains to be available and to keep in touch with Labour MPs - he was, says Morgan (1997: 513, 756), 'a great Commons tearoom operator, with a gift for appealing to the most humdrum, insignificant backbencher and making him a friend for life . . . In the party, he never neglected a detail, never miscalculated the votes, never forgot a face.' All the same, backbench rebels were a constant source of trouble. For three years he struggled through, stitching together majorities in deals with minor parties and helped by the negotiation of the Lib-Lab pact (1977-78) that in truth saw Callaghan give very little away to the Liberal Party (led by David Steel, with whom he had a good relationship and rated highly) in return for their support in the division lobbies (Dorey 2011). There was also a more informal and publicly denied understanding and private dealings with some Ulster Unionist MPs that helped the government manage the parliamentary pitfalls of minority government (Peacock 2018). He was always a highly effective 'backstage' negotiator, conciliator and political poker-player. The Lib-Lab pact effectively gave Callaghan a 20-month breathing space in which Labour could start to benefit from the recovery of the economy, improve its poll ratings against the Conservatives and look like a fairly successful government in the circumstances, one that knew what it was doing.

It was at that point that Callaghan's normally sure judgement and political touch failed him. After three years of severe wage restraint (which had brought inflation down from 25 per cent in 1975 to 8 per cent in 1978), the 5 per cent pay norm he personally insisted upon for 1978-9 was unrealistic and undeliverable. Union bosses and other ministers were aghast but given the chance, he would have been even tougher in the attempt to squeeze inflation out of the system, at times talking about a 0 per cent target for pay increases. With falling real living standards, pressure and resentment on the factory floor and among public sector workers were building up. Then, Callaghan confounded expectations by deciding against calling an election in October 1978 (Dorey 2016). With the benefit of hindsight, this is always seen as a disastrous tactical mistake. From the start there had been some consideration in Number 10 of election timing, in 1976 and 1977, given the absence of a majority and the dangers of defeat on a vote of no-confidence, but with a hung parliament or a Conservative victory looking most likely an early dissolution was ruled out. By 1978 it seemed a more realistic option but over the summer Callaghan carefully studied private polling evidence (particularly in marginal seats) and concluded that the result would be another hung parliament and a minority

Labour government. He had had enough of the messy compromises and muddling-through that involved. The most senior Cabinet ministers, the whips' office and the party organisers in the country were also opposed to an early election, and he thought that the pay policy would work (the unions, he assumed, not wanting to do anything to risk the election of a Conservative government) and that, by hanging on, Labour's prospects would improve with another period of steady administration and economic advance. Calling an early election looked to Callaghan like a high-risk move, a gamble. The three preceding general elections (1970, February 1974 and October 1974) had, after all, all been called early and had delivered poorer results for the incumbent governments than had been predicted by the opinion polls (two defeats for the PMs concerned and one wafer-thin majority).

But then, of course, it all went wrong. The political and economic successes of his government were turned to ash during the strikes, militancy and disruption of the subsequent 'winter of discontent' of late 1978-early 1979 (Shepherd 2013a and 2013b). Callaghan himself seemed indecisive and irresolute - almost paralysed, fatalistic and inert - in the face of the explosion of raw union power that destroyed Labour's reputation as the party that could most effectively 'work with the unions'. It was a failure both of party leadership (with the group he supposedly knew best and had defended when the Wilson Labour government had tried to regulate union power in the 1960s) and of national leadership (an attempt to play the lofty world statesman producing the infamous and lethal newspaper headline 'crisis? what crisis?'). The government finally collapsed after the failure of the devolution referendums (the legislation introduced largely as a reluctant and defensive response to the nationalists' threat to Labour's Scottish base) in March 1979 (Mitchell and Williamson 2022). But the Callaghan government had in effect lost the May 1979 election months before it was actually held.

Conclusion
Had he followed his personal inclination in May 1979 Callaghan

would have resigned immediately as Labour leader, leaving the party to find a new leader. Having been in active politics for over three decades, it would have been a natural time to bow out. Given the Conservative majority of 43 and a likely normal term for the new parliament, he would be over 70 at the time of the next general election. But he was persuaded to stay on and unanimously re-elected. However, his 17 months as Leader of the Opposition were, he would admit, one of the unhappiest periods in his life. He told Denis Healey that he planned to stay on just long enough to 'take the shine off the ball' for him, by which he meant getting the party over the immediate pain and bitterness of defeat, and standing up to the Left, in the hope of smoothing the way for his preferred successor. But the decision to stay on was a mistake and one he later regretted. Callaghan was unable to stop Labour tearing itself apart, with left-right ideological feuding and battles over changes to the party's constitution designed to shackle the party leadership and MPs. Perhaps no one else could have done any better as the Labour Party seemed determined to spiral into extremism and irrelevance – and things got worse in and for the party after Callaghan left the leadership. The left-wing Michael Foot beat Healey for the leadership in November 1980 and it was under Foot that defeat (in 1979) was really turned into disaster (in 1983), helping to give Thatcher the time and political space to undo the postwar consensus policies that Callaghan had stood for, and to remake British politics.

Callaghan became a model ex-prime minister (Theakston 2010). 'He behaved wonderfully well in retirement', as Peter Hennessy said. 'He was an example of how ex-Prime Ministers should behave.' He was a dignified and authoritative voice, an active and respected elder statesman. It was noticeable, however, that after 1994, when Tony Blair, became party leader, Callaghan was not enthusiastic about the direction the Labour Party took (unhappy about the weakening of the union link and the drift to the right). As New Labour distanced itself from the party's past, its traditions and its working-class roots, Callaghan spoke for many in the party when he protested about the much-used 'Old Labour' label, describing himself in a 1996 interview as 'Original Labour'. There was a sense also of New Labour keeping him at a distance to avoid unhelpful reminders of the 'Winter of Discontent'. 'Yes, I've been blotted out of the photographs', Callaghan would say.

Looking at it all in the round, however, and given his economic and political inheritance and context, Callaghan was a better prime minister than he was given credit for in the aftermath of Labour's 1979 defeat. He showed steel and was a canny operator though he paid the price for his misjudgements in relation to the trade unions, pay policy and election timing in 1978-79. The economic record 1974-79 was in many ways better than Labour's critics pretend (Artis et al 1992). Playing 'the calm pilot in the storms' (Morgan 1992: 272), Callaghan's skills as an astute political operator and party manager were just what the situation needed, though he seemed to run out of steam at the end, making fatal miscalculations and blunders in his final year (and he left his party descending into civil war). In a wider sense, however, his premiership had an 'end of an era' feel to it, and he was a politician better equipped for solid 'steady-as-we-go' administration and for conducting a holding operation than for solving the Labour Party's deepening identity crisis or articulating new goals and values. In terms of aims, Callaghan was a 'man of 1945'; as his biographer puts it: 'he regarded Attlee's consensus as his abiding point of reference and always took it as his ideological starting point' (Morgan 1997: 749). But serving as PM at a time when the postwar consensus was unravelling, and recognizing that the old certainties were being challenged and that he could not control or oppose the 'sea change' that he sensed was occurring in British politics (Donoghue 1987: 191; Donoghue 2008: 7), he was not able to chart a new course and his managerial/centrist pragmatism was in the end ineffective. Uncontrollable trade union unrest and the steadily widening ideological cracks within the Labour Party also defeated his attempts to play the stabiliser/balancer. Ultimately, it seemed that Callaghan and his government were just hanging on, hoping to win re-election, but with no strong sense of destination, vision or purpose beyond short-term political survival (Donoghue 1987: 167; Brivati 1998). It was unheroic and, in the end, unsuccessful - but he almost pulled it off, and probably no one else could have done so.

References

Artis, M., Cobham, D. and Wickham-Jones, M. (1992). 'Social Democracy in Hard Times: The Economic Record of the Labour Government 1974-79. *Twentieth Century British History* 3 (1): 32-58.

Brivati, B. (1998). 'James Callaghan' in R. Eccleshall and G. Walker (eds), *Biographical Dictionary of British Prime Ministers.* London: Routledge.

Burk, K. and Cairncross, A. (1992). *'Goodbye Great Britain': The 1976 IMF Crisis.* London and New Haven, CT: Yale University Press.

Byrne, C., Randall, N. and Theakston, K. (2020). *Disjunctive Prime Ministerial   Leadership in British Politics: From Baldwin to Brexit.* London: Palgrave Macmillan.

Callaghan, J. (1987). *Time and Chance.* Glasgow: Collins.

Castle, B. (1980). *The Castle Diaries 1974-76.* London: Weidenfeld & Nicolson.

Donoughue, B. (1987). *Prime Minister: The Conduct of Policy Under Harold Wilson and James Callaghan.* London: Cape.

Donoughue, B. (2008). *Downing Street Diary: With James Callaghan in No.10.* London: Jonathan Cape.

Donoughue, B. (2013). 'James Callaghan Remembered', seminar at Bodleian   Library, Oxford, [https:// podcasts.ox.ac.uk/lord-donoughue-remembers-jim-callaghan]

Dorey, P. (2011). '"A rather novel constitutional experiment": the formation of the 1977-8 Lib-Lab Pact', *Parliamentary history.* 30 (3): 374-394.

Dorey, P. (2016): "Should I stay or should I go?": James Callaghan's decision not to call an autumn 1978 general election', *British Politics.* 11 (1): 95-118.

Lipsey, D. (2012). *In the Corridors of Power: An Autobiography.* London: Biteback Publishing.

Ludlam, S. (1992). 'The Gnomes of Washington: Four Myths of the 1976 IMF Crisis', *Political Studies*, 40 (4): 713-727.

Hennessy, P. (2000). *The Prime Minister: The Office and Its Holders Since 1945*. London: Allen Lane.

Hickson, K. (2005). *The IMF Crisis of 1976 and British Politics*. London: I.B. Tauris.

Hickson, K. And Miles, J. (eds) (2020). *James Callaghan: An Underrated Prime Minister?* London: Biteback Publishing.

Jones, T. (1996). *Remaking the Labour Party*. London: Routledge.

Mitchell, J. and Williamson, C. (2022). 'Choreography of Defeat: The Fall of the 1979 Government', *Parliamentary History*, 41 (2): 342-365.

Morgan, K. (1992). *Labour People: Leaders and Lieutenants - Hardie to Kinnock*. Oxford: Oxford University Press.

Morgan, K. (1997). *Callaghan: A Life*. Oxford: Oxford University Press.

Peacock, T. (2018): *The British tradition of minority government*. Manchester: Manchester University Press.

Seldon, A. & Hickson, K. (eds) (2004). *New Labour, Old Labour: The Wilson and Callaghan Governments 1974-1979*. London: Routledge.

Shepherd, J. (2013a). *Crisis? What crisis?: The Callaghan government and the British 'winter of discontent'*. Manchester: Manchester University Press.

Shepherd, J. (2013b). 'The Fall of the Callaghan Government, 1979', in T. Heppell and K. Theakston (eds), *How Labour Governments Fall: From Ramsay MacDonald to Gordon Brown*. London: Palgrave Macmillan.

Theakston, K. (2010). *After Number 10: Former Prime Ministers in British Politics*. London: Palgrave Macmillan.

Williams, P. (1982). 'Changing Styles of Labour Leadership.' In D. Kavanagh (ed), *The Politics of the Labour Party*. London: Allen & Unwin.

Chapter 10
Margaret Thatcher (1979-90)

Books about British politics in the 1980s with titles such as *The Thatcher Phenomenon* (Young and Sloman 1986), *Mrs Thatcher's Revolution* (Jenkins 1987) and *The Thatcher Era* (Riddell 1991) testified to the way in which Margaret Thatcher, as prime minister, appeared personally and directly to dominate and reshape government, politics and society in that period in a unique way. She gave her name to an 'ism' - Thatcherism. Commentators stressed 'the crucial importance of her personality to what her government does. Her politics proceeds from her character' (Young and Sloman 1986: 142). But following her dramatic fall from power in 1990, sceptics argued that she had been more pragmatic and circumscribed than many pundits (both supporters and critics of Thatcherism) had allowed, and queried the consistency and coherence of her policies and leadership (Beattie 1991). And with a longer perspective, several decades further on from the 1980s, the sense of contradictions within Thatcherism, the complexities of the figure at its centre, and the importance of contingency, circumstances and unintended consequences in understanding her premiership and its legacy remained   strong (Vinen 2010; Moore 2013, 2015, 2019).

Party Leadership
Until it happened, no one (including her) could imagine Margaret Thatcher's rise to party and then national leadership. She became Conservative Party leader in 1975 almost by accident, seizing her chance to run against an incumbent (Heath) who was rejected as an election-loser and whose government (1970-4) had ended in chaos and failure. The old Tory 'magic circle' would never have given the leadership to Thatcher, but a 'peasants' revolt' by demoralised and desperate Conservative backbenchers unseated Heath and she unexpectedly won as other, more heavyweight figures held back (until it was too late to stop her).

This combination of luck and guts was always a significant factor in Thatcher's political success. She was an outsider because of her sex, her modest social origins, and her political position in the Conservative Party. She had been hardworking and determined, but her political progress until then had owed much to political tokenism as the 'statutory woman' and her ministerial experience was narrow. She had been a conventional big-spender as Heath's education minister and had acquiesced in his government's policy U-turns, which the Thatcherites later excoriated as a 'great betrayal'. The notorious 'milk-snatcher' storm only confirmed her limited public and political appeal (the Tory Establishment's doubts in that respect probably not being overcome until after 1982).

Thatcher was clearly on the right of her party but she won the leadership in 1975 probably more because she was 'not Heath' than because of an ideological uprising, though 'negative' factors alone did not account for her victory – ideology and policy stances mattered, with the Tory right strongly backing her while the left of the party supported Heath and then Whitelaw (Wickham-Jones 1997; Cowley and Bailey 2000). Surrounded by former Heathites and in a minority in the Shadow Cabinet, she was of necessity a cautious Leader of the Opposition and while party policy had moved to the right, the Conservatives were by no means committed to a radical 'Thatcherite' programme in 1979 - an election the party won, polls indicated, despite rather than because of her leadership.

Subsequently, throughout her time as PM, and despite her election victories, 'she lacked significant majority support for her projects in the Cabinet, the parliamentary party, and the electorate' as historian Alan Beattie (1991: 8) once observed. Though she had vanquished the Cabinet 'wets' in her first term and was unassailable after the Falklands War and her 1983 election victory, neither the Cabinet nor the parliamentary party ever became 'Thatcherised'. As her premiership went on, she in fact alienated, lost through resignation or dismissed natural supporters and Thatcherite ministers, promoted politicians who were never 'one of us' (e.g. Douglas Hurd and Kenneth Clarke), and fell out with powerful allies-cum-rivals such as Geoffrey

Howe, Norman Tebbit and Nigel Lawson. This was the political equivalent of sawing through the branch of a tree while you are sitting on it. In the end, two-thirds of the Cabinet advised her to throw in the towel when Michael Heseltine challenged for the leadership in November 1990. The bulk of Conservative MPs remained non-ideological party loyalists who supported her only so long as she brought political and economic success. At first, Thatcher – aware of Heath's failings – worked hard to keep in touch with her MPs but as time went on she got more and more remote from them, wouldn't listen and sometimes showed little respect. In 1990 backbench support melted away as the polls indicated that she had become a massive electoral liability, dragging down her party (Wickham-Jones and Shell 1991: Moore 2019: 649).

Ideology and Aims

There is a sense in which 'Thatcherism' existed long before Mrs Thatcher became leader of the Conservative Party in 1975, in that she gave expression to the right-wing views on the unions, public spending and taxation and to the hostility towards the postwar 'Butskellite' consensus that had existed within the party, particularly at rank-and-file level, through the 1950s and 1960s (Green 1999). Although she famously once produced a copy of Hayek's *The Constitution of Liberty* from her handbag, declaring '*this* is what we believe', Mrs Thatcher was always primarily a practical politician - she was not a profound or original political thinker or an intellectual-in-politics (unlike, say, her close colleague Sir Keith Joseph). She saw the importance of ideas in politics, however, and believed that politics should be a battle of ideas between opposed philosophies and moral values. Her own strong beliefs and ideas were more the product of her upbringing, her personal experiences of the 1970s, and her gut instincts, than rational argument or theorising.

She did not burst into the front rank of politics with a well-developed ideology in 1975. 'Thatcherism' was really invented by others - the 'New Right' think tanks and intellectuals - and she was fortunate in coming to power as the ideological counter-revolution was taking shape and gathering strength. Her role was to create political space for that process by mobilising support and controlling the agenda of government. She was good at simplifying complex ideas and relating them to everyday issues and concerns - using ideas for her (populist) political purposes (Campbell 2000). Like Reagan, she expressed and embodied a set of apparently clear and simple ideas (illustrating the argument sometimes made that successful leadership is about leaders telling and embodying persuasive 'stories' about their institutions or countries) (Gardner 1996). But in practice her ideas about economy, state and society were a complex and not necessarily coherent mix, drawing on different strands of the Tory tradition and neo-liberalism (Kavanagh 1990), and her approach was not ideologically consistent (her government's actions often being contrary to free-market dogmas, for instance). Historian Peter Clarke (1996: 367) also captured an important aspect of her personal and political style: 'she was to disappoint the principled exponents of Thatcherism in her own Cabinet when general doctrines about government non-interference clashed with her restless incapacity to refrain from interfering - because she felt she knew best.'

Political Style and Skills

Thatcher was certainly a 'conviction politician' - there was a driving sense of mission, tremendous zeal and energy, moral certainty, a black-and-white view of the world and of people and issues. She was a warrior or crusader type of prime minister, leading from the front, and a powerful and dominating (even domineering and bullying) presence in government: grabbing issues, always master of the details, her sudden and unpredictable interventions keeping Whitehall in a perpetual state of tension. Kenneth Baker, one of her ministers, described her as 'personally dominant, supremely self-confident, infuriatingly stubborn . . . a strange mixture of broad views and narrow prejudices' (Gardener 1996: 238). The prejudices were usually those of the rank-and-file party activists - unlike other Conservative leaders, Thatcher did not feel disdain for the views of the Tory grass roots, but shared and expressed them. But what Malcolm Rifkind   (2000) called her 'phenomenal single-

145

mindedness in the pursuit and use of power' means, as John Campbell put it, that just as much emphasis should be put on the second word of the 'conviction politician' label as on the first. 'She could be brilliantly insincere . . . when the situation required it, and such was her reputation for burning integrity that few could spot the difference. At a number of critical points . . . it was only this which enabled her to skate on some very thin ice and get away with it' (Campbell 2000: 275). The 1986 'Westland affair' provided the most dramatic example of her (and her advisers) sometimes machiavellian methods, and revealed how she was more accomplished at 'the darker political arts' than she liked to admit (Young 2000: 427-57; Moore 2015: 449-96).

Always well briefed, Thatcher regularly made mincemeat of her opponents at Question Time (though she had not done well at PMQs when in Opposition), but she was not in general a good parliamentary speaker (and made as few speeches as possible). 'Her combative belief in her own rightness ensures that she is rarely discomforted and never overwhelmed', said Roy Jenkins, 'but she brings no special qualities of persuasiveness or debating skill which enable her to move minds.' On the other hand, she regularly wiped the floor with television interviewers, working hard to develop her TV skills and image with the aid of her media advisers (Campbell 2003: 452-53, 477-78).

She had a 'rigid cast of mind', says John Campbell (2000: 64), that 'dealt in facts and moral certainties' and was 'intolerant of ambiguity and equivocation'. This was both a source of strength and – ultimately – a limitation. As prime minister, her style was aggressively argumentative not calmly analytical. She had a phenomenal recall of detail and could always find the weak point in a proposal. She had 'instant certainty', it was said, but could be a good listener, though it required expertise, an equal command of detail, and courage to get a case across to her. Crucially, Thatcher argued 'not merely to clear her mind, but to win' (Campbell 2003: 17). One after another 'insider' or minister describes her approach as 'unstructured', 'abrasive', 'illogical' or 'outrageous'. Initially, this style may have been necessary and effective as she struggled to assert her authority and force through radical policies. It was a brutal way of testing policies and testing ministers. But it became counter-productive as her premiership went on and as 'insiders' felt that she became increasingly irrational, harder to deal with and less interested in hearing things that did not support her convictions (Campbell 2003: 16-19, 445-56; Hennessy 2000: 404). Thatcher's displays of anger, triumphalism, contempt and determination to dominate certainly suggest a figure operating at a high emotional temperature. Fatally, in the final phase of her premiership, she was described as 'increasingly willful and tempestuous' and (by one of her ministers) as 'increasingly and damagingly erratic in her behaviour' (Patten 2005: 76).

Thatcher was certainly a dynamic force, aiming by force of will and force of personality to bury the old consensus, fill the ideological vacuum and transform the economy, society and social attitudes. 'Prime Minister, our report is based on the facts', trembling officials once told her. 'The facts. The *facts*. I have been elected to *change* the facts', she shot back (Hennessy 2000: 422). In office, she was able to innovate in policy, pursue her radical vision and set the agenda (for her opponents and her successors). But crucial to Mrs Thatcher's political survival and success (at least up to her third term) was the combination of caution and tactical flexibility alongside strategic vision and purpose. 'She knew exactly what she wanted to accomplish, but she was happy to tack towards her destination when a straight line seemed unachievable' as Michael Portillo (2000), once said.

One of her staff, Matthew Parris (2000), recalled: 'you could never persuade Thatcher that what she wanted was wrong, but you could persuade her that she could not have what she wanted. On gut instinct she was immovable, implacable, confident. But on the risks, the contingencies and the sheer mechanics, she was secretly much less confident. Cornered by events (as in the Falklands or, perhaps, the economic depression of the early 1980s) her resolve hardened and she showed great nerve; but she did not aim to be cornered by events, and if an escape door could be persuasively commended, she took it. She would back out with an ill grace, but back out she did.'

She practised the 'art of the possible', not in the (usual) minimalist sense of doing only what you can or must, but aiming

147

to do 'as much as she could, when she could' says John Campbell (2000: 368-69). She had a well-developed feel for what would go down well with the electorate (or at least 'our people'), when to accept a compromise, when to fight a battle and when to back off. Thus, contrary to her instincts, she compromised over the Rhodesia/Zimbabwe settlement in 1979 and with the Chinese over Hong Kong, and gave way in the face of a threatened coal strike in 1981 (only to crush the miners' union in the 1984-5 dispute). She also accepted a step-by-step approach to trade union reform. Often, she was the last to be persuaded that key 'Thatcherite' policies were politically practicable or prudent. Against all expectations, she was eventually persuaded by ministers and officials into backing the 1985 Anglo-Irish Agreement to deal with the Northern Ireland problem. And on European policy too, John Major argued that for most of her time in government, Mrs Thatcher's actions showed her to be as much a pragmatist as she was a sceptic: taking an abrasive line, complaining loudly and stridently attacking 'Brussels', but in the end accepting - even welcoming - integration on issues such as the Single Market. But this pragmatism co-existed with a visceral anti-EU-ism (and hostility to Germany) that increasingly tended to spill over into public in the late-1980s. Major (1999: 175) suggested that it was when she became less able to keep these two sides of her political personality bolted together that her hold on her government and party started to crumble.

Thatcher showed considerable resilience as prime minister: keeping her nerve through the difficult 1979-81 period (when the Cabinet was deeply divided, her poll ratings falling to historic lows, and the economy plunging into recession); demonstrating courage during the 1982 Falklands War; recovering from another low point after the 1986 Westland crisis (which nearly brought her down). Even more remarkable, was the way in which, over her premiership, her government became more - rather than less - radical and innovative and she was able to continue to provide drive and direction, remaining central to policy development. The privatisation policy, for instance, was not the result of a clear blueprint drawn up in Opposition but developed piecemeal in office and built up momentum as a central and defining 'Thatcherite' policy only after 1983. In other areas (e.g. local government, education), increasingly radical policies were put together as the government struggled to learn from experience, respond to events and keep the initiative (Riddell 1991: 10-11. Thatcher continually challenged the inertial tendencies of Whitehall and never lost her appetite for 'taking on' established interests.

Thatcher's prime ministerial style was distinctive: the downgrading of the Cabinet and Cabinet committee system, the greater use of bilaterals, the increased reliance on personal advisers, the politicisation of some civil servants, 'bouncing' colleagues with off-the-cuff public pronouncements, even signalling dissent from government decisions she disliked. It was an adversarial style - 'Margaret actually liked a good row', according to one of her ministers, Kenneth Clarke (1999) - and civil servants would privately grade her engagements with ministers on the Richter scale. More than any other prime minister, in fact, she seems to have used fear as a political tool; Anthony King (1985: 57-8) called her 'the Lyndon Johnson of modern British politics' for her 'hectoring, cajoling, threatening . . . bullying' style and her willingness to humiliate ministers and officials. She got away with it for a long time but those methods were costly in the end. Partly, all that reflected her temperament. But it was also a matter of the objective situation she was in: in a minority in her own Cabinet (very definitely up to 1982 and - though a larger one - even after 1983) and seeking to drive through an agenda of her own. She was in fact more often on the losing side of the argument and defeated in Cabinet than the mythology allows (King 1985: 116-17). She would have been even more constrained but for her unorthodox methods of governing. As it was, (Lord) Willie Whitelaw exerted a subtle restraining influence as deputy PM (until 1988), and that Nigel Lawson, at the peak of his power as Chancellor of the Exchequer in 1987-88, was able to follow a policy of shadowing the deutschmark contrary to the PM's wishes, also showed the limits to Thatcher's power. In 1989 a Lawson-Howe (foreign secretary) alliance, backed by a joint resignation threat, forced her into making a commitment to join the European exchange rate mechanism (ERM), and a year later an isolated and weakened Thatcher could not block their replacements, John Major and Douglas Hurd, when they insisted on the UK entering the ERM.

Thatcher did reach out for advice and information, appointing at different times high-powered special advisers inside Number 10 on economic policy, foreign policy and efficiency in government. She also tapped a private network of informal advisers from different walks of life – including academics and businessmen – though the problem was that they tended to be committed Thatcherites who reinforced her opinions. It was ultimately to her disadvantage that her two most powerful advisers – Bernard Ingham (press secretary) and Charles Powell (Whitehall private secretary) – became over-identified with her (Kavanagh and Seldon 1999). There are suggestions that in private Powell would argue vigorously with her and sometimes she would concede, but the dominant view (as expressed by Nigel Lawson) was that Powell 'never saw it as his role to question her prejudices, merely to refine the language in which they were expressed' (Lawson 1992: 467, 680) Increasingly, this helped to make her Number 10 'court' something of an echo chamber. After her historic third successive election victory in 1987 there was a definite hardening of the political arteries. Thatcher became increasingly cocooned or cut off by her courtiers from her ministers, backbenchers and the outside world. With the retirement of Whitelaw and the resignation of Lawson (in 1989), there was no minister who could now stand up to her. Thatcher's strengths transformed into flaws and there were increasing signs of authoritarianism, intolerance, inflexibility, recklessness and self-righteousness. The self-inflicted poll tax disaster showed how far hubris had displaced the pragmatic caution of 1975-85 and marked the beginning of the end for her.

A critical and fascinating aspect of this supercharged personality was, of course, Mrs Thatcher's gender (Ribberink 2005). She liked to say it was more important that she was the first prime minister with a science degree than the first woman in that office. Nevertheless, her political colleagues and ministers were well aware of what Douglas Hurd (1993) called 'the extraordinary combination of masculine and feminine qualities which gave [her] such a unique armoury.' Doubtless, much is explained by the fact that she had had to make her way in a male-dominated profession and in a traditionally chauvinistic party - shut out from the clubbable world of the Tory grandees who dismissed her as 'that woman' (Clarke 1996: 359). If she failed, she recognised, 'no chums would save her' (Moore 2019: 856).

But what was once described as her adept 'sexual style flexing' allowed her to use her sex as a political weapon, as circumstances demanded or suited (Genovese 1993: 203-7; Young 1990: 303-12). Thus, on one level she was the 'honorary man' ('the best man among them' it was sometimes said of her Cabinet) or even the tough, confrontational and aggressive 'macho' leader. One official noted how she came across in meetings as though she was 'everyone's mother in a bad temper' (Moore 2015: 4) Fitting the so-called 'Queen Bee' model, she had no time for the feminist movement and did little to advance other women (appointing only one other woman, for a brief period, to her Cabinet). Within her own party, and perhaps in international meetings too, she benefitted from the inability and/or unwillingness of male politicians of a certain age and class, at least at that time, to stand up to a powerful woman and argue back. They seemed equally vulnerable to what different ministers and advisers described as Thatcher's use of 'feminine wiles' and 'her feminine charm' to get her way (Slocock 2018).

A very public relations-conscious leader, she and her advisers worked on her clothes, her hair and even her voice to mould her image and project her personality and power (Conway 2016). From the time in Opposition onwards, they exploited a range of images of women - the housewife, the teacher/headmistress, the nanny - to carry her political message(s), revelling in the 'Iron Lady' gibe flung by the Soviets, and in government appealing to and exploiting British nationalism with Mrs Thatcher cast as 'Britannia', and being transformed into the 'Warrior Queen' after the Falklands War. Mrs Thatcher was undoubtedly a formidable and effective politician, not least for the remarkable way in which her gender was (or became) more of an asset than a liability (Campbell

2000: 408-10).

Context

Context is vital in Thatcher's case, historian John Ramsden (1999: 455) arguing that 'the foundations of her . . . authority lacked real solidity, being dependent on numerous factors outside her control.' She benefitted from the mistakes and miscalculations of Heath in 1975 and Callaghan in 1978-9. Conservative Central Office itself could hardly have invented such inept and/or extreme opponents and enemies as Michael Foot, General Galtieri and Arthur Scargill. North Sea oil came on tap just in time to provide a balance of payments cushion for the Thatcherite 'economic experiment' (Ramsden 1999: 439). The bulk of the press was noisily supportive, and in a wider sense Thatcher (and Thatcherism) were helped also by the perception that they were going with the tide. Domestically and internationally, elite opinion moved to the right in the 1970s, questioning the Keynesian welfare state consensus and supporting monetarism and free markets. In the USA, in Europe and elsewhere in the world, there were similar policy shifts (e.g. on taxation, public spending and privatisation) to those seen in Britain. At the party-political level, Labour's civil war and lurch into unelectability, together with the Social Democratic break-away and the splintering of the opposition, meant that in a first-past-the-post electoral system the Conservatives were rewarded with crushing parliamentary majorities (144 in 1983, 101 in 1987) on around 43 per cent of the vote. All this added up to a favourable environment for a successful statecraft.

The relationship between public opinion and Mrs Thatcher's leadership is complex. It was always the case that more people voted against her and the Conservatives than voted for them. Opinion about her was unusually sharply polarised (King 1985: 107-114), and a 1989 poll is revealing: 67 per cent disliked her, but 63 per cent respected her (Riddell 1991: 214). The 'Thatcher factor' was something of a double-edged sword for the Conservatives: in the early years, the votes gained by her strong personality outweighed those lost by it, but by the third term the balance had shifted the other way (Lawson 1992:

1001). The skilled working class voters (the C2s) of the south of England and the private sector in particular were 'Thatcher's people' and their defection from Labour was crucial in her electoral success in 1979 and subsequently, even as the Conservatives started to see a loss of some middle class support. Ideology and statecraft were shrewdly married, with the popular council house sales policy solidifying support in this key electoral bloc. But Thatcher's election victories were due more to contingent factors such as the state of the opposition and her government's economic record than to the appeal of Thatcherite values. 'Economics are the method', Thatcher once said; 'the object is to change the heart and soul'. The evidence here is that she failed (as polling work by Ivor Crewe [1989] showed) but was able to keep winning elections because while voters' hearts were on the left, their wallets were on the right (Ramsden 1999: 450).

Thatcher herself recognised that public opinion imposed some limits on her. She successfully refashioned attitudes on the unemployment issue, overturning the post-war assumption that presiding over mass unemployment would spell political suicide for a government. On the trade unions, she was able to take advantage of changing opinion, and her government's reforms were popular (Moon 1995: 6). On privatisation, there was more active leadership of public opinion (Sykes 2000: 141-43). But on health policy, Mrs Thatcher was constrained by strong public support for the NHS (Moon 1995:8), disappointed the New Right ideologues, increased spending and introduced a controversial reorganisation scheme only in the third term.

In a premiership as long as Mrs Thatcher's the operating environment was not, of course, static. Politically and economically she was more constrained at some times than at others, facing difficult situations in 1979-81, after the Westland affair in 1986, and again in 1989-90 (made vulnerable because of divisions over Europe, ministerial resignations, the poll tax and economic problems). Post-Falklands and bolstered by the election triumphs of 1983 and 1987, she was in a much stronger position. For much of her premiership, Thatcher was a skilful and resourceful leader in using the tools and powers at her disposal in Number 10. She has been well described by Peter Clarke (1996: 360) as 'a political opportunist in the best sense: always quick to seize the opportunities which came her way and exploit them.' But in the end, she was brought down because she had stretched the elastic too far and could not or would not recognise her need for Cabinet and party support.

Conclusion

As Britain's first woman prime minister, PM for 11 years and winner of three successive general elections, Margaret Thatcher would deserve a place in the record books. But her impact was more profound than that. She was the dominant figure on the British political scene in the 1980s - and her influence was still being powerfully felt through the 1990s and beyond, as both John Major and Tony Blair would testify. She has had a long-term intellectual impact and reshaped the political agenda. The most opinionated and evangelical prime minister since Gladstone in the 19th century (Crewe 1989: 240), she aimed to reshape British society. We can now see that the record of her government was mixed: there were far-reaching changes in the 1980s in the British economy, in the labour market, in industry, in British society and in Britain's international standing. Some of these changes reflected her government's policies and actions; others owed more to the unintended consequences and side effects of those policies and actions; and some reflected broader long-term international trends and influences. The 'bust' - 'boom' - 'bust' economic roller-coster of 1979-90 hardly reversed Britain's relative economic decline: annual economic growth over her premiership averaged 1.8 percent, lower than in the 1960s and 1970s and lower than in other OECD countries. But on any reckoning, Mrs Thatcher stands out as one of the great political 'weather-makers' of postwar Britain (Hennessy 2000: 530), having a transformative and long-term effect on the political landscape and on the terms of political argument. The course of British politics would have been different without her - something that can be said of few politicians.

References

Campbell, J. (2000). *Margaret Thatcher Volume One: The Grocer's Daughter*. London: Jonathan Cape.

Campbell, J. (2003). *Margaret Thatcher Volume Two: The Iron Lady*. London: Jonathan Cape.

Clarke, K. (1999). 'Clarke on Cabinet Government. *LSE Magazine*. 11 (2): 8-11.

Clarke, P. (1996). *Hope and Glory: Britain 1900-1990*. London: Allen Lane Penguin Press.

Conway, D. (2016). 'Margaret Thatcher, Dress and the Politics of Fashion.' In: A. Behnke (ed), *The International Politics of Fashion*. London: Routledge.

Cowley, P. and Bailey, M. (2000). 'Peasants' uprising or religious war? Re-examining the 1975 Conservative leadership contest', *British Journal of Political Science*. , 30 (4): 599-629.

Crewe, I. (1989). 'Values: The Crusade That Failed. In D. Kavanagh and A. Seldon (eds) *The Thatcher Effect*. Oxford: Oxford University Press.

Gardner, H. (1996). *Leading Minds*. London: HarperCollins.

Genovese, M. (1993). 'Margaret Thatcher and the Politics of Conviction Leadership. *Sage Focus Editions,* (153): 177-210.

Green, E. (1999). 'Thatcherism: An Historical Perspective.' *Transactions of the Royal Historical Society*. 6th series (9): 17-42.

Hennessy, P. (2000). *The Prime Minister: The Office and Its Holders Since 1945*. London: Allen Lane.

Hurd, D. (1993). 'Chairing From the Front. *The Spectator*. November 6.

Jenkins, P. (1987). *The Thatcher Revolution*. London: Cape.

Kavanagh, D. (1990). *Politics and Personalities*. London: Macmillan.

Kavanagh, D. and Seldon, A. (1999). *The Powers Behind the Prime Minister*. London: HarperCollins.

King, A. (1985). 'Margaret Thatcher: The Style of a Prime Minister', in A. King (ed), *The British Prime Minister.* Basingstoke: Macmillan.

Lawson, N. (1992). *The View From No.11: Memoirs of a Tory Radical.* London: Bantam Press.

Major, J. (1999). *The Autobiography.* London: HarperCollins.

Moon, J. (1995). 'Innovative leadership and policy change: lessons from Thatcher', *Governance.* 8 (1): 1-25.

Moore, C. (2013). *Margaret Thatcher The Authorised Biography Volume One: Not For Turning.* London: Allen Lane.

Moore, C. (2015). *Margaret Thatcher The Authorised Biography Volume Two: Everything She Wants.* London: Allen Lane.

Moore, C. (2019). *Margaret Thatcher The Authorised Biography Volume Three: Herself Alone.* London: Allen Lane.

Parris, M. (2000). 2000. 'Five Ages of Thatcher.' *The Times.* November 22.

Patten, C. (2005). *Not Quite the Diplomat.* London: Allen Lane.

Portillo, M. (2000). 'The Tories Have Not Left Margaret Behind.' *The Times.* November 22.

Ribberink, A. (2005). '"I don't think of myself as the first woman prime minister": Gender, Identity and Image in Margaret Thatcher's career', in: R. Toye and J. Gottlieb (eds) *Making reputations : power, persuasion and the individual in modern British politics.* London: I.B. Tauris.

Ramsden, J. (1999). *An Appetite for Power: A History of the Conservative Party Since 1830.* London: HarperCollins.

Riddell, P. (1991). *The Thatcher Era and Its Legacy.* 2nd edition. Oxford: Blackwell.

Rifkind, M. (2000). 'Attila the Hen.' *New Statesman.* May 8: 51-3.

Slocock, C. (2018). *People Like Us: Margaret Thatcher and Me.* London: Biteback Publishing.

Sykes, P. (2000). *Presidents and Prime Ministers: Conviction Politics in the Anglo-American Tradition.* Lawrence, Kansas: University of Kansas Press.

Vinen, R. (2010). *Thatcher's Britain.* London: Simon and Schuster.

Wickham-Jones, M. and Shell, D. (1991) 'What went wrong? The fall of Mrs Thatcher', *Contemporary Record.* 5 (2): 321-340.

Wickham-Jones, M. (1997). 'Right Turn: a revisionist account of the 1975 Conservative Party leadership election', *Twentieth Century British History*. 8 (1): 74-89.

Young, H. (1990). *One of Us: A Biography of Margaret Thatcher*. London: Pan.

Young, H. and Sloman, A. (1986). *The Thatcher Phenomenon*. London: BBC.

Chapter 11
John Major (1990-97)

John Major was little known to the public when he suddenly became Conservative prime minister following Thatcher's overthrow in November 1990, and his brand of Conservatism and his political ideas remained opaque and ambiguous. His premiership was turbulent not least because of the bitter divisions over Europe that racked (and wrecked) the Tories as a governing party in the 1990s (Heppell 2006). The crises he faced brought into sharp relief his weaknesses as a political leader (McMeeking 2021). Against the background of Major's inheritance and the difficult circumstances encountered by his government, surviving as prime minister for six-and-a-half years must count as a considerable achievement (Taylor 2006; Williams and Hickson 2017).

Party Leadership

Major rose to the top almost without trace (Seldon 1997: 117). He became prime minister after only eleven years as an MP (compared to Callaghan's 31 years in parliament before becoming PM, Thatcher's 20 years and Blair's 14 years) and after a speedy ascent of the Cabinet hierarchy (moving through three different posts in three and a half years – Chief Secretary to the Treasury, a ludicrously brief stint as Foreign Secretary, and then Chancellor of the Exchequer) that meant that he had little time to make (many) mistakes or enemies. This testifies to his exceptional drive and determination, his intense ambition, and his professional skills in the world of Westminster and Whitehall politics, as well as to a big measure of luck. 'If the ball comes your way, you grab it', he once said. But he would have preferred to have become prime minister a few years later, thinking he would have benefitted from a few more years experience in one of the big offices of state.

Major's prime ministerial slogans of a 'classless society' and 'opportunity for all' spoke to his own experience of family poverty, unemployment and educational under-achievement. He came from a down-at-heel background, his elderly father a music hall performer before running a declining garden ornaments business, the family living in a rented flat in Brixton. He left school at sixteen. Even compared to the lower middle-class Heath and Thatcher, Major's background was an extraordinary one for a leader of the British Conservative Party.

Thatcher was toppled because the Conservatives feared that they would go down to election defeat with her as leader (they were 10% behind in the opinion polls when Major became prime minister). The party did not seek or intend an ideological break with Thatcherism. Tory MPs wanted a change of face and a softer or more emollient public image: 'Thatcherism with a human face'. Major was elected leader because of his perceived capacity to bridge divisions and unite the party through a consensual style of leadership (Heppell 2008). Major was in fact backed by Thatcher and the right (and Eurosceptic) wing of the party, and his election helped to reconcile the right to her downfall, though later she and they were to feel betrayed and to turn against him when they discovered that he was not in practice either very right-wing or an out-and-out Eurosceptic, but instead a pragmatic party loyalist (Dorey 1999: 4).

Major seemed instinctively to take a middle position on most issues. But the Conservative divisions in the 1990s proved to be too serious for his preferred method of handling divisions and dissent - balancing the factions and tactical manoeuvring, not open confrontation - to work (Kavanagh and Seldon 1994: 42-3). Over time, his grip on the leadership seemed increasingly insecure and there were regular rumours of plots to challenge and unseat him. With various rivals marking out positions for the future, Major sometimes seemed almost like a caretaker leader, which weakened his authority. He had to be talked out of resigning after the ERM disaster on 'Black Wednesday' in September 1992. Then, in a unique episode in 1995, he became the only prime minister voluntarily to put his own job at risk by resigning the party leadership and challenging his opponents within the party to 'put up or shut up' (Alderman 1996). Depressed and frustrated by the bitter party infighting and constant sniping at his leadership, he was quite prepared to resign. In the event, he got only three more votes (218) than the minimum he had privately decided would trigger his resignation – a third of Tory MPs refused to back him, either by voting for his opponent (the right-wing, Eurosceptic John Redwood), abstaining or spoiling their ballots – and the manoeuvre did not heal the factional divide. Originally elected leader mainly with the votes of the right, Major survived because he was propped up by the centre and the left of the party. With hindsight, he later (in 2002) said that his 1995 'back me or sack me' challenge had been in vain and admitted that, had he foreseen that the party's electorally-damaging 'factional madness' and 'war of attrition' would continue, he would have resigned outright at that time, handed over to a successor and gone to the backbenches (Theakston 2010: 207). Major's critics and opponents in the party were never strong enough to remove him from office, but were strong enough to limit his authority and capacity for independent action.

Ideology and Aims
Major arrived in Downing Street with very little ideological baggage - a pragmatist who could not be 'labelled' and who had held (or expressed) no unnecessary opinions (Pearce 1991). He had won the leadership by not taking a strong ideological line and because of his chameleon-like appeal (Gilmour and Garnett 1991: 351). No one knew what his views really were and he had had no time to prepare himself to take on the highest office. In practice he was far from being an instinctive Thatcherite, tending to the left of centre on social issues though a free-marketeer on economic issues. Major aimed to get the Conservatives off the hook on the poll tax issue, but in other respects was expected by the Conservative MPs who elected him to consolidate and extend Thatcherism, maintaining and implementing his predecessor's policies. Moreover there was also a sense in which Major was 'second best' for the right-wing and Eurosceptic Conservative MPs - they had voted for him in 1990 to stop Heseltine but were soon disillusioned. He was anxious to win his own mandate but his 1992 election victory – in which he won 14.1 million votes,

the most ever won by a prime minister - did not really strengthen his position.

In some respects there was a shift in style and tone from the stridency of the Thatcher era. The poll tax was abandoned. Elements of 'One Nation' Conservatism seemed to be resurfacing with ideas about 'Civic Conservatism' and a more inclusive, socially-concerned approach being aired, with talk of a 'country at ease with itself'. But Major's government completed the Thatcher agenda in many areas, privatising the coal and rail industries, for instance (though a backbench revolt scuppered plans to privatise the Post Office). However, uncomfortable with ideological or conviction politics, Major did not have the political space to articulate and pursue a distinctive agenda of his own. 'He had an arsenal of basically decent opinions, but never had a vision of where the party should go ideologically or philosophically', as Richard Cockett (1997) put it. Thatcher scornfully derided his 'wavering around all over the place' (Seldon 1997: 560). He backed off attempts to define 'Majorism' or to come up with a 'big idea' - neither the ill-fated 'back to basics' theme nor the Citizen's Charter programme had much purchase in this respect. Major wanted 'back to basics' to mean a focus on traditional values in education, social policy and law and order. But – damagingly – it was instead seen in more moralistic terms and blew up in the government's face with 'sleaze' scandals involving MPs and ministers. The Citizen's Charter (Theakston 1999) brought a welcome and innovative focus on better management, accountability, performance, quality and customer service in the public services (and has had an important long-term influence on the approach of later governments, which built upon it) but the continued resource-squeeze meant that many public services were on their knees by the mid-1990s. Even Major's rhetoric often seemed backward looking and nostalgic (the England of 'warm beer, invincible green suburbs, dog lovers . . . old maids bicycling to communion through the morning mist'), rather than mobilising support for a new agenda and new goals (Seldon 1997: 370; Heppell and McMeeking 2015).

Political Skills and Style

No one would or could look to Major for visionary or innovative leadership. His skills were primarily those of a political manager - his approach was reactive, tactical and problem solving. He had won his reputation as a political technician: a details man, good on short-term tactics, 'micro' politics, one-to-one persuasion, conciliation and man-management. As a former whip, he practised a politics of negotiation and deals, rather than Thatcher-like drive and momentum (Cockett 1997). He showed some skill in 'high' politics - dealing with Kohl, Yeltsin, Clinton and other world leaders and in the handling of complex European negotiations (as seen in his Maastricht success, securing British opt-outs on monetary union and on the social chapter), and also in the initiatives he took in Northern Ireland, which helped build towards the later peace and power-sharing agreement under his successor, Tony Blair, but for which he was given too little credit at the time. But he was not so good on medium- and long-term wider political strategy and objectives. He did not project a clear ideological position or strong sense of policy direction.

Another contrast to Mrs Thatcher was his 'grey' public image. He was a prime minister so colourful, it was said, he would look exactly the same on black and white television. Although he could be incisive, engaging and show subtle personal skills in private and in handling small groups, there was little sense of prime ministerial presence. On his day he could be effective in parliament but he was a poor communicator, a stilted and indifferent performer on television and the public platform, and he hated the 'packaging' of modern media-driven politics. In contrast to Thatcher and Blair, with their tough, centralising and highly 'political' press secretaries and media advisers, Major's approach to the organisation of the media management operation in Downing Street and government (using civil servants, playing a straight bat like Heath had done) was also arguably ineffective. Key Number 10 advisers like Sarah Hogg, a forceful economist who headed the Policy Unit (Hogg and Hill 1995), and the Cabinet Secretary Sir Robin Butler, were able and influential (and Major – in contrast to his predecessor - seemed to trust and work well with civil servants), but Major's staff was increasingly absorbed into short-term crisis management rather than long-term policy planning (Kavanagh and Seldon 1999).

John Major - the consolidator, the balancer, the political manager - was not a conceptual or strategic thinker, but a reactive problem-solver, able to soak up and exploit his always-impressive command of the details. He would sometimes make decisions by listing the pros and cons in two columns on a sheet of paper - not the approach of someone with a clear agenda of his own (Seldon 1997: 94-5). He did not cut a 'presidential' figure and particularly at first – in contrast to Thatcher's approach - ran his Cabinet in a collegiate and inclusive style, trying to carry colleagues with him, reconciling differences and teasing out a consensus. Later on, divisions, factionalism and leaks made collective Cabinet discussion and decision-making much harder to manage. He was very dependent on the Cabinet's 'big beasts' - Kenneth Clarke (Home Secretary, then Chancellor of the Exchequer), Michael Heseltine (a leadership contender in 1990, who was successively Environment Secretary, Industry minister and then deputy prime minister), and Douglas Hurd (Foreign Secretary and another leadership contender) - who were powerful ministerial 'barons'. The departure of Chris Patten in 1992 (who lost his seat) was a blow as he had been a key Cabinet ally and Party Chairman 1990-92.

At first Major's brokerage approach worked well, but in time his unwillingness or inability to assert himself led to charges of weakness, dithering, and letting circumstances and the push and pull of other people determine issues. On some critical occasions he was seen to be overridden by senior ministers and his Cabinet. In 1994, for instance, despite his own serious misgivings about the political effects, Major could not restrain Clarke from pushing through unpopular tax increases on fuel (Seldon 1997: 513). Later, Clarke and a Cabinet majority blocked Major's plans to increase education spending (Seldon 1997: 548). The drift and indecision in the Major years - the lack of a firm personal lead from the top - was acutely felt by experienced Whitehall hands who complained about 'a hole at the centre of the machine'.

As a political operator, Major excelled at networking, the deployment of charm, cultivating personal relationships and friendships - 'planned rational aggression' was never his style, according to Matthew Parris (1993). Major must count, in personal terms, as one of the more genuinely nice occupants of Number 10 - but he found that niceness is not enough in a prime minister. In good times, his public character as a decent, reasonable and capable man, with more of a common touch than the imperious Thatcher, was undoubtedly an asset. But his background seems to have left him with deep personal insecurities and strong emotions and vulnerabilities. There was a thin-skinned over-sensitivity to criticism (media pummelling knocked him off balance) that meant that when the political going got harder (as it did after 1992) he did not have the inner resources and confidence to provide steely leadership.

In terms of character as a political resource, the example of Major shows that the personal factor can in fact be both a strength and a weakness or limitation. The very qualities that made a desperate party turn to him in 1990 were those for which he was later most fiercely criticised. He had won the leadership after a decade of assiduous parliamentary networking, but after 1992 his parliamentary base became increasingly fractious and unreliable, and by the end, the dominant feeling was virtually one of mutual contempt. His 'Honest John' image - that he was trustworthy, likeable, competent, sensible, sincere, unflashy - had been an asset over 1990-92, the perceived contrast to both Thatcher and Labour's Neil Kinnock registering with the public. Paddy Ashdown, the Liberal Democrats' leader, shrewdly described him as a sort of 'suburban Baldwin of our times' (Ashdown 2000: 106). But the broken promises on tax rises (which made the pre-1992 election public spending increases look like cynical vote-buying); the ERM disaster; the apparent inability to deal with the 'sleaze' issue; the way in which Major would try to hang on to ministers in trouble only to let them go when the pressure mounted; his tactical contortions and vacillations - all these made him seem incompetent, ineffective, weak, a loser.

Context

Beyond the differences of personality and style that made Major appear to be a weaker leader than Mrs Thatcher, is the fact that they were prime ministers in very different contexts. Major often seemed trapped by events, not on top of them: 'in office but not in power', as Norman Lamont put it after being sacked as Chancellor in 1993 (Seldon 1997: 378).

Although he enjoyed a political and opinion poll honeymoon period, helped by his successful low-key leadership during the Gulf War (in 1991 polls, he registered as more popular than Thatcher had ever been), until he won the 1992 election against the economic odds, Major lacked an electoral mandate of his own. But after the forced ejection of sterling from the Exchange Rate Mechanism (ERM) on 'Black Wednesday' in September 1992, he was weakened by the Conservatives' nose-diving electoral fortunes, rapidly becoming the least-respected prime minister in polling history. The Tory press turned hostile and was never won back, their bitter and sustained media attacks keeping him always on the defensive. He had inherited an economy moving into recession but derived little electoral benefit (the 'feel good factor') from the economic upturn after 1992, which saw steady economic growth, falling unemployment and low and stable inflation. The ERM debacle, together with the imposition of massive tax increases (contrary to promises made in the 1992 manifesto - but necessary because of the spiralling public spending and borrowing in the two years from 1990), had shattered the Conservatives' reputation for economic competence. This was a key factor in boosting Labour's poll ratings and after 1994 a Tory election defeat always seemed inevitable when Major was faced by one of the most formidable Leaders of the Opposition in modern British politics (Tony Blair) and a rejuvenated Labour Party. When he won re-election in 1992, he had realised that a fifth straight Conservative election victory was unlikely – 'we had stretched the democratic elastic as far as it would go' (Major 1999: 309). In May 1997 the Conservative Party crashed to one of the worst general election defeats in its history losing more than half its MPs (seven Cabinet ministers losing their seats) and being reduced to 165 MPs, while its vote-share fell 11 points to just 30 per cent and its Labour opponents won a huge landslide. Major had – realistically – not expected to win in 1997, but the scale of the wipe out was still a huge shock.

The Conservatives' civil war over the European issue tested to destruction Major's conception of politics and his skills as a political leader. For him it was not a 'gut' issue - he described himself as agnostic, a 'Europragmatist'. It was a question of practicalities, clever negotiation and realism, going for the best possible deal (Major 1999). However, his approach of trying to bridge the party splits by keeping options open could never be a viable long-term policy (Lamont 1999: 499). The Eurosceptic right mistrusted him because they felt that there were no firm personal or political convictions behind the negotiating positions - that he would just go with the flow. The pro-Europeans feared that his instinct was always to trim and to reach a compromise with the sceptics, who would simply bank it and press for more. Anthony Seldon, Major's biographer, notes that 'tactically . . . his policy of keeping the door open left him vulnerable to attacks and manipulation from both sides of the Europe debate' (Seldon 1997: 168). The disloyalty and attacks of his predecessor, and Thatcher's support for the Eurosceptics' opposition and plots, made things worse. 'Anyone who followed Margaret Thatcher was going to have a hell of a job', as the veteran Tory Kenneth Baker once commented, 'particularly after the manner of her departure' (Baker 1999). The corrosive factionalism weakened the foundations of the government and drained the PM's personal authority. The fact that he would talk tough (as over qualified majority voting, or the 'non-cooperation' tactic in the BSE crisis over British beef exports) but then back down, further underlined his apparent weakness. But against the argument that his emollience and prevarications allowed divisions to grow, is the probability that anything other than a balancing act (and any other possible leader) would have split the party even more. By default, Major was the least unacceptable leader for a bitterly divided party.

Major's 1992 election was something of a hollow victory because, while the Conservatives had a 7.5% lead over Labour, it left him with an overall parliamentary majority of only 21 (compared to the 100 plus majorities which had bolstered Thatcher in the 1980s), and this was steadily whittled away by by-election defeats. Backbench rebels could be ignored by Mrs Thatcher's steamroller but Major's room for manoeuvre was limited and he was massively vulnerable to their disruption and blackmail. Moreover, the influx of more right-wing MPs in 1992 ('Thatcher's Children') tilted the balance of the party towards Euroscepticism, something reflected in Major himself moving in a more sceptical direction over 1993-6. But such was the strength of Kenneth Clarke's position as Chancellor of the Exchequer, that Major was unable to abandon the so-called 'wait and see' policy on membership of a single currency.

Conclusion

'Major's leadership style could be argued to have been exactly what was required for the times', was Anthony Seldon's verdict (Seldon 1997: 742-43). The circumstances he faced were particularly difficult and constraining, and the limitations of Major's scope were acute. Major was in many ways a classic 'transactional' political manager. He was a 'healer' not a 'warrior' or 'crusader'. However, he discovered that it was impossible to be a sort of moderate Thatcher when many in his party wanted the 'Real Thing'. Unlike Thatcher, John Major never carved out a strong and distinctive identity of his own. He seemed to have no broad or long-term policy aim other than trying to keep the Conservative Party in one piece, but deep divisions and infighting over Europe, endemic disloyalty and his tactical contortions made him seem weak, defensive and reactive. In his memoirs, Major, while pointing out his successes, seems to regard himself as ultimately a disappointment as prime minister and is candid and self-deprecating about his failures, shortcomings and regrets: 'I rarely found my own authentic voice in politics. I was too conservative, too conventional. Too safe, too often. Too defensive. Too reactive . . . too often on the back foot' (Major 1999: xxi).

Tony Blair's comment that 'John Major isn't the Tory Party's problem. The Tory Party is John Major's problem' (Seldon

1997: 551) emphasised Major's key weakness - an undisciplined, disloyal, divided (even anarchic) and Europe-obsessed parliamentary party, a party at war with itself. Probably no one in the party ever feared Major, but the situation he was in provided few opportunities or resources for heroic, decisive or commanding leadership and offered little scope for much beyond crisis management and fire-fighting. Through three terms of office (1979-90), Thatcherism had maintained a sense of purpose and a radical momentum, and had shown a capacity to renew itself in office. Major consolidated and entrenched Thatcherism (Dorey 1999: 226), and his 1992 victory ensured Labour could not turn the clock back, but during his premiership, the Conservatives increasingly appeared unleadable: directionless, tired, disorganised, accident prone, and doomed to defeat. Major consistently argued after the 1997 meltdown that the Conservatives had to reconnect with and appeal again to 'mainstream voters'. Elections could not be won from the right if the centre was lost, he insisted. He later said he regretted not having taken on the right wing and violently Eurosceptic groups in the party more forcefully when he was prime minister (Theakston 2010: 212).

Ultimately, Major had a difficult inheritance as prime minister and was then overwhelmed. Peter Hennessy (2000: 532) deftly summed up Major's premiership: 'he could be good on his day and where circumstances were propitious, but . . . he succumbed to the political weather rather than made it.' His vacillations, his inability to impart a clear sense of direction and failures of communication all suggested a politician out of his depth. He was sunk by 'events beyond his control as well as by blunders for which he must take responsibility' judged *The Economist* on the eve of the 1997 election (Economist 1997). Given the situation, probably only an exceptional leader could have done much better and imposed him or herself on the Conservative Party and on events (Sewldon 1997: 741). Major could not, and so his leadership ability was tested in the harshest possible way in the 1990s and found to be wanting.

References

Alderman, K. (1996). 'The Conservative Party Leadership Election of 1995', *Parliamentary Affairs.* 49 (2): 316-332.

Ashdown, P. (2000). *The Ashdown Diaries Volume 1: 1988-1997.* London: Allen Lane.

Baker, K. (1999). 'He let the bastards grind him down', *The Guardian,* 17 October.

Cockett, R. (1997). 'Major: The Verdict of History', *The Independent on Sunday,* 11 May.

Dorey, P. (ed) (1999). *The Major premiership : politics and policies under John Major, 1990-97.* London: Palgrave Macmillan.

Economist. (1997). 'John Major: The End is Nigh', *The Economist,* 22 March.

Gilmour, I. and Garnett, M. (1997). *Whatever Happened to the Tories: The Conservative party Since 1945.* London: Fourth Estate.

Hennessy, P. (2000). *The Prime Minister: the office and its holders since 1945.* London: Allen Lane.

Heppell, T. (2006). *The Conservative party Leadership of John Major 1992-1997.* Lampeter: Edwin Mellen Press.

Heppell, T. (2008). *Choosing the Tory Leader: Conservative Party Leadership Elections from Heath to Cameron.* London: I.B. Tauris.

Heppell, T. and McMeeking, T. (2015). 'The oratory of John Major', in R. Hayton and A. Crines (eds). *Conservative orators from Baldwin to Cameron.* Manchester: Manchester University Press.

Hogg, S. and Hill, J. (1995). *Too Close to Call: Power and Politics - John Major in No.10.* London: Little, Brown.

Kavanagh, D. and Seldon, A. (eds) (1994). *The Major Effect.* London: Macmillan.

Kavanagh, D. and Seldon, A. (1999). *The Powers Behind the Prime Minister.* London: HarperCollins.

Lamont, N. (1999). *In Office.* London: Little, Brown.

Major, J. (1999). *The Autobiography.* London: HarperCollins.

McMeeking, T. (2021). *The Political Leadership of John Major: A Reassessment Using the Greenstein Model*. London: Palgrave Macmillan.

Parris, M. (1993). 'It's fine being friendly, but...'. *The Independent on Sunday*, 4 April.

Pearce, E. (1991). *The Quiet Rise of John Major*. London: Weidenfeld & Nicolson.

Seldon, A. (1997). *Major: A Political Life*. London: Weidenfeld & Nicolson.

Taylor, R. (2006). *Major*. London: Haus Publishing.

Theakston, K. (1999). 'A Permanent Revolution in Whitehall: the Major governments and the civil service', in P. Dorey, (ed) *The Major premiership : politics and policies under John Major, 1990-97*. London: Palgrave Macmillan.

Theakston, K. (2010). *After Number 10: Former Prime Ministers in British Politics*. London: Palgrave Macmillan.

Williams, B. and Hickson, K. (eds) (2017). *John Major: An Unsuccessful Prime Minister? Reappraising John Major*. London: Biteback Publishing.

Chapter 12
Tony Blair (1997-2007)

In electoral terms, Tony Blair was by some way the most successful ever Labour prime minister, winning three successive general elections - two with huge, landslide majorities and the third with a substantial majority - and clocking up ten consecutive years in Number 10. His personal dominance of British politics, together with his strong and visible leadership style as prime minister, makes comparisons with Margaret Thatcher inevitable. Both were portrayed at times as quasi-presidential, also pursuing a 'big picture' politics of vision and moral certainty. Both became global celebrity figures. Blair admired her 'conviction' approach; he was also heavily influenced by the idea that her success rested on the building and maintenance of a populist 'hegemony' over suburban, centre-ground, aspirational 'middle England', and he aimed to appropriate that political territory for New Labour (Rentoul 2001: 276-77; Gould 1998). However, it is not clear that his strategy and policy aims were as well defined as hers, or that his policy legacy will be so enduring.

Party Leadership
Blair was elected Labour leader in 1994 at the age of 41. He had not even been a member of the Labour Party at the time it had last won a general election (in 1974). Blair was not born into the Labour Party, as he once said - he chose it. Historically, some other Labour leaders were also middle-class professionals from Conservative family backgrounds, who attended public schools and Oxford, but none were so much the 'outsider', distant from and impatient with the party's traditional culture and ethos. Paradoxically, as Anthony King (1998: 201) noted, this made Blair 'the perfect leader for the Labour Party in the 1990s. He might almost have been a product of computer-aided design. He was young. He was classless. He was squeaky clean. He had no ties to the trade union movement. He carried virtually no

ideological baggage. Above all, he was persuaded, in a way that John Smith had never been, that change in the Labour Party had to be root-and-branch.'

The Labour Party's crisis was Blair's opportunity. Successive electoral defeats had left Labour looking like a party of permanent opposition, unable to break out its declining working class and regional bases. Neil Kinnock (party leader 1983-92) had done much to jettison unpopular left-wing policies, overhaul party machinery and campaigning, and move Labour back to the European social-democratic mainstream, but Blair and other 'modernisers' believed that the party had not changed enough and were frustrated by the 'safe and steady' leadership style and the 'one more heave' political caution of John Smith (leader from 1992 until his death in 1994).

Blair was a dazzlingly successful Leader of the Opposition in the 1994-97 period (McAnulla 2012). He completed and went beyond what Kinnock and Smith had started in terms of refashioning Labour's policies, image, organisation and appeal. Blair talked of 'taking on' his party and giving it 'electric shock treatment' (Gould 1998: 216, 218). Crucial to his reinvention of the party was the audacious and symbolic break with its past marked by the abolition of the ideological sacred cow of 'clause IV'. The strategy was to reposition Labour and widen its appeal as a moderate, pro-business, 'catch all' party, which was safe for 'Middle England' to vote for. The political priority was therefore on the projection of reassurance and competence, insisting that New Labour could be trusted and would not repeat Old Labour's mistakes on the key issues of taxation and public spending, economic management, and union power. A strong anti-Conservative tide, and a desire for change, helped to win the 1997 election, but Blair was committed only to cautious and incremental changes in policy.

Once in Downing Street, Blair's relationship with his own party and its affiliated trade unions often appeared distant and uncertain. The wider party's culture and ethos remained 'Old Labour' rather than 'Blairite'. Trade union leaders were kept at arm's length; power was drained away from the party conference and its national executive committee. There were pronounced 'control freak' tendencies, Blair running New Labour and the government through a small cabal (Minkin 2014). Veteran left-winger Tony Benn pointedly joked that New Labour was a strong party because all its members were in the Cabinet. But Blair was not sustained by a mass base of support in the wider party, and he failed to re-create the party in his own image or enthuse its members. On the other hand, he was not so constrained by the party as previous Labour leaders (including Wilson and Callaghan) had been, and he did not have to laboriously stitch together backroom deals or cope with internecine left-right internal party struggles. However, personal feuding within the New Labour high command sometimes destabilised the government. In this vein, John Davis and John Rentoul's book on the Blair government highlights a crucial fracture by treating it as if it was in some ways a coalition between Blairite and Brownite parties (Davis and Rental 2019).

Ideology and Aims

Blair was described by one 'insider' as 'very good at the wide sky - the big picture - and very good at handling tomorrow. It's the bit in between that's the problem' (Hennessy 2000: 8). Many of his problems in achieving the reforms he wanted can be traced back to the failure to provide a strategic sense of direction or a broad philosophical coherence for his government, and to a tendency towards what one critic called 'waffle and cliché' (Seldon 2004: 148). Blair's long-term ideological goals remained opaque, and New Labour was ideologically vapid. In contrast to Thatcher he struggled to define a clear and coherent 'narrative' or ideological 'story' with which to communicate and mobilise support. 'Blairism' could seem to be just whatever the New Labour government did; it was a practice in search of a philosophy (Rawnsley 2000: 312-13). Blair's early rhetoric about his ambition to shape a new 'progressive century' and realign centre-left politics was not matched by significant practical action. His 'Third Way' slogan did not give clarity or consistency to government, boiling down to a pragmatic approach to choosing 'what works' and makes or keeps you popular.

Similarly, the 'modernisation' mantra did not give a clear policy-steer or sense of direction (Rose 2001: 228-30).

Blair saw himself as a unifier, opposed to class conflict and division, was impatient with what he dismissed as tribal party politics, and despised ideology and dogma. Politically, he was variously described as a Thatcherite, a post-Thatcherite, a one-nation Conservative, a European-style Christian Democrat, a social-democratic moderniser, and an unprincipled, 'spin'- and image-obsessed opportunist. Blair was clearly not a socialist, but clinging to the ethical goal of a fairer society nor was he really a Thatcherite, though he believed that Labour had to accept much of the economic and social legacy of the Thatcher era. In practice, his administration's policies were mildly social-democratic and redistributive (showing the influence of Gordon Brown on welfare policy), supporting a market economy but not a market society, and active but not old-style 'big' government.

Massive public expectations were aroused in 1997, but the landslide paradoxically strengthened Blair's caution and unwillingness to take risks with the government's popularity. Later he felt he had rather wasted the opportunity of his first term in which the main focus was on securing re-election. The government stuck to the Conservatives' spending plans for its first two years but thereafter pushed through massive increases in public expenditure in the years after 2000. To the extent that he then began to shape and articulate a domestic policy agenda through his second term, it owed more to the legacy of Thatcher and Major than it was comfortable to admit, and there was resistance to his policy ideas about 'choice and diversity' in the reform of public services like education and health within the government and the Labour Party, though he kept up the pressure and the reform impetus to the end, being perhaps most radical in his final truncated term 2005-7.

On a different level, the pursuit of power, winning and then retaining government office, were central aims for Blair and New Labour. Historically, Labour's statecraft has been less determined and less successful than the Conservatives' (Brivati 1997). Under Blair there was an emphasis on discipline and unity, and on tight control from the centre both in Opposition and in government. The Blairites learned from Clinton and from the experience of the Major government about the need to control the media and dominate the agenda in an era of continuous campaigning, though arguably fighting so strongly and constantly for the headlines adversely affected policy development. Always keeping an anxious eye on the movements of public opinion, Blair was the first prime minister to have regular weekly meetings with his top pollster (Philip Gould). Previous Labour PMs' election timing had often been poor; Blair's eye was always on the second term and he got his timing right in 2001 and then in 2005. Crucially also, Blair and Brown understood from their reading of the history of previous Labour governments the importance of achieving and maintaining a reputation for competent management of the economy, something that became central to New Labour's success after 1997 with a stress on stability, rules and prudence in economic policymaking.

In terms of overseas policy goals, Blair wanted Britain to play a more constructive role in Europe and wanted to enter the euro, but in practice he proved unwilling to take on Gordon Brown and the Treasury, the Eurosceptic press and public opinion, and failed to seize his moment or to press the argument sufficiently strongly. His support for the United States military action in the Middle East also cost him friends in Europe. But that was an inevitable outcome of his strong commitment to the 'Special Relationship', and the close ties he forged with successive US presidents, Bill Clinton and then George W. Bush. It also followed on from his moralistic approach to foreign affairs, framed in terms of the theory of humanitarian intervention, of the 'war on terror' and action against 'rogue' regimes, and seen 'on the ground' in Kosovo, Sierra Leone, Afghanistan and – most controversially of all - Iraq (Dyson 2009). The exposure of the flawed decision-making process and the faulty intelligence material central to the latter, and the way events developed in that country after the overthrow of Saddam, massively damaged Blair's political capital and reputation in his own party (139 Labour MPs voting against the war) and in the country.

Political Style and Skills

From the start, Blair's leadership was 'presidential' in style and intent; his model was Thatcher, not Major: the strong leader driving through a radical programme (Foley 2000: 98-99). Like Thatcher, Blair was a populist, claiming a direct line to 'the people', and also a sophisticated, calculating politician. Crucial to the success of both Thatcher and Blair was the way they were able to redraw the map of electoral politics, detaching key blocs from their predecessor's constituency and annexing them to their own coalition, as David Marquand perceptively commented: 'Each [coalition] was assembled by a politician of genius, with a capacity to reach out, across familiar ideological boundaries, to the core constituency of the opposing party. Both the politicians concerned were curiously rootless figures, cut off - in one case by gender and in the other by upbringing - from the cultures of their respective parties. Above all, each coalition owed as much to a revulsion from old attachments as to the attractions of new ones' (Marquand 1998: 23).

Blair was telegenic and charismatic, and came across as likeable, idealistic, intelligent, persuasive and sincere, personifying New Labour's cross-class appeal. A consummate political actor - one Clinton aide said he was a politician with 'perfect pitch' - his feel for the country's emotional pulse was displayed most brilliantly at the time of the death of Princess Diana (Rawnsley 2000: 62). He has strong religious convictions and moral views, and related to that was sometimes a 'preachy' style of pulpit-politics. He was a skilful negotiator and conciliator (as seen in the making of the 1998 Good Friday peace agreement and then the 2007 power-sharing settlement in Northern Ireland), almost Rooseveltian in his political use of personal charm. Unlike Thatcher, however, he did not have an all-consuming interest in or appetite for the details of policy, though this developed in office to some extent; his strength and his feel was more for the 'big picture' and for strategy, values and images (Riddell 2001: 35, 38).

He was a complex and contradictory character. In the pursuit of his aims he could come across as determined, innovative and confident: a bold 'pathfinder' leader seeking to lead his party and country in a new direction (Kavanagh 2001: 4). But he was also calculating, could be cautious and risk-averse and conflict-averse, and crab-like in the way he sometimes approached difficult decisions - an insecure politician, media-obsessed and frightened about losing control (Rawnsley 2000). He was criticised for jumping from subject to subject as they became more or less pressing rather than applying himself to pushing through strategies to a conclusion. 'He intervenes, persuades and then forgets', it was said (Bevir and Rhodes 2006: 681). But as a 'war leader' - particularly over Kosovo, post-9/11 and Iraq - he seemed like a cross between Gladstone and Churchill with his combination of courage, commitment and a moral fervour and certainty that looked like hubris to his critics.

Blair was communicator-in-chief in the most media-conscious British government ever. William Hague often worsted him at Question Time (1997-2001) but Blair usually showed enough skill to perform adequately in parliament, which he did not anyway see as the most important political stage. Anthony Seldon (2004: 58) pointed to Blair's 'thespian skills' and his 'extraordinary persuasive and presentational skills'. Being telegenic, persuasive and able to project sincerity helped Blair to win his party's leadership in the first place. Dennis Kavanagh's (2005: 17) verdict was that he showed 'a remarkable capacity to communicate with the electorate, to demonstrate empathy at key moments and present himself as a "regular sort of guy"'. However, as time went on, Blair's communication skills were increasingly seen in a negative light: there were controversies over 'spin', a perceived mismatch between rhetoric and substance in policy achievement, and divisions over Iraq produced a haemorrhaging of trust. If Blair's media machine was more effective at the short-term battle of the headlines than the longer-term winning of hearts and minds, the final responsibility for that approach to political communications was his.

Blair himself worked in a highly personal and informal way - he thought politically but not organisationally, and having never previously been a minister or run a government department was impatient with the constraints and slow-moving ways of bureaucracy and collective government. Whitehall 'insiders' felt he didn't know how to properly use the machinery of government to make things happen. He created a 'command premiership', building up a 'presidential' apparatus in Downing Street, or what one adviser called 'a more Napoleonic system', to counter the Whitehall 'baronies' (Powell 2010). There was a whole array of special units and groups, frequently reorganised, with a greatly increased number of special advisers staffing the Strategy Unit, the Prime Minister's Delivery Unit, the Social Exclusion Unit, the Strategic Communications Unit and others; and the Cabinet Office was pulled towards working more directly for the prime minister, particularly but not only on foreign policy and security issues (Seldon and Meakin 2016). But it was a weakness that most of the key and powerful figures in Blair's Number 10 were focused more intensely on presentation and short-term political management than on policy (Seldon 2004: 437). Nor, as Seldon (2004: 692) pointed out, 'did he listen to powerful, independent-minded intellects who offered alternative solutions and who were able to convince him of unpalatable truths.'

As his premiership went on, he increasingly practiced what critics dubbed 'sofa government': he disliked big, formal meetings and relied on a small group of close aides at Number 10. Some talked of 'court politics' in Downing Street, while Seldon (2004: 692) labelled it 'denocracy' saying that, damagingly, his advisers 'rarely asserted countervailing advice or opinions on foreign policy, but tended to affirm Blair's own positions, either because they did not think it their job to question policy . . . or because they often agreed with him.' He went much further than even Mrs Thatcher did in terms of ignoring or bypassing the traditional collective model of Cabinet and Cabinet committee governance, preferring instead bilateral meetings with key individuals. Where previous Labour PMs like Wilson and Callaghan had to bring ministers together and thrash out key policies through lengthy meetings, Blair's Cabinet sessions were short and perfunctory. It was a centralised and personalised regime in which Blair's unelected 'court' of Number 10 advisers (including figures like Alastair Campbell, Blair's media and communications chief; Jonathan Powell, his chief of staff; Sally Morgan, his political secretary; and policy advisers like Andrew Adonis and Michael Barber, head of the Delivery Unit) had more power and influence than most Cabinet ministers. This whole approach to government came under the spotlight in a hugely negative way in the different inquiries (the Butler and Chilcot reports) criticising the lack of formality, structure and collective deliberation in the decision-making in relation to the Iraq war (Davis and Rentoul 2019).

Much was decided in private bilateral meetings between Blair and Chancellor of the Exchequer Gordon Brown, who was an 'Iron Chancellor' with an unprecedented power and policy scope inside the government. The government was often likened to a 'dual premiership' because of the way that they dominated in separate spheres. Blair's main interests and concerns were foreign and defence policy, Northern Ireland, schools and health; Brown was effectively in charge of economic policy, welfare reform and broad swathes of the domestic agenda, and exerted massive leverage through the Treasury's control of public spending and public service agreements. The longstanding and complex political and personal relationship between Blair and Brown was the central axis of New Labour and of the government. Other ministers had to steer between the two, or join-up as 'Blairites' or 'Brownites'. While both were strengthened by this unique political 'marriage', and when they worked together they were formidably effective and got their way in the government, there were also deep splits and sometimes disabling tensions over policy and the succession, accompanied by vicious semi-public infighting between their rival advisers and cliques, and the relationship became increasingly acrimonious and dysfunctional. Feeling boxed in, frustrated and constrained, Blair was occasionally tempted to move or fire Brown, but always backed off – fearing the explosive consequences and understanding his strengths and what he brought to New Labour and to the government.

Context

Blair always recognised that New Labour's support was wide but shallow. Labour's 1997 vote share of 43.2 per cent was not high in historical terms and its 179 seat parliamentary majority was based on half a million fewer votes than Major had won in 1992. In 2001 Labour lost six seats and the Conservatives gained only one, Blair winning another crushing majority of 167, though overall turnout slumped (from 71 per cent in 1997 to 59 per cent in 2001) and Labour's vote-share fell to 40.7 per cent. Even after Iraq, however, he was able to win a third election in 2005 with a comfortable majority of 66, though Labour's vote-share was down to just 35.2 per cent.

The Blair government was operating in a very favourable context. It inherited a strong economy and there was continued economic growth, high employment, low inflation and low interest rates during Blair's decade in power, providing the resources for higher spending on public services and helping the government win the 'economic competence' argument that previous Labour governments had usually lost. The government's parliamentary position was on paper impregnable though it was increasingly difficult to control the party and Labour MPs rebelled more frequently than ever before, unhappy with Blair's rather autocratic style of leadership and neglect of parliament (he thought he didn't need it). New Labour was supported by most of the press (for the first time in the party's history). The Conservative Opposition was - until after 2005 – weak, unpopular and inept, and Labour remained ahead in public opinion polls until 2006. Blair's personal approval rating plummeted, however: he last had a positive (+2) net satisfaction rating in April 2003 (this compared to +12 in January 2002 and +60 when he was first elected in 1997). When Blair left office 60 per cent of voters said they were dissatisfied with the way he was doing his job, with only 33 per cent saying they were satisfied (a net rating of -27, a figure the same as John Major's at the end of his premiership, but not as bad as Mrs Thatcher's -46 at the end of her time in office). Basking in his wide popularity at the start, Blair in his last few years in Number 10 rather made a virtue of not caring what people thought about him, insisting that he was motivated more by 'doing the right thing'.

Conclusion

The end of Blair's premiership was a long drawn-out process. (Theakston 2010: 214-15). Blair's party did not in a formal sense force him out, in the way that Thatcher was overthrown in a direct leadership challenge, but he was deposed by it all the same after facing considerable and mounting pressure to step down. Gordon Brown and his supporters fought a sort of war of attrition from a fairly early stage and Blair's wider position in the parliamentary party very much weakened after the Iraq war. Brown believed that they had an agreement (dating from Brown's decision not to stand for the party leadership in 1994) that Blair would make way for him at some point in the second term, expecting a 2004 handover. After the 2001 election, he reportedly thumped the table, shouting, 'When are you going to move off and give me a date?' and 'I want the job now!'

Blair had never settled in his mind how long he would serve, telling Alastair Campbell (2007: 628-9) at one point that two terms or eight years 'was about all you get in the modern world' and 'you have to know when to go.' Under continued pressure from Brown, he 'wobbled' in the spring of 2004 and came close to quitting, but recovered his confidence, zest and appetite for office. There are claims that he would have left office before the 2005 election had Brown played along more, either by supporting his public sector reforms or by letting him take the country into the Euro. Brown would not agree but, equally, seemed ultimately willing to wound but not kill - letting his supporters pile on the pressure and destabilise Blair but flinching from finally pulling the trigger himself. Then in September 2004 Blair announced he would fight the next election and, if re-elected, serve 'a full third term' before stepping down; he did not, however, specify a date for his departure. The move did not satisfy the Brownites, however, and dissent and plotting continued, culminating in the so-called 'September coup' in 2006, after which Blair bowed to the inevitable and announced that that year's party conference would be his last, privately assuring a still disbelieving Brown that he would go in the summer of 2007. Brown desperately wanted his endorsement, which Blair in the end gave after toying about a possible alternative, notably David Miliband, but recognising that there was no real alternative and, at some level, feeling that – despite all they had gone through – he owed the succession to Brown and wanted him to have it, so long as he would continue to support the New Labour project. Seldon (2007: 573) described Blair as leaving at 'more or less the moment of his choosing' but it is hard to deny that there was a party, or at least Brownite, revolt and if he could have stayed on a year or so longer, he would surely have done so.

In 1997, Blair had been the least experienced PM for 70 years, having never sat behind a ministerial desk before in his career. He proved to be remarkably adept in the exercise of power - critics were not able to say (as they had of John Major) that he was not up to the job of being prime minister. He stamped his authority on his party and on his government ('Tony wants . . . ' becoming the most potent words in Whitehall). He displayed a remarkable strategic ruthlessness in relation to the Labour party, confronting it with the need to change but probably winning heads and not hearts. Blairism's shallow roots in the party were a crucial weakness over the longer-term – arguably, one reason why Corbyn became party leader in 2015 was because Blair failed to permanently reshape the politics of the Labour Party (as he later admitted), actively manage it as a proper bastion of support, or finish off the left when he had the chance.

Blair wanted to lead one of the great reforming governments, and there were real policy achievements and social gains in the New Labour years, but there remained a suspicion that, as Clare Short (2004: 136–137) put it, his idea of 'reform' was actually one of 'constant announcements, headlines and eye-catching initiatives. They call it modernisation but it is a mania for change which keeps the whole system in a constant state of flux.' Another criticism is that while Blair had a great feel for public opinion, in relation to it, however, he was in his early years in particular much more the 'preference-accommodator' than the 'preference shaper' – often following the consensus, reluctant to confront powerful interest groups, trying to be all things to all people, and in thrall to the focus groups and opinion polls. But by the middle of his second term, he had become just as much a driven 'conviction' leader as Thatcher, massively so (but not only on) on foreign policy. He had entered Number 10 on a wave of great enthusiasm, high hopes and goodwill – all of which evaporated by the time he left office, leaving him mistrusted and his reputation greatly tarnished, with the Iraq war casting a dark cloud (McAnulla 2011; Bower 2016). The dominating 'presidential' figure had become the 'unfulfilled prime minister', to quote the title of one book on his time in office and legacy (Riddell 2005). He had made Labour electable again after nearly two decades in the wilderness, but left behind a successor about whose style, instincts, policies and electability he harboured serious doubts – which turned out to be correct – and a party that seemed increasingly antagonistic towards his political approach and dismissive of his record.

References

Bevir, M. and Rhodes, R. (2006). 'Prime Ministers, Presidentialism and Westminster Smokescreens'. *Political Studies.* 54 (4): 671-690.

Bower, T. (2016). *Broken Vows: Tony Blair: The Tragedy of Power.* London: Faber & Faber.

Brivati, B. (1997). 'Earthquake or Watershed?", in B. Brivati and T. Bale (eds). *New Labour in Power.* London: Routledge.

Campbell, A. (2007). *The Blair Years: Extracts from the Alastair Campbell Diaries.* London: Hutchinson.

Davis, J. and Rentoul, J. (2019). *Heroes or Villains? The Blair Government Reconsidered.* Oxford: Oxford University Press.

Dyson, S. (2009). *The Blair Identity: Leadership and Foreign Policy.* Manchester: Manchester University Press.

Foley, M. (2000). *The British Presidency.* Manchester: Manchester University Press.

Gould, P. (1998). *The Unfinished Revolution: How the Modernisers Saved the Labour Party.* London: Little, Brown.

Hennessy, P. (2000). *The Prime Minister: The Office and Its Holders Since 1945.* London: Allen Lane.

Kavanagh, D. (2001). 'New Labour, New Millennium, New Premiership', in A. Seldon (ed), *The Blair Effect.* London: Little, Brown.

Kavanagh, D. (2005).'The Blair Premiership', in A. Seldon and D. Kavanagh (eds). *The Blair Effect 2001-5.* Cambridge: Cambridge University Press.

King, A. (ed). (1998). 'Why Labour Won - At Last', in A. King et al., *New Labour Triumphs: Britain at the Polls.* Chatham, NJ: Chatham House.

McAnulla, S. (2011). 'Post-political poisons? Evaluating the 'Toxic" dimensions of Tony Blair's leadership.' *Representation.* 47 (3): 251-263.

Marquand, D. (1998). 'The Blair Paradox', *Prospect.* May: 19-24.

Minkin, L. (2104). *The Blair Supremacy: a study in the politics of Labour's party management.* Manchester: Manchester University Press.

Powell, J. (2010). *The New Machiavelli.* London: The Bodley Head.

Rawnsley, A. (2000). *Servants of the People.* London: Hamish Hamilton.

Rentoul, J. (2001). *Tony Blair: Prime Minister.* London: Little, Brown.

Riddell, P. (2001). 'Blair as Prime Minister', in A. Seldon (ed). *The Blair Effect.* London: Little, Brown.

Riddell, P. (2005). *The Unfulfilled Prime Minister: Tony Blair's quest for a legacy.* London: Politico's Publishing

Rose, R. (2001). *The Prime Minister in a Shrinking World.* Cambridge: Polity.

Seldon, A. (2004). *Blair.* London: The Free Press.

Seldon, A. (2007). *Blair Unbound.* London: Simon & Schuster.

Seldon, A. and Meakin, J. (2016). *The Cabinet Office 1916-2016.* London: Biteback Publishing.

Short, C. (2004). *An Honourable Deception? New Labour, Iraq, and the Misuse of Power.* London: Simon & Schuster.

Theakston, K. (2010). *After Number 10: Former Prime Ministers in British Politics.* London: Palgrave Macmillan.

Chapter 13
Gordon Brown (2007-10)

Gordon Brown was often compared to various characters from Shakespeare, and his career and embattled premiership were sometimes seen as a sort of Shakespearean tragedy. Thus he was like Macbeth, bloodily clawing his way to power and then ruling alone and in fear. Or he had the paranoia and destructive jealousy of Othello, it was said, or the (in)decisiveness and hesitation of Hamlet. Or he had the poor judgement of King Lear, lashing out in all directions, a desperate figure clinging to the vestiges of power. Someone compared him to Coriolanus: principled but inflexible, unsympathetic, and temperamentally unsuited for popular leadership. Another comparison, this time to one of Shakespeare's comedies, was to the stiff and wooden Malvolio in *Twelfth Night*, attempting to discard his serious and melancholic personality and 'smile' – but with unfortunate results. Perhaps it would take our greatest playwright to do justice to this complex and tortured personality and his turbulent and traumatic time in power.

Party Leadership
After being overtaken by Blair in 1994, Brown had been leader-in-waiting for fully 13 years, something testifying to his ambition, staying power and ruthlessness. He was a powerful and commanding chancellor of the exchequer for ten years. But he never forgave Blair for supplanting him, always insisted that Blair had promised to make way for him after no more than two terms as PM, and his bitterness and plotting destabilised the New Labour government and diminished its achievements. Any likely rivals for the top job were politically killed off or backed off from standing against him, and Brown had a 'coronation' in 2007, with 88 per cent of Labour MPs nominating him, rather than facing a contested election for the party leadership.

Brown did have the ability to attract and retain tribal support as a sort of 'clan chieftain' in the Labour Party (Bower

2007: xiii), winning and keeping the backing of a network of 'Brownite' MPs and ministers on the road to Number 10. But overall Brown was not good at party management and had to work with a large number of MPs who owed him little or nothing. The Labour Whips' Office did not work well in 2007-2010, and backbench dissent and rebellions reached a higher level than in any previous post-war parliament. Labour's party machine was also decaying in terms of organisation, staffing and finances, something that would hamper its election performance.

As prime minister Brown did reach out to senior Blairites, giving some of them Cabinet positions, and even made some 'big tent' gestures (offering former Lib-Dem leader Paddy Ashdown a Cabinet post and bringing in outside recruits at junior minister level – the 'GOATS' – to what was dubbed a 'government of all the talents', though few of them made much of a mark). But he remained a suspicious and cliquish figure rather than genuinely pluralist (Rawnsley 2010: 461-465).

Brown faced seemingly annual attempts to topple or remove him from Number 10. Bringing back Peter Mandelson in 2008 was an audacious move that reflected the weakness of Brown's political position, supplying much-needed presentational and strategic skills to the centre of government while also providing a prop and ally in the face of plots against the prime minister, but at the cost of making Brown dependent on his former bitter enemy. The June 2009 Cabinet resignations and coup attempt further underlined Brown's vulnerability – he could not move senior ministers (like Alistair Darling or David Miliband) to other posts against their will and his premiership could have been finished if they too had resigned. There was a final abortive coup attempt in January 2010, advertising Labour disunity and undermining Brown's standing again just months ahead of the general election.

Ideology and Aims

Brown had little time for Blair's 'third way' and it suited him in the years before 2007 to seem a bit more to the left and more authentically 'Labour' or social-democratic than Blair. Some of this was political tribalism, some of it was about maintaining party support and his stranglehold on the succession, but some of it reflected his deeper understanding of Labour's socialist traditions and doctrines and stronger roots in the party than Blair (who delighted in 'taking on' his party and attacking its sacred cows). Some thought or hoped that he would break from Blairism and New Labour and eagerly anticipated radical new ideas and bold plans from a man who described himself at the start of his leadership as a 'conviction politician', someone strongly concerned with social justice and with a 'moral compass' (Hughes 2010:11). Religion was, incidentally, very important to him and he later wished he had been more open about his faith and beliefs when in office (Crines and Theakston 2015). He had a strong international vision, concerned about issues of development and global institutions and challenges, but lacked an overarching domestic vision.

Brown, as Peter Watt, Labour's general secretary, put it, 'had been so desperate to become Prime Minister, and had plotted so meticulously and ruthlessly to get to No. 10, that we all assumed he knew what he was going to do when he got there.' However, it soon emerged that there was 'no vision, no strategy . . . [no] grand plan . . . Gordon was simply making it up as he went along' (Watt 2010: 7-8). In contrast, Steve Richards (2010) argues Brown *did* have a plan, which was to govern in a sort of steady, statesmanlike 'father of the nation' style for a year, and then hold an election in 2008, after which he would introduce reforms in public services and the constitution – but the problem was he got blown off course by the mistake over the non-election of 2007 and never recovered the political capital, credibility or space needed to pursue his ideas after that.

In any case, as a co-architect of New Labour from the start, and with his powerful influence from the Treasury over economic and social policy after 1997, Brown – for all he positioned himself as 'not Blair' or even 'anti-Blair' - could hardly be expected to disown the past and engage in a complete ideological and policy redirection. In the post-war period, mid-term successions and changes of prime minister without a change of party have not usually resulted in significant shifts in policy direction. Broad policy continuity rather than a radical break or 'fresh start' is the usual pattern (Griffiths 2009: 55). There were plenty of so-called 'initiatives' from Brown ('too many' according to one former minister) but, overall, an incoherent policy agenda and an inability to plant a firm enough idea of what he stood for (Hughes 2010: 213, 231). There was no 'strategy for government', as a Number 10 aide admitted. Brown seemed to have 'run out of ideas, seemed to have run out of big projects', argued Vince Cable, something putting his government at the mercy of events. Tony Blair was reportedly concerned that Brown 'hasn't got a plan' (Rawnsley 2010: 526-7). Peter Mandelson (2010: 15, 451) felt that Brown had a 'tendency to react to events' and to short-termism, and argued that while he did 'see the big picture', he tended to look to create 'tactical opportunities' rather than 'a strategy to advance it.' Brown's government, as Beech and Lee put it, 'suffered from the prime minister's failure to adequately articulate his vision . . . the general lack of an ideological narrative . . . hampered his effectiveness [as prime minister].'

Brown cited the need for more time to spell out his 'vision for Britain' as one of the key reasons for not calling an early election in the autumn of 2007 (Hughes 2010: 134). Two years later, critics were still claiming that he 'doesn't know what he believes in' (Kettle 2009). His constitutional reform proposals disappeared without trace, and only in his last year did he develop a proper agenda for public services reform, that owed more to Blairism than he would admit, and came too late to make much difference. He has been labelled variously as a statist and social engineer, a technocratic Treasury centraliser, the heir to Thatcher, the heir to Blair, a man of the left or at least the centre-left, a practitioner of 'cautious Blairism' (Hughes 2010: 126), and someone whose personal political philosophy has been more influenced by market liberalism and the ideas of US thinkers (including neo-conservatives) than by European social-democracy, becoming increasingly distant from the Labour Party's mainstream ideas (Lee 2007). Brown's failure to set out a plausible 'narrative' about what he was doing and trying to achieve – communicating a strategic sense of direction – damaged his credibility and weakened his leadership.

Political Style and Skills

As a communicator, Brown suffered through comparison with Blair and with David Cameron – both telegenic, persuasive, able to reach out to the public, sell their ideas and project empathy and sincerity. He tried to make a virtue of his lack of slickness, purporting to scorn the politics of celebrity and image – 'not flash, just Gordon'. At first, his more subdued style appealed to some as a welcome change from Blair's prime-minister-as-actor-on-the-screen approach. But 'as time went on, it became increasingly evident that Brown lacked the range of presentational skills required to be a successful modern leader' as Andrew Rawnsley (2010: 525). put it. 'He's crap at communication', a Labour minister summed up bluntly, 'and the role of a leader is to communicate' (Sylvester 2008).

Brown could pack a real intellectual punch with his speeches – some drawing on and quoting a tremendous range of sources and heavyweight thinkers. But his speechmaking style was often monotone and relentless, usually involving a barrage of statistics, facts and lists of achievements. His style and public personality were not well suited to the business of connecting with a modern electorate through television. 'I've got all the policy, all the ideas', Brown would insist (though this claim is debatable). 'I just can't communicate it. 'I'm good at what politics used to be about, about policies', he once said. 'But now people want celebrity and theatre' (Mandelson 2010: 6, 14). Attempts to lighten or to humanise his image often ended up backfiring and making things worse, as with an infamous 'YouTube' appearance.

Any idea that the Brown premiership would bring 'the end of spin' was never credible given the aggressive media management he and his entourage had long practised (Price 2010: 394-5). He was in fact obsessed by headlines and the need for a constant stream of eye-catching announcements (Mandelson 2010: 15). The real criticism was that Brown did not have a proper media strategy and his Number 10 media operation could have been more effective, with the lack of a political heavyweight with hard-edged journalistic experience at the PM's side.

Brown's Number 10 was often labelled 'chaotic' or 'dysfunctional'. Some of his appointments – such as that of Jeremy Heywood as the first Number 10 permanent secretary to pull together the civil service side, problem-solve and progress-chase – were successful. But on the political, media and strategy sides there were more problems, and a succession of staff changes and infighting that damaged the effectiveness of his administration, particularly during Stephen Carter's ill-fated time as strategy director, when he clashed with the old Brown political clique (Price 2010: 409). It was always his preference to work through a small and tight inner group of trusted courtiers but one official argued that Brown 'surrounded himself with people who amplified his weaknesses rather than compensated for them' (Rawnsley 2010: 520). He had filled Number 10 with 'apparatchiks and spinners' it was said (Hughes 2010: 211). Moreover the Brown coterie were reported to be 'very reluctant to tell him when he was wrong. None of his people liked to contradict him' (Rawnsley 2010: 524). He expected and required total loyalty while also licensing close aides like Ed Balls, Charlie Whelan and Damian McBride to act as thuggish behind-the-scenes hatchet men, spinners, attack-dogs and assassins (McBride 2013). Brown was never squeamish about or reluctant to resort to the political black arts or what one critic called methods of 'terrorism' (Bower 2007: 191). The likes of Balls, Whelan and McBride did what they thought Brown wanted them to do, raising questions about his judgement and political style in terms of whom he chose as close allies, how he dealt with opponents and rivals, and his approach to the media. This was the 'dark side' of the purportedly 'ideologically serious, morally driven statesman.'

A return to collective Cabinet government was promised but the controlling and micro-managing Brown - a poor manager of his ministerial team - could hardly reinvent himself as an Attlee-esque chairman of the Cabinet. There were claims (Mandelson 2010: 442-3) that discussions around the Cabinet table were initially longer and more substantial under Brown than they had been under Blair, but his obvious impatience often suggested he would rather be elsewhere. Geoff Hoon felt that neither Blair nor Brown had 'any time for ministers'. The difference was, he went on, that Blair 'broadly let you get on with it [and] wasn't much interested unless something went wrong', whereas Brown 'wants to interfere in everything. He's temperamentally incapable of delegating responsibility' (Rawnsley 2010: 523). Relations with his Foreign Secretary, David Miliband, and his Chancellor, Alistair Darling (whom he would have liked to replace with his longtime adviser and right hand man Ed Balls), were strained. Brown, as prime minister, was deeply wary of the Treasury and its stance on economic policy and the deficit in particular. He himself chaired two key Cabinet committees: NEC, the National Economic Council – a successful organisational initiative - handling economic policy and the financial crisis (Blair had not chaired his own government's economic policy committee), and NSID, the lead committee on national security, international relations and development.

At the start, Brown was depicted as a dominating figure. Blair had had to share power with Brown, running a sort of rival government from the Treasury, but there were said to be no 'big beasts' or obvious, credible and weighty 'alternative prime ministers' in Brown's Cabinet (Hughes 2010: 30). The Cabinets of other post-war premiers had contained ministers with reputations and power-bases of their own, and there had been some heavyweight ministers under Blair (Brown himself, but also John Prescott, David Blunkett, John Reid, Charles Clarke). However, the picture of a hegemonic prime minister could hardly be sustained as events, mistakes, party unrest and Cabinet plots engulfed him. The return of Mandelson in 2008 provided a vital political shield but the stories of Cabinet ministers (including Jack Straw, Alistair Darling and Harriet Harman) forcing a string of concessions on policy and strategy from the prime minister after the third coup attempt in January 2010 spoke eloquently of dependency, not ascendancy, in Brown's position in the core executive and of his lack of deep support at Cabinet level.

Brown was certainly never going to be able to emulate Blair's almost Rooseveltian political use of personal charm to 'schmooze', persuade, win people over and avoid conflict (Rawnsley 2010: 57). Brown was more the 'big clunking fist', as Blair himself put it; 'Stalinist in his ruthlessness' in the way that he operated, according to a former Cabinet Secretary. It was almost as if he would rather be feared than loved. He was described as having a 'mastery of machine politics' and using 'faction boss methods'. His negotiating style was 'bone-crunching'; he 'steam-rollered' and intimidated rather than reasoned or persuaded. Other Cabinet ministers had come to regard him as 'secretive, cliquish and vengeful' at the Treasury, a political bruiser and a brutal operator (Rawnsley 2020: 69, 74, 434, 461; Bower 2007: 4, 109-110).

In more positive terms, Brown was depicted as the 'consummate strategist', 'the biggest political brain in the Labour Party' with 'the ability to see where the politics of something is going', the 'great chess player of British politics, the man who always thought a dozen moves ahead' (Hughes 2010: 75, 209; Rawnsley 2010: 510). But he was also 'the scheming fixer . . . the petty infighter . . . [and the] endlessly prevaricating, indecisive, fiddling tactician' (Hughes 2010: 3). His aim was always to carve out 'dividing lines' with opponents that exposed their vulnerability. His 'time horizon' was described as 'extraordinarily short'. 'He's always thinking how do we get ourselves out of a corner and put someone else in a corner' (Rawnsley 2010: 58, 585).

However, the build up to and the procrastination over the 'election that never was' in the autumn of 2007 – allowing expectations to run out of control before deciding finally not to go to the country when the opinion polls suggested Labour would have a much smaller majority - exposed both 'tactical foolishness' and 'strategic stupidity', as Rawnsley (2010: 510) describes what was arguably Brown's biggest political mistake as prime minister.

Where Blair was 'a much more instinctive decision-maker', according to Jack Straw, Brown's approach was slow, cautious and often disorganised (Rawnsley 2010: 523). Brown had a deeper grasp of policy than Blair. But critics argued that his long years at the Treasury were perhaps not a good preparation for the premiership. As chancellor, policies could be carefully planned and reviews instituted, giving him time to make up his mind. Chancellor Brown only rarely had to do the spontaneous and the immediate, but as prime minister the unpredictable and the press of events gave him no choice. Moreover, he was someone who wanted to concentrate on issues one at a time, refusing to consider other questions until he had thoroughly gone through the options and the details, considered all the angles and all the risks, and had finally come to a decision. A prime minister has to be able to deal with multiple problems and fast-moving crises, and Brown's ponderous and inflexible style was not suited to the day-to-day demands and pressures of Number 10 (Rawnsley 2010: 522).

While Brown burned the midnight oil, constantly demanding more papers and information, he came to seem indecisive, vacillating and dithering. On one matter after another (the 'non-election' of autumn 2007, the 10 pence tax rate, the parliamentary expenses scandal), there seemed a crippling 'inability to make big decisions' (Watt 2010: 174). Worse still, once Brown had made a decision, it was said to be incredibly difficult to get him to unmake it. Conviction that he understood the issues more deeply than anyone else bred stubbornness, inflexibility and a damaging unwillingness to change course or compromise in the face of public discontent, media criticism or backbench pressure (Hughes 2010: 211). Brown was said to dislike open debate or challenge; he had 'difficulty distinguishing between disinterested advice and a stab in the back', complained one official (Bower 2007: 213). Knowing that he responded badly to unwelcome advice, ministers and advisers could be reluctant to offer it.

It was frequently argued that Brown showed less emotional literacy than Blair or Cameron. He admits in his memoirs (Brown 2017) that he was not comfortable with the more 'touchy-feely' side of modern politics. On a human level, Brown, who is a shy man, was often described as thin-skinned, buttoned up, unsure of himself, and – to put it mildly - as not possessing an easy manner (Mandelson 2010: 16). Alastair Campbell is supposed to have labelled him 'psychologically flawed'. Labour MP Frank Field said he had 'no empathy with people' and allowing him into Number 10 was 'like letting Mrs Rochester out of the attic.' Austin Mitchell (2018: 73), a Labour MP, compared him to a Dalek. He could be charming, warm and humorous in private life but was driven, intense and highly volatile. Tom Bower's (2007) biography ruthlessly dissected Brown's character, depicting him as a 'brooding volcano', a man of 'demons and grudges', 'tantrums and offensive behaviour', 'consumed by hatreds', insecure and suspicious, awkward and uneasy, with poor social skills and a ferocious temper. Anthony Seldon calls Brown 'the most damaged personality' to have been prime minister since the war (Seldon and Lodge 2010). Brown displayed stamina and resilience, and had great integrity and a sense of moral duty, but a more even temperament would have been an asset and helped him to weather the demands of office and lead his government more successfully.

Context

Brown was an unlucky prime minister in that he faced a very hostile operating environment or context (Buller and James 2015). Anthony Seldon has argued that had Brown taken over earlier – perhaps during Labour's second term, when the government was in a stronger political and economic position – his 'personal peculiarities' would have proved 'less of an obstacle' to positive achievement (Hughes 2010: 109). Brown in fact always feared that he would get the premiership too late to make a success of it (Rawnsley 2010: 280). In the event, he ran up against a whole range of problems that typically handicap multi-term governments and challenge 'tail-end' prime ministers following dominant and long-serving predecessors: longevity in office and the associated boredom of the electorate; a depleted stock of able ministers; loss of reputation for economic competence; an increasingly hostile media; internal divisions over policy and the succession; and a revived and credible Opposition (Hughes 2010: 110; Heppell 2008). Ironically, Blair's personality and skills might have been better suited to dealing with and finding a response to some at least of these problems had *he* succeeded Brown rather than the other way round.

Brown had a brief 'honeymoon' in the summer of 2007 when he seemed to deal calmly and competently with a terrorist incident, foot and mouth disease, and a flooding crisis. His poll ratings were for a short while good. But his judgement was soon called into question over the fiasco of 'non-election' that autumn, he became massively unpopular, and thereafter he seemed reactive, hit by one thing after another, and never really on top of events.

There is one big exception to that verdict. In handling the global financial and banking crisis from 2008 onwards, Brown seemed more confident and at home than in discharging the normal political and public duties of prime-ministerial leadership. His decisive action and the sense that he had the experience to make him the right man for the situation may have helped him stave off leadership plotters. David Miliband or Alan Johnson, for example, would not have known how to respond to the crash; nor would Blair have been able to handle so well an economic crisis of that order. Normally portrayed as a cautious ditherer, he took bold and swift initiatives. 'He's really good in a crisis in a subject he understands', admitted a senior civil servant. 'He's energised by it' (Rawnsley 2010: 586).

Brown performed better and was rated more highly on the world stage than on the domestic one, and he was in his element in the negotiations and meetings of world leaders (the G20) in 2009, responding to the global financial crisis. He took the lead in coordinating international action that rescued the banking system and headed off a world depression. Both Obama and Sarkozy praised Brown's skills and the role he played in the high-level economic summitry. As Rawnsley (2010: 634) put it, he enjoyed and was better at being 'Chancellor of the World' than prime minister of Britain. His 'no time for a novice' line worked cleverly against internal party rivals and the Tory opposition, but the political pay-offs with the electorate at home seemed less clear, particularly in the face of criticism that he had not addressed the longer-term economic and financial problems that built up during his time as chancellor. Moreover, Conservative framing of responsibility for the crash and attacks on the mushrooming budget deficit were hitting home, even though Britain was moving out of recession over 2009-10, and the government was in fact increasingly split on economic policy, with other ministers and the Treasury thinking that Brown was burying his head in the sand by sticking to his line of 'Labour investment' versus 'Tory cuts'.

Conclusion

Brown has been described by critics as 'overwhelmed by a job that was much harder than he anticipated' and as 'defeated by so many of the challenges of leadership', by a ministerial ally as lacking the 'skill-set' for prime minister, and as admitting privately himself that he was not 'a good Prime Minister' (Mandelson 2010: 13, 489). He was disorganized and a poor decision-maker. Brown's experience also shows that modern politics demands more from leaders in terms of communication skills and emotional intelligence than it did in the past. Deborah Mattinson, a New Labour pollster, argues politicians now have to be likeable to be successful. In the 1980s Thatcher could get away with being respected as a leader but disliked. But attitudes to leadership, she says, have changed and attributes such as empathy have become more important. 'Is it possible to be a successful politician nowadays without attracting some level of public warmth? My judgement would be that it is not' (Mattinson 2010).

But besides the argument that Brown was simply unsuited to the job of being prime minister, he was also clearly very unlucky in terms of the daunting circumstances he faced during his time in Number 10 (Seldon and Lodge 2010; Richards 2010; Theakston 2011). He can be credited with saving the economy from complete collapse and for his response to the global financial crisis – but none of that saved his premiership.

After his first few months, Brown was widely expected to lose the next election and a big Conservative majority was expected in 2010. His poor election campaign performance seemed to seal his fate. Labour had its worse result since 1983, with just 29% of the vote and losing 91 seats (Heppell 2013).

The hung parliament that resulted instead almost gave Labour another chance and Brown was even willing to step aside as Labour leader and prime minister if that helped put together a 'progressive coalition' - but the Liberal Democrats were not interested. There is a strong suspicion that but for his shortcomings Labour might have scraped a slightly higher vote and some more seats, and thereby changed the coalition arithmetic. He would still personally probably have been finished, but the other 'what ifs...' in that scenario are tantalising.

References

Beech, M. and Lee, S. (2009). 'In conclusion: The prospects for Brown' social democracy', *Policy Studies*, 30 (1): 101-106.

Bower, T. (2007). *Gordon Brown*. London: HarperCollins.

Brown, G. (2017). *My Life, Our Times*. London: Bodley Head.

Buller, J. and James, T. (2015). 'Integrating structural context into assessment of political leadership: philosophical realism, Gordon Brown and the great financial crisis', *Parliamentary Affairs*. 68 (1): 77-96.

Crines, A. and Theakston, K. (2015). '"Doing God" in Number 10: British Prime Ministers, Religion and Political Rhetoric.' *Politics and Religion*. 8 (1): 155-177.

Griffiths, S. (2009). 'The public services under Gordon Brown - Similar reforms, less money', *Policy Studies*. 30 (1): 53-67.

Heppell, T. (2008). 'The degenerative tendencies of long-serving governments: 1963...1996...2008?', *Parliamentary Affairs*. 61 (4): 578-596.

Heppell, T. (2013). 'The Fall of the Brown Government, 2010', in T. Heppell and K. Theakston (eds), *How Labour Governments Fall: From Ramsay MacDonald to Gordon Brown*. London: Palgrave Macmillan.

Hughes, C. (ed) (2010). *What Went Wrong Gordon Brown?* London: Guardian Books.

Kettle, M. (2009). 'An October revolt is plotted: Brown's head is not safe yet.' *The Guardian*. 3 September.

Lee, S. (2007). *Best for Britain? The Politics and Legacy of Gordon Brown.* Oxford: Oneworld.

Mandelson, P. (2010). *The Third Man.* London: Harper Press.

Mattinson, D. (2010). *Talking to a Brick Wall.* London: Biteback Publishing.

Mitchell, A. (2018). *Confessions of a Political Maverick.* London: Biteback Publishing.

McBride, D. (2013). *Power trip: a decade of policy, plots and spin.* London: Biteback.

Price, L. (2010). *Where Power Lies: Prime Ministers v the Media.* London: Simon & Schuster.

Rawnsley, A. (2010). *The End of the Party.* London: Viking Penguin.

Richards, S. (2010). *Whatever It Takes: The real story of Gordon Brown and New Labour.* London: Fourth Estate.

Seldon, A. and Lodge, G. (2010). *Brown at 10.* London: Biteback.

Sylvester, R. (2008). 'It's not about Mr Brown's flaws, but Labour's', *The Times.* 3 June.

Theakston, K. (2011). 'Gordon Brown as Prime Minister: Political Skills and Leadership Style', *British Politics.* 6 (1): 78-100.

Watt, P. (2010). *Inside Out: My Story of Betrayal and Cowardice at the Heart of New Labour.* London: Biteback.

Chapter 14
David Cameron (2010-16)

When David Cameron became prime minister on 11 May 2010 the prime-ministerial record books had to be updated. He was (at 43 years and 7 months) then the youngest prime minister since 1812. He was the first Old Etonian prime minister since Alec Douglas-Home back in 1964. He had got to Number 10 after the shortest length of service as a Member of Parliament (nine years) since 1783. (Rishi Sunak, in 2022, has subsequently broken both of Cameron's records in terms of age and prior parliamentary service as PM.) He was the first prime minister to have been a special adviser. And he was the first PM heading a peacetime coalition government since the 1930s. Subsequently, in 2015, he won the first Conservative parliamentary majority since 1992, and then went on to log a more dismal entry in the record books, becoming the first British prime minister to resign after calling and losing a referendum on a major issue of policy (Britain's membership of the European Union).

Party leadership
Cameron's election as party leader in 2005 showed that, after three successive crushing election defeats and the failure of three different Leaders of the Opposition, the Conservatives were at last waking up to the fact that they were in a deep hole and needed to stop digging. Cameron had only become an MP in 2001, and had spent a couple of years as a shadow minister, though he had earlier had 6 years 'inside operator' experience as a party staffer and a ministerial special adviser in the late 1980s/ early 1990s before working as a communications executive for the media company Carlton. The obsession with his elitist social class and education background led some to ignore or underestimate the political professionalism acquired through this apprenticeship – though it was perhaps more a political technician's professionalism, while in terms of substantive ideas or political purpose he was arguably much more under-

developed (Elliott and Hanning 2012; Ashcroft and Oakeshott, 2016). Though not the initial favourite, and by far the least experienced contender, he won the Tory leadership (coming first among MPs and in the wider party membership vote) because he was a fresh face, his communication skills and voter appeal, and because of his broad base of support across the factional groups (including the Eurosceptic Thatcherite right and the more Europhile moderate left) (Heppell 2007).

Cameron's self-styled 'modernisation' strategy in opposition between 2005 and 2010 attempted to 'detoxify' the Conservative brand and image in order to make the party electable again (Bale 2016). In terms of general election results, he was successful, though helped to a great extent by the mistakes and failures of Labour (in government under Brown before 2010 and then in opposition up to 2015 under Ed Miliband) and by economic circumstances. His party's seat gain (+108 seats) in the election that ousted Labour in 2010 was its largest in nearly 80 years, albeit on a fairly modest vote gain (+3.7 per cent) and resulting in a hung parliament and a coalition rather than a majority Conservative government. Then, in 2015, contrary to expectations, the Conservatives gained another 25 seats and Cameron was able to form the first majority Conservative government for 23 years, as the first Tory PM in 60 years to increase his party's vote share (+0.8 per cent). His overall majority (12 seats) may have looked relatively small, but Labour was left trailing the Conservatives by 6 per cent of votes and nearly 100 seats. Cameron's Liberal Democrat coalition partners were also smashed in 2015, losing nearly two-thirds of their vote share and being reduced to just 8 seats, victims of a huge slump in support after 2010 and then of the ruthless Tory targeting of their seats.

Despite these electoral successes, Cameron's relationship with his own party was often problematic. He faced significant party management issues, with discontent and suspicion among Conservative MPs who felt neglected or ignored, and who complained about the leader and his inner circle being remote, exclusive and arrogant, and about the failure to win an outright election victory in 2010 and the need for a coalition. The Tory right were especially unhappy and restive; 'these people will never love you', one of his aides told him, they would 'tolerate' him in a sort of contractual relationship only so long as he was a winner (Cameron 2019: 237; Fall 2020: 20). The parliamentary party was much more ideologically Thatcherite (combining increasingly 'hard' Europhobia and social conservatism) than Cameronite (softer Euroscepticism and social liberalism) – the 'Cameroon' modernisers were always in a minority. Cameron himself has admitted to 'failures' in party management and wished he had done better at taking his party with him (Cameron 2019: 238, 249). Forming the coalition (with a combined majority of over 70 in the Commons) freed him to some extent from his party's right-wing die-hards, gave him some freedom of manoeuvre, and made his government after 2010 more stable and secure than a minority Tory administration would have been. But the unprecedented high level of backbench dissent and rebellion, and the way Cameron was pushed into conceding an EU referendum, showed the limits of his authority and support in his party. Cameron's social liberal initiatives (such as on same-sex marriage) also exposed and aggravated divisions in the party and alienated many MPs and the grassroots (Heppell 2019). Indeed, for many in his party, Cameron seemed an inauthentic voice of Conservatism. Yet, without a consensus on a replacement and the failure of a well-organised faction to gain ascendancy, Cameron escaped a leadership challenge, though he was frequently suspicious of the ambitions and manoeuvring of Boris Johnson.

Ideology and Aims

Cameron can hardly be said to have provided the sort of radical policy vision and driving sense of mission or direction that Thatcher did in the 1980s. Cameron was often described – and described himself – as an instinctive, non-ideological, pragmatic, 'whatever works', type of 'One Nation' Conservative. 'I don't like grand plans and grand visions', he once said (Jones 2008: 43). 'I don't believe in isms.' He has been described in various ways (see: Theakston 2012: 204-5): as like a centrist 'Macmillan Conservative', as a 'progressive Conservative' (socially-liberal, fiscally-conservative, tolerant and internationalist), as the heir to Blair, as the heir to Thatcher, as a neo-Thatcherite or a post-Thatcherite. He rather dodged around describing himself as a Thatcherite, but never disavowed the fundamentals of Thatcherism, saying she was right on 'the big things' but that 'some of the rough edges needed to come off', and claiming that his premiership owed a huge debt to her but also marked a break from her (Cameron 2019: 416). Meanwhile, some observers thought 'he never goes the whole way on anything' or 'he believes things, but nothing too much', and some talked of simple opportunism (Theakston 2012: 204). He was alleged to have said, 'I'd like to be prime minister because I think I'd be good at it' – as if the aim was to just have the job not *do* something with it. The question was how far his personal ambition was matched by any larger purpose (Ashcroft and Oakeshott 2016: 375-378).

From the start of his leadership, however, Cameron insisted that he wanted to be as radical a social reformer as Thatcher had been an economic reformer (Jones 2008: 315; Evans 2010). He declared that fixing the 'broken society' was his defining purpose and his party's 'central mission'. He talked of 'modern, compassionate Conservatism'. The 'Big Society' was Cameron's 'Big Idea', and was consciously designed to chart a new 'third way' of sorts between the Thatcherite individualism of his party's past and the statism of New Labour, emphasising social responsibility, the voluntary sector and community: 'there is such a thing as society, it's just not the same thing as the state.' But its policy implications were imprecise and contested, and even some close allies like George Osborne were not really sold on it. Critics claimed it was just a cover for public sector funding cuts, as his government prioritised 'austerity', and certainly the idea seemed to fade from government policy and rhetoric after the first couple of years or so.

Cameron's Conservative critics and enemies were always suspicious that he seemed far too comfortable with his enforced cohabitation with the Liberal-Democrats. And broadly speaking, the lineage of his government's public service, education and welfare policies could in many ways be traced back to New Labour. In some ways, Cameron pursued what might be understood as 'Blairism after the crash': policies that a re-elected Labour government could, out of necessity, have found itself pursuing in a climate of straitened public finances (Byrne et al 2017). It was striking that his impatient and iconoclastic adviser Steve Hilton left Downing Street in 2012 frustrated that Cameron was a reactive and tactical politician, at best an evolutionary reformer, at worst someone who just wanted to be re-elected, rather than a vision-driven, strategic and transformative leader.

Political Style and Skills
Cameron excelled at the public communication aspects of political leadership. He was the government's most effective communicator, and a confident and highly-accomplished 'frontman'. Cameron was more like Blair than like Brown or Major in terms of self-assurance, media savvy, presentation skills, and knowing how to handle the media to sell and promote himself and his policies, and to reach out, connect with and persuade the wider public. Good on television, he was also accomplished and statesmanlike at big set-piece occasions. Cameron was very good at appearing 'prime-ministerial'. He was also quick on his feet, sharp, confident and effective in the gladiatorial jousts at PMQs but sometimes, when rattled and annoyed, was accused of coming across as an aggressive 'Flashman' figure.

In terms of organising and running Number 10 and the government, Cameron initially turned his back on the methods of Blair and Brown. He had declared before the 2010 general election that he wanted a more collective Cabinet government style of policy-making and decision-taking, building a strong team and trusting his colleagues to get on with the job. The imperatives and dynamics of coalition to some extent made that a necessity and affected the sort of role he could and needed to play as prime minister (Bannister and Heffernan 2012; 2015). The coalition 'brought back Cabinet government' it was often argued. Cameron always chaired the Cabinet and ran meetings in an effective and business-like way. But the Cabinet – then as later - was not really a body that originated policy or took more than a small proportion of government decisions (the decision to hold a referendum on membership of the European Union did not go to it), and the level of serious collective discussion in the Cabinet declined throughout the government's term of office. Cabinet committees were more important decision-making bodies, particularly the National Security Council (chaired by Cameron himself, and bringing together key ministers and defence, foreign policy and intelligence advisers), the Home Affairs Committee (chaired by Nick Clegg) and the Europe Committee (chaired by William Hague when he was Foreign Secretary). During the Libyan intervention in 2011 the National Security Council (NSC) morphed into a 'War Cabinet', meeting over sixty times. Cameron's use of the NSC contrasted with the more informal 'sofa government' methods that arguably served some of his predecessors in No. 10 so ill (as seen with Blair and Iraq).

The key group functioning as a sort of inner Cabinet was the so-called 'Quad'. This consisted of Cameron and George Osborne for the Conservatives and Clegg and Danny Alexander (chief secretary to the Treasury) for the Liberal Democrats. This handled issues relating to the operation of the coalition, holding things together and working out agreements on the big policy disputes, and it also dealt particularly with major tax and public spending issues (Seldon and Snowden 2016).

Cameron entered office determined not to copy Gordon Brown's (ineffective) control-freakery, micro-management and meddling. He had little interest in tinkering with the machinery of government and also thought the frequent ministerial reshuffles favoured by other prime ministers were absurd and damaging. He initially let his ministerial 'barons' run their fiefdoms with a very large degree of independence. But a modern prime minister needs to look 'strong' and cannot detach himself too much without provoking media and political criticisms when things go wrong. Cameron's relaxed, broad-brush and hands-off approach was arguably a factor in the coalition government's difficulties and problems with issues like the controversial big NHS reorganization, votes for prisoners and other policy U-turns and wobbles. In consequence, after the first year or two Cameron became rather more of a 'chief executive' than a 'chairman' figure.

The prime minister's No. 10 back up was scaled down after the 2010 election. It soon became clear, however, that No. 10 needed to strengthen its policy expertise and its oversight and control over the rest of Whitehall, and sharpen up its political operation. In 2011, therefore, a new Policy and Implementation Unit was created (its dozen-strong staff a mix of civil servants and outsiders from the private sector). The Conservatives in opposition had talked of cutting back on the number of politically-appointed special advisers working for the prime minister and other ministers but in the event ended up appointing more than there had been in the outgoing Brown government. Like other prime ministers over the last couple of decades, Cameron came to believe that he needed a strong No. 10 to drive and coordinate policy and manage crises.

There were some criticisms, however, of cliquishness and of a tight and exclusive 'court' around Cameron at Number 10. He had a close-knit team of aides and advisers. His chief of staff, Ed Llewellyn, was influential as a foreign policy adviser to the prime minister, making the personal connections and lubricating the relations between Cameron and other leaders, particularly in the EU. Kate Fall, deputy chief of staff, functioned as Cameron's 'gatekeeper' (Fall 2020). Steve Hilton was described variously as the prime minister's chief 'policy guru', 'the director of blue skies thinking', 'a wild Catherine wheel man of ideas' and an 'impatient revolutionary' (Theakston 2012: 198). As strategy chief up to 2012, he was the brains behind the 'Big Society' and was active in dreaming up ideas on public service reform. But he had a counter-productive, antagonistic style, and it was not just Liberal Democrat ministers in the coalition who reportedly found his ideas often 'madcap' or 'off the wall' (Laws 2016: 66). Hilton also did not work well together with Andy Coulson, Cameron's director of communications from 2007 until he resigned in 2011. Coulson, a former tabloid editor with populist right-wing instincts, acted as something of a counterweight to Hilton, the long-term big picture thinker, in Cameron's team, and their relations were sometimes difficult. In 2011 Craig Oliver (formerly a TV editor, producer and executive) replaced Coulson. On the civil service side, Jeremy Heywood was the key official, first as Downing Street permanent secretary (as under Brown) and then from 2012 as Cabinet Secretary. Heywood was 'the indispensable man' and Cameron's 'enforcer', crucial to the day-to-day running of the government, sorting out blockages in Whitehall and coalition disputes, and driving the delivery of key policy priorities. 'Heywood spots the problems', one close observer said, 'and is called in to deal with them' (Theakston 2012: 198).

Insiders were impressed with Cameron's personal political skills even when he was a young special adviser, testifying to his astute political antennae and tactical nous. Observers of Cameron as a political leader admitted that he could be cunning. More emphasis, though, tended to be put on the way in which he was very good in small groups, like Blair using his courtesy, charm and social skills to great effect. Where Thatcher was abrasive, provocative, strident and confrontational, Cameron was a more emollient and consensual personality, something that helped in the 'detoxifying' of the Conservative brand in Opposition and also suited the coalition context.

Cameron's skills were seen to good effect in the successful negotiation of the challenges of coalition government, both in terms of his cunning poker-play in achieving a favourable settlement for the Conservatives in the initial negotiations of May 2010, and then in handling his Liberal Democrat partners to keep the coalition government together for a full parliamentary term. Cameron certainly looked comfortable and at ease at the head of a coalition, and seemed equipped to deal with the politics of a coalition, in a way that it was difficult to imagine Thatcher or Brown being, for example. Positive personal chemistry at the top is essential for coalition governments to work. From the start, Cameron and Nick Clegg, deputy prime minister, were reported to get on well together and to have a close rapport. They had regular bilateral meetings, and seemed to get on better than Tony Blair and Gordon Brown did under Labour. Clegg was certainly given more information and consultation about the Budget than Blair usually got when Brown was at the Treasury. But after the coalition's first year, and with the weakening of the Liberal Democrats' political position after their big election losses and defeat on the AV referendum in 2011, there were signs that inter-party and ministerial relations became rather more 'transactional', formal and business-like, with less trust and more tensions, hard bargaining and airing of party differences and conflicts of view (D'Ancona 2013; Laws 2016).

The other key personal and political partnership at the heart of the government was between Cameron and George Osborne, the Chancellor of the Exchequer. They worked collaboratively and were very close confidants and political allies to a degree not seen in the modern history of prime minister-chancellor relations. Cameron did not get into the details and pretty much left economic policy to his Chancellor. Osborne was Cameron's closest lieutenant and he ranged across all areas, not just the economy, being a key figure on political strategy and party management. Osborne attended the two key daily Number 10 meetings at 8.30 am and 4.00 pm with Cameron and the PM's inner team of aides and advisers (and which William Hague also often attended) that set the government's agenda and coordinated its message. Clegg did not attend those meetings. It strengthened Cameron that there was no alternative leader in the Commons or the Cabinet with the stature and popularity to threaten him. Osborne accepted he was number two and therefore a rival next door in No. 11 did not menace Cameron, as Blair was threatened by Brown.

As a decision-maker, the nimble Cameron was very different from his immediate predecessor in Number 10, who had been obsessed by details, ponderous, inflexible and vacillating. Having got those around him to outline the arguments on all sides of a question, Cameron generally made up his mind fairly quickly. He had more of a broad-brush style even than Blair, who could master policy details like a barrister when he needed to. 'Themes not details' were said to be his forte, and Cameron himself emphasized that 'being a good prime minister is about making the right judgements' (Jones 2008: 104). He was said to pick up ideas quickly and to be intelligent but also to be more interested in resolving problems and making things happen than in underlying philosophy or theories. A close observer once described him as 'a good examinee in the Oxford PPE style', suggesting breadth and quickness rather than depth. There were reports that a 'laid-back' inattention to policy detail and an 'essay crisis' style of leadership sometimes worried his aides (in other words, letting things drift before getting a grip on them) (Theakston 2012: 205-6).

Cameron scored highly in terms of the emotional intelligence now widely recognized to be an important component of successful political leadership. The contrast to Gordon Brown seemed strong. Cameron came across as untroubled by inner demons and well adjusted. He seemed reasonable, balanced, emotionally secure, self-confident and comfortable with himself. He had an easy manner, was optimistic, cool and usually calm under pressure, and he could keep things in proportion. Underneath the personal charm and ease, however, he was also tough, determined, and could be ruthless when necessary.

Context

In terms of the cycles of 'political time', Cameron encountered a political and economic order more vulnerable than any time since the 1970s (Byrne et al 2017). Central to this vulnerability were the effects of the 2008 financial crisis. The economic recession this produced proved longer than any since the 1930s. Living standards only slowly recovered. There were wider social and political problems and tensions too. There was a perception of disconnection between elites and the public and deepening distrust of politicians. The dominance of the SNP in Scotland and the 2014 independence referendum challenged the UK's territorial integrity. The threat from Nigel Farage's UKIP testified to a constituency of disaffected 'left behind' voters and mobilised disaffection against the EU and immigration policy.

A key reason for the Conservatives' political success under Cameron was the way in which they were able to redefine the economic argument after the 2008 financial crash. They claimed to have the worst economic inheritance of an incoming government for at least 60 years. Though the real scale of the problem was exaggerated, tackling the deficit and 'austerity'

208

worked as a statecraft strategy because it undermined Labour's reputation for economic competence and boosted the Conservatives' own credibility on that crucial battlefront, even though George Osborne had mixed success in practical terms and missed his target to eliminate the deficit (Gamble 2015; Evans 2021). Cameron and Osborne consequently enjoyed a significant opinion poll lead on economic matters throughout the 2010-15 parliament with voters assigning primary responsibility for the UK's economic difficulties to Labour. The Liberal Democrats were locked into this strategy as part of the coalition agreement, which meant that for all the sharing of power and ministerial posts after 2010, the Conservatives effectively dominated the overall political agenda of the coalition and had to give up little of real substance in policy terms (Heppell 2014; 2019).

Economic growth slumped after Cameron took office and it took until 2014 for the economy to surpass its pre-crisis peak. But growth had strengthened, inflation was low and unemployment had fallen significantly in time for the 2015 general election. The fact that the Conservatives went into that election ahead of Labour on the two crucial counts of economic competence (who was most trusted to manage the economy) and political leadership (which party had the best leader) was a better guide to the eventual outcome than the (misleading) general party choice opinion poll figures that dominated the media headlines.

In 2015 Cameron was the least-worst alternative for many voters and his success rested upon his opponent's misfortunes: his Lib-Dem coalition partner's electoral collapse and Labour's rout in Scotland. Cameron appealed to 'safety first', stressing competence and exploiting concerns about Labour's economic management and the threat of instability posed by the SNP. He was lucky he did not confront more dynamic, convincing or capable Leaders of the Opposition. If some Conservative-supporting newspapers were hostile to Cameron, they directed even greater vitriol at Ed Miliband (and after 2015, Jeremy Corbyn).

Cameron's party often seemed restive and unhappy. The 2010-15 parliament was the most rebellious since 1945, with

35% of all divisions witnessing rebellions by coalition MPs. Many of these had little lasting significance but several demonstrated growing divisions within Conservative ranks. Large-scale rebellions on an EU referendum and the EU budget signalled the hardening of Eurosceptic opinion. There were 91 backbench rebels against House of Lords reform, which damaged relations with the Lib-Dems. Defeat on military intervention in Syria undermined Cameron's authority on foreign policy. He needed Labour and Lib-Dem votes to pass the same-sex marriage legislation because his own party was split down the middle. In the second term, 2015-16, party management remained a headache, not least because the government possessed a smaller Commons majority than that of the coalition – one of only 12 seats.

At the same time, Cameron struggled to find an effective strategy to counter UKIP. Nigel Farage posed as a tribune for those alienated from mainstream parties and the existing regime. Cameron worried that UKIP's appeal to disgruntled Conservative voters, grassroots members and (potentially defecting) MPs could only get stronger. Here Farage outbid Cameron with a demand for an immediate EU referendum and was well positioned to attack missed immigration targets.

The 2014 Scottish independence referendum was a much closer call than Cameron would have liked, but it at least temporarily averted the breakup of the Union while seriously damaging Labour in electoral terms in what was until recently its Scottish redoubt. But no assessment of Cameron's leadership could fail to place centre stage the decision to stage an EU referendum, and the subsequent defeat of the 'remain' campaign in the 2016 referendum. Cameron (2019: 398-415) has claimed that an in/out referendum was becoming necessary and inevitable, and was the only way to keep the UK in the EU. He admits there was massive party pressure on him over the issue, and his critics maintain *that* was actually the key factor – that the decision in 2013 to grant a referendum was taken largely for reasons of party management, to buy-off the Eurosceptics in his party and to 'shoot the UKIP fox' into the bargain. Cameron thought his leadership might be at stake if he did not offer it. But the absence of a strong positive case being made for Britain's EU membership by the prime minister and other 'remainers', and the limited achievements of Cameron's attempted renegotiation of the terms of membership, did for the lacklustre 'remain' campaign, leaving it with nothing to say on the crucial issue of immigration in particular. The result, inevitably, meant the abrupt end of Cameron's premiership, leaving behind a degree of uncertainty and division unknown in British politics since the 1970s, perhaps even since the 1930s.

Conclusion

At a time of great economic and political danger in 2010, David Cameron moved quickly, decisively and imaginatively in a way that took his party back into power and provided an unexpectedly stable and effective government (Heppell and Seawright 2012; D'Ancona 2013; Seldon and Snowden 2016). But for all his achievements as a successful coalition prime minister, and then as an unexpected election winner in 2015, his reputation and place in history seems destined to be defined by Brexit and his calling and losing the referendum. Critics immediately bracketed him with the likes of historic 'failed' prime ministers like Neville Chamberlain and Anthony Eden.

The referendum disaster exposed the side of him that was careless and complacent, a gambler and a risk-taker rather than the cool and careful pragmatist priding himself on his supposedly sound judgement. Critics argued it was symptomatic of wider failings relating to his manipulative approach, his style of leadership and his short-term horizons – an obsession with tactics, presentation, and opportunistic moves rather than the longer-term and the strategic; as Ashcroft and Oakeshott (2016) said: 'doing what was needed to get through the immediate crisis, and banking on his own ability to cope with the next one when it arose.' In the end, his luck ran out. He had feared being the prime minister who 'lost Scotland' and 'broke the Union', and while he avoided that fate, the referendum there helped to boost the SNP, and Scotland's future is still far from settled. Instead, he is the prime minister who inadvertently took Britain out of the EU.

Cameron aimed to change and modernise his party, but in retrospect we can perhaps see how fragile, shallow and unfinished that modernisation actually was. Resulting first in a coalition and then only a slim Conservative majority, the modernisation strategy was never as electorally successful as it needed to be to silence Cameron's critics or give him the scope to 'remake' his party. Europe had long divided the Conservative Party, helping to bring down his two Conservative predecessors in No. 10, Thatcher and Major. Cameron did not (and did not want to) challenge its policy stance over Europe. He was himself a self-confessed Eurosceptic but believed being in the EU was better for Britain than leaving. He sought to appease and quieten down the hard-line Eurosceptics, buy time and head off the threat from UKIP, thinking he would in the end win through and hold things together, as Harold Wilson had in the 1970s. But he under-estimated the strength of anti-Europeanism in his party and more broadly in the country, and over-estimated his own ability to persuade, meaning that strategy failed – a career-closing calamity for him, and one unleashing huge and divisive challenges for his successor(s) and his country.

References

Ashcroft, M. and Oakeshott, I. (2016). *Call me Dave : the Unauthorised Biography of David Cameron.* London: Biteback Publishing.

Bale, T. (2016). *The Conservative Party From Thatcher to Cameron.* Second edition. Cambridge: Polity.

Bennister, M. and Heffernan, R. (2012). 'Cameron as Prime Minister: The Intra-executive Politics of Britain's Coalition Government', *Parliamentary Affairs.* 65 (4): 778-801.

Bennister, M. and Heffernan, R. (2015). 'The limits to prime ministerial autonomy: Cameron and the constraints of coalition', *Parliamentary Affairs.* 68 (1): 25-41.

Byrne, C., Randall, N., and Theakston, K. (2017). 'Evaluating British prime ministerial performance: David Cameron's premiership in political time', *British Journal of Politics and International Relations*, 19 (1): 202-220.

Cameron, D. (2019). *For The Record.* London: William Collins.

D'Ancona, M. (2013). *In It Together : the Inside Story of the Coalition Government.* London: Viking.

Elliott, F. and Hanning, J. (2012). *Cameron : Practically a Conservative.* London: Fourth Estate.

Evans, S. (2010). 'Mother's Boy: David Cameron and Margaret Thatcher', *British Journal of Politics and International Relations.* 12 (3): 325-343.

Evans, S. (2021). 'Speaking in her language: Cameron, Thatcher and Deficit Reduction under the Coalition Government 2010-2015', *Parliamentary Affairs.* early view.

Fall, K. (2020). *The Gatekeeper.* London: HQ.

Gamble, A. (2015). 'Austerity as statecraft'. *Parliamentary Affairs.* 68 (1): 42-57.

Heppell, T. (2007). *Choosing the Tory Leader: Conservative Part leadership elections from Heath to Cameron.* London: I.B. Tauris.

Heppell, T. (2014). 'Ministerial selection and portfolio allocation in the Cameron government', *Parliamentary Affairs.* 67 (1): 64-79.

Heppell, T. (2019): *Cameron: The politics of modernisation and manipulation.* Manchester: Manchester University Press.

Heppell, T. and Seawright, D. (eds). *Cameron and the Conservatives: The Transition to Coalition Government.* London: Palgrave.

Jones, D. (2008). *Cameron on Cameron: Conversations with Dylan Jones.* London: Fourth Estate.

Laws, D. (2016). *Coalition: The Inside Story of the Conservative-Liberal Democrat Coalition Government.* London: Biteback Publishing.

Seldon, A. and Snowden, P. (2016). *Cameron at 10 : The Verdict.* London: William Collins.

Theakston, K. (2012). 'David Cameron as Prime Minister', in T. Heppell and D. Seawright (eds). *Cameron and the Conservatives: The Transition to Coalition Government.* London: Palgrave Macmillan.

Chapter 15
Theresa May (2016-19)

Theresa May was still a schoolgirl when, it is claimed, she announced she wanted to be the first female prime minister of Britain. Six or seven years later, in 1979, Margaret Thatcher beat her to it. It took another 37 years before, in July 2016, May became the second woman to assume that office. Her inheritance would have been a hugely demanding one for any prime minister - not least with the challenges of Brexit, which defeated her - but May's short and turbulent premiership also starkly revealed that, in the end, she simply 'wasn't up to it' and was 'found out' in office (Seldon 2020: 660, 671).

Party leadership
Comparative political science research suggests that across a range of different countries women are more likely to be selected as party leaders in conditions of political crisis, and when challenging circumstances make the post least attractive and successful tenure most uncertain (Beckwith 2015). Margaret Thatcher's emergence as Conservative opposition leader in 1975 fits that picture, as does Theresa May's sudden and dramatic elevation to the Conservative leadership and the premiership in 2016, in the aftermath of David Cameron's resignation following his defeat in the EU referendum.

In terms of age (59), and service in parliament (19 years) and in the Cabinet (6 years), May also conformed to the pattern that new leaders selected by parties in government tend to be older, senior and more experienced in office than those breaking-through in opposition (compare, for instance, Callaghan and Brown to Blair and Cameron). First elected in 1997 (when she was one of only 13 female Conservative MPs), May's route to Number 10 involved a long slog through a series of middle-ranking shadow Cabinet posts in opposition – including a stint as the first woman to be Conservative Party chairman, when her brutally frank remarks about the Tories being seen as 'the nasty party' identified her as a moderniser but did her no favours with her colleagues. Ambitious, competent, the proverbial 'safe pair of hands' and hard-working, she was never part of the Tory leadership inner circle under Michael Howard (2003-05) or David Cameron (after 2005). But she got a lucky break in 2010 when – putting together the Conservative and Lib-Dem coalition – it became important and necessary to have a woman in one of the top jobs, and May thus unexpectedly became Home Secretary. She held that post – one of the most difficult and toughest in government, and often a poisoned chalice for its holder's career-hopes – for six years, showing a steely determination, taking a hard line on issues such as immigration, security and the need for police reforms, and often clashing bitterly with other ministers (in both the coalition parties). If not much liked, she earned grudging respect as 'a bloody difficult woman', to use Ken Clarke's words – a label that helped rather than hindered her in the 2016 leadership election (Prince 2017).

May had more senior ministerial experience than Thatcher (with four years as Education Secretary) had when she became Conservative leader. Her long stint as Home Secretary helped her project an image of experience, competence and security that paid off in 2016. Later as prime minister she performed strongly on security issues, such as terrorism and handling the Salisbury poisoning attack by Russian agents. But she had survived at the Home Office by being 'controlling, careful and uncollegiate' (Sylvester 2020: 495), and the strengths and qualities she developed there turned into a weakness – even a liability - later in Number 10. Moreover May's apprenticeship was narrow in another sense (and a contrast to Thatcher's in this respect). She was the first prime minister for half a century with no experience as either Leader of the Opposition or Chancellor of the Exchequer - roles requiring high-level performative skills and a grasp of the interconnections of policy and politics across the board. This background perhaps concealed her limitations and made the step up to the multifaceted leadership challenges of the top job even harder for her (Seldon 2020).

The 2016 Conservative Party leadership contest has been described as 'a chaotic bloodbath of recrimination, backbiting and betrayal' (Prince 2017: 331) One Tory MP said it was like 'student politics' – 'I want a grown-up' was how he explained his backing for May (Prince 2017: 341). She benefitted from the divisions and feuding among her opponents, including Boris Johnson's withdrawal from the race after being denounced by his erstwhile campaign manager Michael Gove, and the splitting of the 'Leave'-supporting Brexiteers between socially-liberal backers of Gove and socially-conservative supporters of Andrea Leadsom. After two ballots of Conservative parliamentarians, May had the support of 60.5 per cent of her party's MPs – a stronger mandate than that won by any of her predecessors since the introduction of elections for the leadership in 1965, and a bigger parliamentarians' vote than Johnson later got in 2019, with Leadsom trailing in second place among MPs, with only 25.5 per cent. Surveys of the wider rank-and-file party membership (two-thirds of whom were ardent Brexiteers) suggested May was favoured over Leadsom by 63 to 31 per cent, but the latter's withdrawal meant there was no grassroots ballot, and May was crowned leader as 'the last woman standing' (Quinn 2019; Jeffery et al 2018).

May clearly trumped Leadsom on competence and ministerial experience by a huge margin; tellingly, over 80 per cent of ministers were estimated to have voted for her, and most of the Tory whips' office reportedly worked on her campaign. As one minister put it, her appeal was as 'a serious woman for serious times' (Duncan 2021: 49). But also vital was the way in which she seemed best placed to unite the party. She had been a 'Remainer' but presented herself as an unenthusiastic and reluctant one, and played hardly any part in the EU referendum campaign. Her 'Brexit means Brexit' slogan signalled she accepted the result and could be trusted to deliver it. That helped win her significant support across the party her rivals lacked. While 56 per cent of Tory MPs had supported 'Remain' in the referendum, 42 per cent backed 'Leave' – and May was backed by nine out of ten of the 'Remainers' and by over a third of 'Leavers'.

The truncated leadership election meant that the party and country were spared a two-month campaign season that may have prolonged the political instability after the shock of the referendum result. But, equally, May was not 'road-tested' out on the hustings as a campaigner and communicator – when her weaknesses in those respects would have been exposed - and was also not really required to spell out what she stood for, her political philosophy and policies or to elaborate in detail on what Brexit might mean in practice, and the problems, choices and trade-offs involved. She had not won an intellectual argument or a policy argument with the party and the mass membership that might have strengthened her authority in government and given her a clearer mandate to lead (Ross and McTague 2017: 53). She had no real time to work up a proper agenda and strategy for government. Her limitations and the drawbacks of this lack of policy definition and articulation were to become apparent only later.

Ideology and Aims
'There is no "Mayism"', Theresa May herself once said (Prince 2017: 390). She has in fact been described as a politician with strong views rather than a strong ideology, and as someone more driven by a moral compass than operating within an ideological framework (Spencer 2017). 'There's no interest in ideas', commented a Conservative who worked for her (Shipman 2017: xxvi). May talked about the impact of her Christian upbringing and faith, and like a number of other recent prime ministers (Thatcher, Blair, Brown and to a lesser extent Cameron), her religious views – deep-rooted but understated and not flaunted - seem to have helped frame or inform her general thinking and approach, and underpin the very strong sense of public service and duty that was widely commented on (Spencer 2017; Crines and Theakston 2015). She believed strongly that politics isn't a game, it's a serious business - a point she would make to emphasise the difference between her sort of politics and that of the likes of Cameron, Osborne and Johnson. But she was not well equipped to provide a strong sense of purpose or a new defining vision for her party and government.

In trying to 'place' her within the Conservative Party, William Hague viewed her as coming from the moderate wing, not the anti-EU right, and believed she backed Ken Clarke in the

1997 leadership election (Prince 2017: 83). She once said 'there is more to life than individualism and self-interest', distancing herself from Thatcherite ultras by suggesting that the Tories lost office to New Labour in the 1990s because people felt they were promoting the individual too much at the expense of the wider community or society as a whole (Prince 2017: 374; Spencer 2017: 312-313). But although a so-called 'moderniser', May seemed to the right of Cameron not least because she was more of a social conservative than a metropolitan liberal on the social-cultural values and issues divide.

Launching her leadership campaign, she spoke of a 'different kind of Conservatism', and a key influence on her here seems to have been her aide and adviser Nick Timothy, a devotee of the late-19th/early-20th century politician and social reformer Joseph Chamberlain. In this vein, May talked about 'the good that government can do', the need for the state to step in when markets were not functioning as they should, and the scope for 'a new industrial strategy', a substantial house-building programme and an end to corporate excess. The idea was to broaden the party's appeal across class and geographical divides to 'the just about managing', tackling unfairness and injustices, making Britain a 'country that works for everyone', and putting the Conservatives back in touch with 'ordinary working people' rather than – in a swipe at the Cameroons – just the 'rich and the privileged' (Espiet-Kilty 2018; Prince 2017: xii, 184, 238; Shipman 2017: 17; Seldon 2020: 45-6).

All this meant that some described May's approach as a combination of 'reforming capitalism' with a 'populist agenda pitched on the side of working families' (Worthy 2017); others described it as 'blue-collar Toryism', designed to appeal to communities that felt left behind and might have once voted Labour but had recently been attracted by UKIP and had voted 'leave' (Hayton 2017). Certainly, under May the Conservative party produced in 2017 its most 'left-wing' general election manifesto since 1964 (Allen and Bara 2019). In the context of what may be an ongoing electoral and party realignment, driven by major economic, social, class and cultural changes, May's attempt to open up questions about the distributive effects of neo-liberalism could be interpreted as an effort to build (or re-build) a Conservative electoral coalition that incorporated small 'c'-conservative working class voters (a strategy successfully carried further by Boris Johnson in 2019).

However the danger was that the 'burning injustices' agenda could cede ground to Labour, who polls suggested were believed to be more convincing and trusted to 'deliver' on social problems and issues. In any case the follow-through in terms of practical policies and programmes seems to have been limited and stuttering, and actions did not live up to words – partly because of internal ministerial differences and resource constraints, partly because of the loss of May's momentum and authority after the 2017 election, and partly because dealing with Brexit absorbed so much attention and energy, leaving little 'bandwith' in government and the civil service for anything else. The promises of an 'end to austerity' (in May's 2018 conference speech and the 2019 budget) marked a recognition that the Conservatives needed to have a positive strategy for a future general election and that the government was about more than delivering (and feuding about) Brexit. But there were obvious risks, after a decade of restraint and cuts, with pent-up expectations, and with the public finances and the state of the economy so dependent on what sort of Brexit deal could be reached, not to speak of the danger of always being out-promised by the left populism of the Corbynite Labour opposition. In the end, May ran out of road before she could make any progress with a broader agenda. It is likely that she will be historically defined and remembered primarily – perhaps even exclusively – in terms of Brexit rather than for other policy ideas and achievements or for 'remaking' Conservatism.

Political Style and Skills

May was widely described as a third-rate communicator and a mediocre media performer. Steve Richards (2019: 352-3) says that more than a failure to communicate, May's indifference to communication or the 'teaching' function of a political leader was a fatal flaw. Her job, as she saw it, was getting decisions right and making policy, not talking to the media and communicating what the government was doing. But her House of Commons performances were described by one Labour opponent, Yvette Cooper, as 'steady and serious. She is authoritative in parliament – superficial attacks on her bounce off' (Cooper 2016). With the media and the public presentation side of politics, however, and in front of the television cameras or audiences of ordinary people, she was rightly called 'unremarkable, wooden, frankly boring' (Sparrow 2018). Her style was defensive and remote: she was reluctant to give interviews, answer questions or open up, and was apparently not good at thinking on her feet. Her stilted, scripted, emotionless and robotic manner led to her being described as the 'Maybot'. Putting her at the centre of an exceptionally personalised or presidential-style general election campaign in 2017 was clearly a huge and costly mistake by the Conservatives. And in national terms, the challenges of Brexit were not made any easier to deal with by the presence in Number 10 of someone so poorly equipped for, and shrinking from, the difficult job of engaging, educating, connecting with and persuading the public and shaping a narrative about where Britain was headed – though admittedly these tasks would have been difficult enough for a leader with better communication skills.

As an incoming prime minister in 2016, May acted decisively (even brutally) to reshape the government – more so than most of her predecessors among the post-war mid-term successor PMs (Allen 2017). Six of Cameron's Cabinet ministers were demoted and seven sacked; there were eleven new faces round the Cabinet table. May paid-off some personal scores and grudges by immediately firing George Osborne and Michael Gove. Only a quarter of the new Cabinet were 'Leavers' but they occupied three key posts – Boris Johnson as Foreign Secretary, David Davis at the newly created Department for Exiting the European Union (DExEU), and Liam Fox heading the new Department for International Trade. These changes underlined May's commitment to Brexit and also tied-in Brexiteers who now had to 'own' the result they had fought for and take responsibility for implementing it. They were perhaps more political gestures to the party and to the Brexiteers than sensible or well thought-out machinery of government changes, however, and the relationship between DExEU, Number 10, the Foreign Office and other departments did not work smoothly. Another political motive perhaps was that Johnson was seen as a threat and so part of the plan was to appoint him to a role where he could to some extent be sidelined, reveal his shortcomings and discredit himself – as indeed he did before resigning in 2018, along with Davis, after a split over the developing plans for a Brexit deal. She soon lost her second Brexit minister, Dominic Raab, and in fact the May government saw an unprecedented and disruptive number of ministerial resignations on policy/political grounds, compared to other governments over the last 40 years.

Unlike, for instance, David Cameron with George Osborne and William Hague, May did not have very senior and heavy-weight lieutenants working closely with her, and supporting and sustaining her in government (Barwell 2021: 419), though Damian Green and then David Liddington did useful behind-the-scenes coordinating work on domestic policy as de facto deputy PMs based in the Cabinet Office. Complicating and complicated by the need to balance and manage the Cabinet over Brexit was the difficult relationship between May and her Chancellor, Philip Hammond. Poor in personal terms and with differences over policy (Hammond was a cautious and economically-dry Thatcherite), this was one of the most difficult and occasionally even counter-productive prime minister/chancellor relationships for decades. Sources close to the chancellor dismissed the prime minister as 'economically innumerate' (Duncan 2021: 162), while there was speculation that May would sack him after her anticipated general election triumph – but instead he had to be kept on and his position was strengthened.

With May's personal political capital massively depleted after the 2017 general election, she had to bring back Michael Gove, then she botched a reshuffle in January 2018 when she could not move any of the 'big beasts' and some other ministers refused to switch jobs. Had the senior figures in the Cabinet all rallied around one candidate, they could have forced her out after the general election debacle. But there was no consensus about a successor, and tension and rivalries among possible opposing contenders. In the event, there were many and growing signs in an increasingly deeply divided Cabinet after 2017, and in an endemically 'leaky' atmosphere, that government ministers were more able and willing to assert themselves over policy and decision-making, at many times showing open insubordination and ill-discipline, little loyalty to the PM, paying scant regard to the convention of collective Cabinet responsibility, and clearly manoeuvring for position in a future leadership race.

Also among the victims of the general election were Nick Timothy and Fiona Hill, who had been the powerful joint-chiefs of staff in Number 10. They had worked closely with her in the Home Office, moulded her for and helped propel her to Number 10, and provided ideas and strategies that she often seemed unwilling or unable to provide herself. In Downing Street 2016-17 they operated a highly centralised, domineering, dictatorial and top-down regime, marked by abrasive, aggressive, mistrustful and bullying attitudes and actions towards others (whether ministers, civil servants or other advisers). It was a toxic and destructive environment, likened by some to a 'reign of terror' or a bunker mentality (Shipman 2017; Seldon 2020). The political and policy consequences were bad. Decision-making was slowed down, as everything had to go through the two 'chiefs'. Other viewpoints – including unwelcome official advice - were shut out. Ministers became resentful. There was minimal consultation with her Cabinet over the development of Brexit policy in this period – the 'red lines', the 'hard' Brexit and the triggering of Article 50 were all decided in a secretive process by a small inner group around the prime minister. Timothy, a longstanding Eurosceptic, was a powerful voice on Brexit, and he masterminded the 2017 manifesto and dreamed-up the controversial and electorally damaging social care policy plan (the so-called 'dementia tax') that was promptly abandoned in middle of the campaign.

It was not surprising that Cabinet ministers demanded the immediate removal of the two 'chiefs' after the general election. Their replacement, Gavin Barwell (a former minister and MP), operated in a more conventional, low-key and lower-profile fashion, trying to set a different tone, and he worked more on a team basis with the civil servants and other figures at the centre, aiming also to improve Number 10's relations with MPs (Barwell 2021). Meanwhile, at an early stage the senior civil servant Oliver Robbins (a bogeyman figure for the 'hard' Brexiteers) was established as the key official adviser on Brexit, initially also heading the DExEU department, but then shifting across to be based in the Cabinet Office and working directly for the prime minister. The illness and early retirement of Cabinet Secretary Jeremy Heywood (who died in 2018) removed a powerful presence at the centre of a Whitehall machine under unprecedented strain, someone who had been a key adviser, fixer and solution-finder for Blair, Brown and Cameron. His replacement – Mark Sedwill – was more in the mould of 'securocrat', with a background in foreign policy before working closely with May at the Home Office and then as National Security Adviser.

At the centre of it all was the rather enigmatic figure of Theresa May herself. She was someone who in one sense appeared the sensible, normal, voice of 'Middle England' - unflashy and cautious but also safe, serious, competent, dutiful and professional. She was once neatly described as a 'first-rate second-rank politician' (Barnett 2017). She was supposedly on top of the details, a tough negotiator, systematic, tenacious and conscientious, with a remarkable resilience and the ability to just keep plodding on – the 'do your homework' rather than the 'essay crisis' prime minister, to make a comparison with Cameron (Runciman 2019: 190). Quiet, shy, gauche and reserved, a very un-extrovert and private person, something of a loner – 'unclubbable', as the saying goes - she had very few political friends outside her inner circle. She wanted to do the right thing and decide issues on their merits, it was said, rather than being a transactional deal-making sort of politician (2017: 118).

But this was also someone who was reportedly cold, secretive and untrusting, and hard to get to know properly. 'You can't talk to her like a normal person', commented one of her Cabinet ministers, Amber Rudd (Swire 2020: 322), while another minister, Alan Duncan (2021: 181), said May's 'social skills' were 'sub-zero'. She had a vengeful streak, too, alienating people and making enemies more easily than allies, which did not help her when her authority drained away. She was also described as lacking intellectual confidence and ideas of her own, as being narrow-minded and unimaginative, poor at delegating and sharing with other people. One official commented that she did not like discussions in front of her where aides debated and disagreed with each other – she wanted 'the advice', one viewpoint put to her (Rogers 2020). Another criticism was that she was slow to make decisions and then stubborn, rigid, inflexible and difficult to budge, and a micro-manager, once she had decided something, someone who tried to prevail by grinding people down and wearing them out. The exasperated leader of one EU country reportedly said she was 'devoid of the basic human skills you need to be a political leader.' At no point in the Brexit process did she successfully privately engage with any of the main European leaders. She was on occasion capable of taking bold or wilful decisions - but more often she took her time, played for time, and didn't. But as with other prime ministers, her personal strengths and weaknesses were coterminous, their political significance (for good or ill) depending on context and the wider play of political forces and events.

Margaret Thatcher had believed she could do anything a man could do - only better – but scorned feminism and allowed no political space for other women. In contrast, May had declared herself a feminist and had a record of hard work and achievement in championing women's involvement in political life, being one of the leading figures in the 'Women2Win' organisation that helped women as candidates and produced a step-change in terms of Conservative female parliamentary representation after 2010. Also unlike Thatcher, May's Cabinet included a significant proportion of women ministers – in July 2016, eight out of 27 Cabinet ministers, including the PM herself (and nine out of 29 in 2019). Theresa May was, of course, a female prime minister in a rather different social and political context to Mrs Thatcher, with for instance 32 per cent of all MPs being women after the 2017 election (compared to only 3 per cent when Thatcher first entered Number 10), and with other parties also led by women, along with many more other women leaders around the world. On the negative side, there is some evidence, however, that media coverage of May was more gendered than that of Thatcher, albeit in the context of a trend towards more personalised and celebritised media coverage of politics than in the 1980s (Williams 2021). May's Number 10 press office apparently had to field constant media questions about when she had cried (Gillard and Okonjo-Iweala 2020).

Described initially in the press as 'the new Iron Lady' or 'another Maggie', May was always irritated by comparisons to Thatcher and insisted, 'I do things my way.' However, Tory critics were soon privately mocking her as 'Old Ma May' (Swire 2020) or criticising her for not measuring up against their heroine: 'Theresa May: You're no Margaret Thatcher' complained Norman Tebbit in 2018, in one of his *Daily Telegraph* columns. Interviewed by former-Australian prime minister Julia Gillard for a book about women political leaders (Gillard and Okonjo-Iweala 2020), May herself seemed not to think she was treated differently in parliament because she was a woman, or that there was a strong gender dimension to her rise to power or her experience in Number 10. But the reference to her not having children and therefore being somehow less fit to hold office made by Andrea Leadsom in the Tory leadership race was a particularly overtly sexist judgement. And later, in 2019, when she apologised to aides for getting choked up on the steps of Number 10 while announcing her resignation, she said 'the papers will use those pictures differently because I'm a woman', suggesting that she had learned from sexist media reporting that showing emotion led to women being regarded differently to men and seen as weak (Barwell 2012: 384).

At one level the obsessive media interest in Mrs May's shoes and clothes could be seen as rather trivialising, but in another sense it was perhaps a way in which she was able to safely display something of the personal or 'human' side she was otherwise uncomfortable about revealing. Equally, there was clearly something about gender and leadership going on when May could be labelled 'an Ice Maiden' for being no more cold, reserved and bloodless in personal style and manner than many men in political life over the years. Similarly, when she was mocked for dancing on to the stage to Abba music to give one of her party conference speeches, there were arguments she was being unfairly criticised because of her gender – a male politician parading their love of pop music would, it was claimed, be described as 'authentic' and cool.

Gender analysts point to a sort of double bind or double standards affecting women at the top of politics. There are tensions between leadership roles and expectations and gender roles and expectations. Leadership is traditionally associated with masculinity but women who display 'masculinist' leadership qualities or styles are criticised as 'unfeminine'. At the same time successful leadership is depicted as unemotional, but women are supposedly more emotional and empathetic and therefore vulnerable to being seen as either weak leaders or (if deficient in those respects) somehow flawed as a woman (Harmer and Southern 2018: 238). However, this sort of analysis underplays the extent to which emotional intelligence and empathy are nowadays seen as vital ingredients of successful political leadership generally – something needed by men as well as by women leaders. But the problem was that May 'just cannot project empathy', as one minister complained: 'she is emotionally incompetent' (Duncan 2021: 188, 195). In that light, the criticisms of May as apparently lacking warmth and compassion (in contrast to Jeremy Corbyn) in her response to the Grenfell fire disaster in 2017 (with 'show us you care' headlines) arguably saw May being criticised for failings both as a leader and as woman.

Context

No recent peacetime 'takeover' prime minister has faced a more challenging in-tray or a more intimidating set of circumstances and issues to handle than Theresa May. Also, few have suffered such a huge and dramatic change of fortune. Whatever the strengths and limitations of her character, style and approach, the changing wider political context and the constraints on her freedom of manoeuvre explain much about May's premiership and what happened during it.

If Theresa May appeared to be a much weaker leader than Margaret Thatcher, for instance, that was not just because of differences in style and personality but also because they were prime ministers in very different contexts. Crucially, May was prime minister at a different point in 'political time' compared to Thatcher - they faced different opportunities, challenges and constraints. In terms of the 'political time' model, coming to power against the background of the crisis and breakdown of the post-war consensus 'regime' in the 1970s, Thatcher had the political space and opportunity to be a bold 'reconstructive' leader, opposing the old political and economic order, and constructing a new coalition around an alternative policy and governing framework. In contrast May, like Brown and Cameron before her, was an affiliate of a vulnerable and dysfunctional 'regime' facing many acute challenges, and as a 'disjunctive' leader was on the defensive and had severely limited options and room for manoeuvre (Byrne et al 2021).

Economically, May was more constrained than Thatcher had been, with the continuing effects of the prolonged period of austerity after the financial crisis, relatively low economic growth (averaging 1.5 per cent a year 2016-19, barely half of that achieved in the boom Thatcher years of 1981-89), and the economic uncertainties triggered by Brexit. Politically, at first she had a narrow parliamentary majority of just 16, a position rendered more precarious still by the prospect of continuing fractious Tory divisions and dissent over Brexit. On the other hand, the collapse of the Liberal Democrats in 2015, internal Labour Party conflicts and infighting over Jeremy Corbyn's leadership, and the implosion of UKIP all eased the pressure on her. To that was added a surge in the Conservatives' opinion poll ratings and the party's lead over Labour, and in particular a massive personal lead for her over Corbyn in polls on who would be the best person as prime minister (and with May being more popular than her own party in the polls).

Then in April 2017 she gambled everything by calling an early general election (having previously insisted she wouldn't) -

a fateful decision that almost bankrupted her in political terms. With a 20 per cent lead in the polls, she had hoped and seemed on course for a greatly increased majority, which she wanted to bolster her position in parliament and her own party, and with the EU, as she negotiated Brexit. But the electorate refused to co-operate. Although the Conservatives' vote increased in the June 2017 election by over 5 per cent to 42.4 per cent (May won a similar vote share to that achieved by Thatcher in the 1980s) they suffered a net loss of 13 seats, ending up with 317 MPs. Labour did better than expected, finishing up only 2.4 per cent behind the Tories in vote terms (albeit still fully 55 seats behind). May was left clinging on by her finger nails in Number 10, heading a minority government, thanks to a Conservative revival in Scotland (gaining 12 more seats to add to the one already held there) and after putting together a 'confidence and supply' deal with the Northern Ireland MPs of the Democratic Unionist Party (allowing, in theory, a working majority of 13 on key issues). Calling an unnecessary early election turned out to have been a catastrophic misjudgement. The claims and promises of 'strong and stable' leadership now looked hollow, the prime minister becoming a lame duck overnight, labelled a 'dead woman walking' and 'in office but not in power'.

The 2017 election result inevitably set a limit on May's premiership and on what she could achieve. It finished any hopes she might have had of redefining modern Conservatism, being a big social reforming prime minister leaving a domestic legacy, and repositioning her party. 'I am the one who got us into this mess and I'm going to get us out of it', she told her MPs: 'I will serve as long as you want me.' But the idea of her fighting another general election campaign horrified her MPs. The 'hard' Brexit rebels failed to oust her in a formal vote of no confidence in her leadership in December 2018 (200 MPs voted to support her while 117 opposed her), and before the vote she was compelled to promise to stand down as leader before the next general election. The result was a pyrrhic victory, revealing the scale and depth of Conservative Party divisions but doing little to strengthen the fundamentals of her position.

The diehard Brexiteers continued their opposition to the prime minister and their plotting and manoeuvring to overthrow her, with even her pledge to stand down and leave Number 10 before the next phase of the Brexit negotiations if they backed her failing to win over enough of them to get the March 2019 withdrawal deal she had negotiated with the EU through parliament. The Conservative Party became unleadable - fissiparous and bitterly faction-ridden, descending into ungovernability and seemingly intent on retoxifying itself. Tony Blair (Parker 2018) described her as 'a pretty reasonable person surrounded by a lot of unreasonable people', and John Major (2018) said that the situation she faced with the Brexit fundamentalists (the hard Brexiteers of the European Research Group (ERG), acting as a party within a party) was worse than the one he endured with the Eurosceptic 'bastards' in the 1990s, when party infighting and disloyalty, together with governing incompetence, led to a landslide defeat and 13 years in opposition.

The realities of the parliamentary arithmetic also imposed their own constraints, seen starkly in the series of huge Commons votes against her planned deal in 2019, the government's loss of control, the deadlock with no majority for any particular form of Brexit, and the need to delay the UK's date of departure from the EU. Economic realities always pointed to one sort of future arrangement, while internal Tory politics pushed in another direction. But by aligning herself with the 52 per cent who backed 'leave' and taking early on a pretty 'hard' Brexit stance – for understandable reasons in terms of short-term internal Conservative Party politics and her perceived need to underline her own Brexit credentials – May, who was always a strongly tribalistic and dyed-in-the-wool Conservative, arguably missed an opportunity to set herself up as a unifying national leader, bringing the country together by reaching out at the start, when she was at her strongest, to the 48 per cent that voted 'remain', constructing and selling a reasonable cross-party compromise and, as it were, trying to achieve as 'moderate' a Brexit as possible, based on a rational, open and honest discussion of the real trade-offs the country faced in terms of political control, trade and economic consequences, Ireland, freedom of movement, the position and interests of the EU 27, and so on.

When she did try to reach out to other parties in April 2019, it was too late and proved fatal for her. It was always difficult to see the talks with Jeremy Corbyn and Labour succeeding because there was by then too little trust or willingness to compromise, and Labour had little incentive to share responsibility or get the government and the Conservative Party out of a hole. There was also the problem of a probable huge Tory backlash and party split if she were to attempt to make concessions, work with Corbyn and force through an agreement with Opposition votes. In the end, with her authority shot to pieces, mounting party pressure on her and Cabinet support collapsing, she ran out of options and announced her decision to quit in late-May, leaving office in July 2019.

Conclusion

The central problem Theresa May always faced was the absence of a simple, easy or pain-free Brexit solution that could simultaneously be acceptable to the EU and command majority support in the Cabinet, in her party, in parliament and in the country. May's approach often seemed to involve dithering, prevarication, obfuscation, appeasement and double-talk – a lack of leadership. But in the circumstances she faced, it may have been a rational strategy to play for time, avoid being pinned down on specifics for as long as possible, to look for 'transitional' fudges and force last-minute choices. This could be defended as a sort of painful education in the reality that any deal was going to be sub-optimal - because there could be no deal that was demonstrably better than the deal Britain had as a full member of the EU - though the Brexit hardliners were uneducatable in those terms, and these methods did not alter the parliamentary arithmetic.

May liked to insist that her approach was to just 'get on with the job' when the situation the country faced after 2016 - in one of the critical moments of post-war British history - arguably demanded a leader with the ability to think more widely,

230

imaginatively and creatively about how to use the job. But beyond the limitations of character and vision, the political context and pressures May faced were tremendously constraining, and the challenges huge and nationally divisive.

When she left office commentators largely damned her achievements and legacy, and labelled her as one of the worst prime ministers in British history. It would be hard to dispute that May's premiership was a failure. But it is arguable that the problems of May's premiership may be too readily and easily written-off in terms of her personal weaknesses. As prime minister she certainly had serious shortcomings, and often made poor choices and made situations worse – but she was making decisions in conditions of unique constraint. Theresa May, to a degree not encountered by other recent prime ministers, confronted, with the challenges of Brexit and a party at war with itself, an almost impossible leadership situation in which division, disappointment, disillusionment and failure were probably inevitable (Byrne et al 2021).

References

Allen, N. (2017). 'Brexit, Butchery and Boris: Theresa May and Her First Cabinet.' *Parliamentary Affairs*. 70 (3): 1-12.

Allen, N. and Bara, J. (2019). 'Marching to the Left? Programmatic Competition and the 2017 Party Manifestos.' *Political Quarterly*, 90 (1): 124-133.

Barnett, A. (2017). *The Lure of Greatness: England's Brexit and America's Trump*. London: Unbound.

Barwell, G. (2021). *Chief of Staff: Notes From Downing Street*. London: Atlantic Books.

Beckwith, K. (2015). 'Before Prime Minister: Margaret Thatcher, Angela Merkel and   Gendered Party Leadership Contests.' *Politics and Gender*. 11 (4): 718-745

Byrne, C., Randall, N. and Theakston. K. (2021). 'Theresa May's disjunctive premiership: choice and constraint in political time.' *British Journal of Politics and International Relations*. 23 (4): 699-716.

Cooper, Y. (2016). 'Theresa May helped to divide Britain. She won't heal it.' *The Guardian*. 7 July.

Crines, A. and Theakston, K. (2015). '"Doing God" in Number 10: British Prime Ministers, Religion and Political Rhetoric.' *Politics and Religion*. 8 (1): 155-177.

Duncan, A. (2021). *In the Thick of It: The Private Diaries of a Minister*. London: William Collins.

Espiet-Kilty, R. (2018). 'Cameron and Big Society. May and Shared Society. Same Party: Two Visions?' *Observatoire de la Societe Britannique*. 21 (1): 213-233.

Gillard, J. and Okonjo-Iweala, N. (2020). *Women and Leadership*. London: Penguin.

Harmer, E. and Southern, R. (2017). 'More Stable than Strong: Women's Representation, Voters and Issues'. In J. Tonge, C. Leston-Bandeira and S. Wilks-Heeg (eds.), *Britain Votes 2017*. Oxford: Oxford University Press.

Hayton, R. (2017). 'A fundamentally Conservative document: what have we learnt from   May's manifesto?' *LSE British Politics and Policy*. https://blogs.lse.ac.uk/politicsandpolicy/what-have-we-learnt-from-the-conservative-manifesto-2017/

Jeffery, D., Heppell, T., Hayton, R. and Crines, A. (2018). 'The Conservative Party   Leadership Election of 2016: An Analysis of the Voting Motivations of Conservative Parliamentarians.' *Parliamentary Affairs*. 71 (2): 263-282.

Major, J. (2018). 'Sir John Major: May faces more "hardline" rebels over Europe than I ever did - and they could spark an autumn election.' *ITV News*. 17 July. https://www.itv.com/news/2018-07-17/sir-john-major-brexit-rebels-theresa-may

Parker, G. (2018). 'Theresa May, a political survivor cornered by Brexit.' *Financial Times*. 7 December.

Prince, R. (2017). *Theresa May: The Enigmatic Prime Minister*. London: Biteback Publishing.

Quinn, T. (2019). 'The Conservative Party's leadership election of 2016: choosing a   leader in government.' *British Politics*. 14 (1): 63-85.

Richards, S. (2019), The Prime Ministers. London: Atlantic Books.

Rogers. I. (2020). Interview: Brexit Witness Archive, UK in a Changing Europe. https://ukandeu.ac.uk/interview-pdf/?personid=43562

Ross, T. and McTague, T. (2017). *Betting the House: The Inside Story of the 2017 Election.* London: Biteback Publishing.

Runciman, D. (2019). *Where Power Stops: The Making and Unmaking of Presidents and Prime Ministers.* London: Profile Books.

Seldon, A. (with Newell, R.) (2020). *May at 10.* London: Biteback Publishing.

Shipman, T. (2017). *Fall Out: A Year of Political Mayhem.* London: William Collins.

Sparrow, A. (2018). 'Politics Live.' *The Guardian.* 23 July.

Spencer, N. (2017). 'Theresa May.' In N. Spencer (ed), *The Mighty and the Almighty: How Political Leaders Do God.* London: Biteback Publishing.

Swire, S. (2020). *Diary of an MP's Wife.* London: Little, Brown.

Sylvester, R. (2020). 'Theresa May'. In I. Dale, *The Prime Ministers.* London: Hodder & Stoughton.

Williams, B. (2021), 'A Tale of Two Women: a comparative gendered media analysis of UK Prime Ministers Margaret Thatcher and Theresa May', *Parliamentary Affairs,* 74(2): 398-420.

Worthy, B. (2017). 'Theresa May: leaking leadership capital?'. Birkbeck Perspectives. http://blogs.bbk.ac.uk/bbkcomments/2017/06/08/theresa-may-leaking-leadership-capital/

Chapter 16
Boris Johnson (2019- 22)

Boris Johnson undoubtedly finds it deeply wounding and frustrating that he sits well down the league table of British prime ministers arranged by length of tenure - his 3 years and 44 days putting him in 32nd place out of 55, though ahead of Callaghan, May, Brown, Eden and Douglas-Home among the postwar premiers. That his great 'frenemy' David Cameron managed 6 years and is in 23rd place in that table probably makes it worse. Johnson's premiership may have been a relatively short one, and ended in humiliating circumstances, but it was historically and politically consequential because of Brexit and the pandemic. And the personality at the centre of it all - Johnson himself - is a hugely compelling and controversial part of the story, something neatly captured in the sub-titles of various books about him: *A Tale of Blond Ambition* (Purnell 2012); *The Gambler* (Bower 2020); *Media Creation, Media Clown, Media Casualty?* (Mair 2022); *The Rise and Fall of a Troublemaker at Number 10* (Gimson 2022).

Party Leadership
Boris Johnson's route to Number 10 was an unorthodox snakes-and-ladders journey. Unorthodox because he built and developed his political character and reputation not through the usual channels of parliament, the opposition front bench and/or solid experience in government and as a Cabinet minister. He never seemed to fit in well or enjoy parliament, or make much impression as an MP in the House of Commons. He had two short stints as a junior opposition spokesman, being fired from one of them for lying to his party leader. Later, he was a mediocre and disloyal Foreign Secretary for two years (2016-18). Instead, he established himself on the national stage as a media celebrity and controversialist through his polemical journalism and television work, and in his two terms as Mayor of London (2008-16). For all his Eton and Oxford 'establishment'

credentials, this profile meant he was the maverick semi-outsider and never a 'safe', dull and dutiful 'insider'. Along the way to the top, there was an extraordinary series of gaffes, scandals and embarrassments – personal and political – that would have finished-off anyone else but which he shamelessly managed to shrug off or bounce back from. In the end, that is what brought him down and ended his premiership - but it is amazing how long he got away with it all. 'Boris Johnson: his rise, fall, rise, fall and rise' was the title of one BBC profile of him. (BBC 2016). He was helped by the way that media cheerleaders largely indulged him as a 'character' rather than really turning the flame-thrower on him, laughing along with his stunts and antics instead of seriously scrutinising his character, actions and record.

Johnson was obviously ferociously ambitious, convinced of his own greatness and his destiny, self-serving and opportunistic. But he lacked real backing from allies, followers, friends or a faction in the Conservative Party. The Cameroons mistrusted him and Theresa May loathed him. Fellow Brexiteers had doubts about Johnson's commitment to their cause, and his support on the backbenches was relatively thin in 2016 when Michael Gove declared him unfit to lead and his leadership bid collapsed. What made the difference three years later was the failure of the May premiership and the sense that the Conservative Party was facing an existential crisis and had run out of options. With the Brexit process log-jammed in parliament, and Nigel Farage's Brexit Party steaming ahead to top the vote in the 2019 European elections, in which the Tories came fifth and won just 9 per cent of the vote (their worst result in any election in 200 years), traumatised Conservative MPs swallowed their doubts and swung to Johnson because they feared for their seats in a meltdown and thought that, in the situation they faced, he would be a star campaigner and less of a risk than another 'safe pair of hands' figure (leadership rival Jeremy Hunt being described as 'Theresa May in trousers') (Elliott 2019).

Johnson was elected as leader not on the basis of a record as a successful or competent administrator (most Conservative

235

MPs, including many who voted for him, would have said that his ministerial record was the least distinguished of the serious contenders), but as the person who could marginalise Farage and reunite the Leave coalition. Strongly leave-supporting MPs, who had opposed May's deal and made her life hell, backed Johnson, while Hunt ultimately won the support of only a quarter of Tory MPs. And Johnson appealed to the mass membership as a charismatic true believer (his resignation from May's Cabinet crucial in that respect) who would deliver Brexit.

Although he won a decisive victory in the party leadership election (winning 92,000 votes, 66 per cent of the total), Johnson was clearly a divisive figure, significantly less popular with the wider public (a net favourablity score of -27) than Theresa May was when she became prime minister in 2016 (a net score of +12 then, though she had slumped to -37 by the time she left office). Often described as a 'Heineken' politician, able to reach parts of the electorate other Conservatives cannot, Brexit made him (to his own surprise and discomfort) into more of a 'Marmite' character, though with the advantage that initially his main opponents (Farage and Corbyn) were even more polarising and overall less personally popular. It is sometimes overlooked that Johnson's popularity ratings at the time of his general election victory were actually lower than May's had been in 2017 - the crucial difference was that Corbyn's poll ratings were abysmal by 2019 (Ford et al 2021).

Not someone who had spent years cultivating deep reserves of loyalty among Tory MPs, Johnson found that the forces that had carried him to power constrained and undermined him. Backbench pressure, rebellion and insurrection had forced Cameron to hold the referendum that drove him from office and subsequently had toppled May. It was always going to be difficult for a politician who had done his own thing and been congenitally disloyal to different leaders to then impose party discipline himself. Rather than a solid parliamentary faction or tribe behind Johnson, support was mainly transactional and anchored in his perceived ability as an election winner. But there seemed little lasting gratitude for the delivery of an 80-seat majority with one MP commenting that backbench support was 'a mile wide and an inch deep' (Colville 2020). Beyond Johnson's own carelessness and lack of feel for party management, the contempt for backbenchers displayed by Dominic Cummings, Johnson's chief adviser for his first 18 months in office, hugely aggravated matters. MPs, one complained, felt 'completely neglected, ignored, under valued and disconnected from what is going on' (Hardman 2020). Subsequently, the Number 10 machine tried to be less high-handed and to reach out more to MPs and the party, but all the signs were that Conservative backbenchers could not be counted on to fall automatically or easily into line - in fact the rebellion rate after the 2019 general election was (with 44 per cent rate of Tory MPs rebelling at least once in parliamentary votes) more than double that under Cameron in his final 2015-16 term.

The ruthlessness in expelling from the party 21 MPs (including senior and well-known figures) who had in September 2019 voted against crashing out of Europe without a deal could not provide a sustainable model for running things, fostering loyalty or keeping the peace in the party – party management-by-purge simply not being a viable long-term option in a parliamentary system. Fractious, restless and disenchanted MPs made their unhappiness known with revolts over housing and planning reforms, policy towards China, the handling of the pandemic and lockdown restrictions, trade and other issues. Within a year of the bumper 2019 victory, the position almost seemed to call to mind the Major years of instability and party feuding. Adding to the trouble, Conservative factionalism became more organised with groups like the Northern Research Group and the Covid Recovery Group copying the methods and tactics of the revolt-addicted European Research Group fundamentalists, and the 'Red-Wallers' of the 2019 intake increasingly making their distinctive voice and interests known. Backbench rebellion tends to be habit-forming and contagious, and corrosive of prime-ministerial authority. Though there had been signs of an upswing in mood on the backbenches as part of a wider 'vaccine bounce' in 2021, that did not last. Buyer's remorse and concerns about Johnson's shortcomings were never far below the surface, with the prime minister seeming almost on probation with his party rather than someone empowered by his big majority. In the end, in 2022, the elastic snapped as MPs finally lost patience with Number 10's handling of 'sleaze' and wider character issues involving the PM, and were spooked by the government's collapsing poll ratings and their electoral prospects if things continued, but party management failings and problems had been there from the start as a serious constraint on Johnson.

Ideology and Aims

Boris Johnson, it has been said, is 'a one–off. There are not many ideological Johnsonites' (Kettle 2020). But it is not clear that Johnson himself is an ideological anything. Even measured against the many prime ministers who have been largely pragmatists of one sort or another rather than vision-driven leaders, he seemed lacking in serious interest in political principles or policy, and ideologically negligible. It was almost as if there was an intellectual hole at the centre of Johnson's politics. Supporters and apologists, such as biographer Andrew Gimson (2016: 343-44), described his stance as 'adventurous pragmatism', saying he boldly 'sketches daring enterprises, and will fill in the details later', being able to react 'at lightening speed to unexpected events . . . expressing the public mood before the public even knows what its mood is.' In this sense, Johnson could be seen as a 'post-ideological politician' (Worthy et al 2019: 32) or a 'shape-shifting' figure – adaptable, open, travelling light and lacking explicit or fixed doctrine (Sylvester 2020). Michael Heseltine called Johnson 'the most flexible politician in modern times' (Parker and Bounds 2020).

But to his critics, it is and has always been all been about himself: Johnson as a pure opportunist, driven by personal ambition and calculations of self-advancement - of what will make and keep him popular, and help him win and keep power - with his views and opinions adjusting to suit. In this vein, Heseltine described Johnson as the sort of politician 'who waits to see the way the crowd is running and then dashes in front and says, "Follow me"' (Guardian 2019). Johnson himself once joked he had 'no convictions, apart from one a long time ago for speeding' (Finklestein 2019). As Groucho Marx said, 'these are my principles, and if you don't like them, I have others.' This also calls to mind Lloyd George – a prime minister of whom it was said, 'he did not seem to care which way he travelled providing he was in the driver's seat' (Gimson 2016: 343). This meant that where he headed or ended up depended greatly on the balance of political pressures he faced, the advice and agendas of competing advisers, and the impact of external events.

Exhibit number one for the prosecution here tends to be the way Johnson, after allegedly 'veering all over the place like a supermarket trolley' on the subject (Gimson 2016: xi), came out for Brexit in the 2016 referendum. Although he had long been stoking the flames and cultivating Euroscepticism, a couple of year earlier he had privately told the journalist Anne Applebaum (2020: 70) that 'nobody serious wants to leave the EU'. Rather than being a genuine hardline 'outer', it is claimed he believed that Brexit would lose but that campaigning for it would position him to win the support of the rabidly Eurosceptic Tory grassroots in a future leadership contest. Given what was at stake, it is not surprising that what Johnson liked to describe as having it both ways, or having his cake and eating it, was to his critics insouciance and bad faith carried to the point of duplicity and irresponsibility.

It is hard to pin down what sort of conservative Johnson is – and some question whether he is really a conservative at all. When Thatcher was overthrown in 1990, Johnson was apparently found with tears in his eyes saying it was as if 'someone had shot Nanny' (Gimson 2016: 102). He later talked about her 'colossal' achievements (Johnson 2013) and defended inequality, elitism and capitalism and stuck up for the bankers, but also remarked that 'there is such a thing as society' – a way of signalling some distance from Thatcherism, as Cameron also did. And he described himself as a 'Brexity Hezza' (Sylvester 2020), conjuring up Thatcher's *bête noire* and nemesis, to express support for state activism and intervention, increased spending and the end of austerity, in a way that would put him to the left of Cameron and George Osborne. At one point he even invoked Franklin D. Roosevelt and his 'New Deal' – not usually a Tory hero – something consistent with his clear appetite for *grands projets* and grandiose, eye-catching initiatives.

Johnson's conservatism has been called 'elastic and ambiguous' (Worthy et al 2019: 32). This is perhaps another way of saying that he has not been a conviction politician of strong and fixed views, but has improvised and reinvented himself as circumstances and political situations and needs have changed. He does fit into a deeper pattern here because such adaptability and ability to renew itself in office has long been the Conservative Party's 'secret weapon', and key to its extensive history of electoral success. As mayor of London he paraded his libertarian inclinations and presented himself as a liberal, compassionate, cosmopolitan Conservative – with views on immigration, lower taxes, and a higher minimum wage to match. One biographer (Gimson 2016: 345) argued that Johnson represented a sort of 'Merry England conservatism' – vulgar, brash, optimistic, cheerfully magnanimous. Another commentator talked about him offering 'a Tory social democracy rooted in national pride and delivered with a spoonful of humour and entertainment' (Sullivan 2019).

Johnson's 2019 general election manifesto was only half the length of Labour's, and relatively vague and sketchy on detail. Talking about the 'forgotten people' and the 'left-behind towns', and pledging to spread opportunity and to 'level up' Britain (Richards 2020: 400), he sometimes claimed to be a 'One Nation' Conservative, though the moderate pro-European MPs from that tradition who he purged might dispute that, and that label may anyway be so malleable as to be pretty meaningless except as a sort of unifying bromide.

Contradictory objectives abounded: in favour of large-scale infrastructure investment and higher public spending but also saying he favoured low taxation (though he pushed through tax increases to pay for NHS and social care reforms); standing for free trade yet pushing a Brexit policy that increased trade barriers with the UK's largest overseas market (and will mean slower economic growth also making 'levelling up' harder); a liberal stance on immigration as mayor of London that morphed into the anti-immigration dog-whistling populism of the Brexit campaigner. Perhaps 'Johnsonism', if it existed at all, was a combination of English nationalism, an interventionist and somewhat left-leaning economic stance, and a right-leaning stance on issues of culture, identity and social values. But crucially, Johnson was open to the charge that his approach avoided 'candid acknowledgement of policy trade-offs and hard choices' (Bush 2020) and denied the existence of difficulties, meaning that he was always more comfortable campaigning than governing.

Political Style and Skills

Johnson has long been praised as an outstanding communicator with a rare ability to reach the more politically uninterested or averse parts of the public, and also to fire-up the Conservative rank-and-file as the darling of the Tory party conference. His showmanship and theatricality, media skills, colourful language and unique 'Borisisms', and his wit and humour have all been crucial parts of the act in this respect. Johnson, it has been said, 'speaks like a bloke telling jokes in a pub' and that may have been part of his appeal and success as a vote-seeking politician. But being a clever Oxford Union debater, 'fake news' journalistic provocateur, and jokey *Have I Got News For You* panellist did not translate across into effective leadership performance as a political teacher or public educator and persuader, as prime ministers need to be. Though Johnson in his biography of Churchill praised the great war-leader for being 'straight' with the British people and 'frank about the challenge[s] facing the country' (Johnson 2014: 96), he did not compare well when considering his struggles to set a tone and find a mode of address commensurate with the gravity of the pandemic crisis, for instance, or as a framer of serious and honest arguments about, and a persuasive vision for, the future and the renewal of the country, as opposed to superficial boosterism and what was dubbed an 'empty rhetoric of exhortation' (Shrimsley 2021).

As an MP, minister and then prime minister, Johnson was often unimpressive in the parliamentary arena, his style and techniques not working so well in that forum. His trademark gags, flannel, bluster and one-liners did not go down well as a response to serious or forensic questioning by MPs and political opponents. It seemed that he wanted just to make a broad case or vague promises, or put up a smokescreen, and appeared uncomfortable and failed to engage with direct criticism and detailed scrutiny (Dommett 2015). It is also striking how, in his leadership campaign and in the 2019 general election, his minders kept him away from the media as much as possible, in an effort to control the message and avoid challenge and hard questioning.

Johnson never showed much interest in or understanding of the machinery of government, policy-making processes and executive arrangements. His approach was alway to delegate the detailed work on policy and making things happen to his team and various lieutenants. There were suggestions that, consciously or unconsciously, Johnson allowed or actually stirred up conflict and tension in his team to air different options and help him make up his mind (Forsyth 2021). But both as London mayor and as prime minister, his operation often seemed chaotic and dysfunctional. Some people from his time as mayor followed him into Downing Street, including his adviser Eddie Lister (who left in 2021) and Munira Mirza, who became head of the policy unit (before resigning in disgust with the PM's conduct in 2022). He imported a hardline Brexiteer as his EU negotiator - David Frost, who was given a peerage and subsequently and controversially was also lined up as a political appointee as National Security Adviser, but ended up instead as a Cabinet minister handling post-Brexit policy and relations with the EU until, unhappy with the government's general policy direction, he resigned in late 2021. But for Johnson's first year and a half, through 2019-20, the dominant figure was Dominic Cummings, a strange and toxic mix of Rasputin, Dr. Strangelove and Malcolm Tucker, and a man who thought that there should be more 'weirdos and misfits with odd skills' working as advisers in Number 10 (Syal 2020).

Cummings imposed a hugely centralized, top-down and controlling system, with a culture of fear and bullying, and insisted that all ministerial special advisers reported to him. Holding the civil service, parliament, judges, the media, the

Conservative Party and most ministers in contempt, Cummings was a maverick, and an aggressive, confrontational and uncompromising disruptor, rule-breaker and iconoclast, pursuing a strategy of 'creative destruction'. He declared war on Whitehall and wanted to sideline the civil service, with a number of top mandarins forced out. Johnson seemed in thrall to him, expending huge political capital to keep him when Cummings flagrantly broke the government's pandemic lockdown regulations. Perhaps he was dependent on his powerful aide for ideas and for policy drive and definition that he could not provide himself, but with Cummings also usefully playing the role of prime-ministerial hatchet man or 'bad cop', and to some extent possibly also serving as a human flak jacket for his political master, absorbing some of the fury and fire directed at the government.

In the end, advisers are always dispensable, and inevitably, it would only be a matter of time before the pros, from Johnson's point of view, of having such a figure as his key adviser and right-hand-man, were outweighed by the associated political costs of the fear, loathing and turmoil he generated. In November 2020, Cummings was forced out in a sort of internal palace coup, taking with him his ally Lee Cain, the PM's communication chief. More conventional, calm and even technocratic figures were then brought in – realists and reformists, not revolutionaries with agendas of their own - including Simon Case, a classic Whitehall operator, as Cabinet Secretary and Dan Rosenfield, with a Treasury, banking and corporate background, appointed as chief of staff to try (with only limited success) to introduce more order and process in the Number 10 set-up. In another move back to a more orthodox set up, the top civil servant at the Ministry of Defence was appointed National Security Adviser. And reviving a sensible Blair-era initiative that improved Whitehall performance, rather than further Cumming-style insurgency and conflict, a Number 10 delivery unit was created in 2021 to push through policy and progress chase on implementation.

In Johnson's shambolic and scandal-ridden final period in office in 2022 there was another clear-out and yet a third Number 10 set up, with Steve Barclay, an MP and minister, appointed as chief of staff, a new director of communications (Guto Harri), along with other senior staff changes, as the PM struggled to survive, prop up relations with his MPs, and throw 'red meat' to his party. It was no way to make good policy, or run a successful government or Downing Street operation. Throughout the Johnson years, in fact, there were endless stories about a febrile atmosphere in the Number 10 'court', as competing groups and factions jostled for position and vied for the PM's attention, with Carrie Symonds, Johnson's fiancée and then wife, and herself a political communications professional, said to be an influential figure in her own right and portrayed in the more lurid accounts as a sort of Lady Macbeth of Downing Street (Ashcroft 2022).

The *Economist* (2020) described Johnson not so much as *primus inter pares* (the traditional description of a prime minister in relation to their Cabinet colleagues) but as primus inter poodles. He certainly proved himself a good butcher, with a ruthless reshuffle on becoming prime minister in July 2019 (when over half of May's Cabinet were sacked - 11 ministers dismissed while 6 others resigned – the most extensive Cabinet purge by a new mid-term successor PM in postwar history), followed by other reshuffles in February 2020 and September 2021, with a final one in July 2022 needed to put together what was effectively a caretaker government before leaving office in September 2022. Leadership rival Jeremy Hunt refused a ministerial demotion in 2019 and left the government; Dominic Raab became Foreign Secretary before being later replaced by Liz Truss and demoted to Justice Secretary; Priti Patel was made Home Secretary; Michael Gove, whose clout and ability to deliver Johnson recognized while not fundamentally trusting him, had an influential behind-the-scenes role as Cabinet Office minister before being made Minister for Levelling-up. (Johnson later sacked Gove in a final act of Godfather-like vengeance as his government fell apart in 2022). Overall, Johnson appointed a pretty rightwing, Brexiteer Cabinet – one that could be guaranteed to be loyally behind the prime minister on the big decisions, albeit with some lightweight figures of limited competence. One insider called it 'a Potemkin Cabinet' (Parker

2020); 'the most underpowered cabinet in living memory' was another description (Jenkins 2019) - one that mostly rubber-stamped rather than took decisions, and was controlled from Number 10.

Arguably the sign of a weak and insecure leader, Johnson was said to be unwilling or unable to tolerate challenge, competition, disagreement or criticism from his ministerial team. His first chancellor of the exchequer, Sajid Javid, quit in February 2020 after clashes with Johnson and Cummings over public spending plans and economic strategy, and after refusing to have his special advisers merged into and controlled by Number 10. However, his successor, Rishi Sunak, proved he was far from being a sort of prime-ministerial glove puppet, seeming to rise more successfully to the level of events in the face of the pandemic and its economic shocks than Johnson was able to, and quickly being talked of as a possible successor. But with Sunak more of a Thatcherite than a 'Johnsonite' in terms of his views on the role of the state, tax and spending, there were tensions and strains in the Number 10/Number 11 relationship, and arguments over policy and the direction of the government. In the end, of course, Sunak's resignation (along with Javid's from Health) helped start the avalanche of government and ministerial resignations that finally toppled Johnson.

It is perhaps difficult to assess Johnson's character and style as a political figure and prime minister by the ordinary standards (Bower 2020). One biographer, Sonia Purnell (2012), called him 'the most unconventional, yet compelling politician of the post-Blair era.' Yet again Lloyd George, another extraordinary political personality and leader, comes to mind - of whom it was said by J.M. Keynes (1933) 'if Mr Lloyd George had no good qualities, no charms, no fascinations, he would not be dangerous.' Johnson's 'big' personality, charm, wit, intelligence, charisma, optimism, positivity, and ability to connect to and entertain the public are clearly on one side of the ledger here. He was a household name and a national celebrity figure long before he became prime minister. But at the same time the 'Boris' we think we know is an act, a brand, a constructed persona, underneath which there is a certainly harder-edged but perhaps essentially unknowable personality. On one side is the buffoonish performance, making people feel good, persuading people to like him. But there was also the 'fox disguised as a teddy bear', as one acquaintance put it (Bower 2020: 69): the cunning and calculating operator who is arrogant, unprincipled and amoral, the seeming 'authenticity' concealing a political guile, ruthlessness, huge selfishness, and narcissism.

Rory Stewart (2020), a former Conservative minister and leadership contender, called Johnson 'the most accomplished liar in public life' – someone who is dishonest, plays fast and loose with the truth, telling people what they want to hear, perhaps believing it himself at the time he says it. A former French ambassador described him as an unrepentant and inveterate liar, who used lies 'to play a game . . . [and] as an instrument of power' (Bermann 2022: 120). Many people who have worked for him or close to him (including his former close aide Dominic Cummings, who publicly turned on Johnson after leaving Number 10) believe Johnson to be a cynical and unreliable charlatan, chancer and risk-taker, someone who trusts nobody and is not a team player, who would bend, stretch or break the normal rules, who would duck responsibility, and would always betray you or let you down. Other critics (see Bower 2020) point out that underneath the surface public bonhomie, there is an insecure loner and someone who is actually deeply unpleasant and a bully, with a sharp temper and a strong vindictive streak. Also on the negative side of the balance sheet are the criticisms of his laziness, inattention to details, short-termism and a fundamental unseriousness or carelessness. Civil service aides were reportedly ordered to send him shorter memos – not more than two pages long - and to reduce the number of documents in his red box to make sure he read them. Avoiding the dangers of 'micromanagement' might be one thing, but showing little interest in the governance or ethical norms of institutions or in the complexities of long-term projects, agreeing with contradictory advice from different sources or at different times, constantly changing his mind and finding it hard to make and stick to decisions, and apparently being obsessed by the media, loving the spotlight and preferring the 'fun' stuff but not liking to hear bad news or about problems and difficulties were all more problematic things in the make-up of the nation's chief executive.

Of course while politicians need to be remarkable and lucky to get to Number 10, they do not necessarily have to be likeable or admirable in a conventional sense to lead and govern successfully as prime minister. While many critics argued that Johnson was unsuited to and lacked the skills for the office of prime minister (and some went further and said - surely correctly - that he was morally unfit for it), the Conservative commentator and Thatcher biographer Charles Moore (2020) perhaps identified the real puzzle when he said that Johnson's 'ambiguities' were 'his weapons', and that he was simultaneously 'alarmingly unsuited to high command' *and* had 'unique leadership capacities'. This mix inevitably made the conduct and performance of Johnson's premiership even more of a high-wire act than is usually the case, and underlines how much its ups and downs, successes and failures, could be traced back to, and could not be explained without reference to, the character, attitudes and attributes of the singular figure at its head.

Context

The first four or five months of the Johnson-Cummings regime were an exercise in aggressive confrontation, provocation, manipulation and manoeuvre to try to break out of the stalemate situation created by the 2017 election and the years of Brexit trench warfare under May. In some respects this was a high-risk strategy as the government had no majority, expelled 21 of its own MPs, tried to close down parliament but was thwarted by the Supreme Court, had a possible no-deal exit from the EU vetoed by MPs, and there was speculation that Johnson could end up becoming one of the shortest-serving prime ministers. But he secured an EU withdrawal agreement essentially by accepting what May had rejected two years earlier and what he had said he would not do, in the process betraying the DUP who were opposed to it - namely, the creation of an economic border in the Irish Sea in order to facilitate greater divergence between Great Britain and the EU. And then the opposition parties, rather than continuing to exploit the blocking potential of the hung parliament, weakly and ineptly gave him what he wanted in the shape of an early, pre-Brexit, general election.

The result was a triumph for Johnson (Ford et al 2021). The Conservatives won 43.6 per cent of the UK vote and an 80 seat parliamentary majority, with 48 net gains. There was only a modest 1.2 per cent Tory vote gain compared to 2017, but Labour's share fell by almost 8 per cent of the vote, to 32.2 per cent, and it lost 60 seats. It was the Conservatives' best result since Thatcher's 1987 victory, and Labour's worst result since 1935. Six months earlier, the Conservatives had been 23 per cent behind Farage's Brexit Party at the European elections; now Johnson had reunited the Leave vote behind his 'Get Brexit Done' mantra and the Brexit Party threat had been eliminated, the Faragists falling to just 2 per cent of the vote. While there were a variety of short-term factors helping Johnson and the Conservatives (particularly the voter-repellent leadership of Jeremy Corbyn, Labour's tensions over Europe, and the poor Liberal-Democrat campaign), the election outcome also reflected crucial longer-term shifts in the tectonic plates of British politics, the social and demographic changes and realignments that have eroded old loyalties and shaped new divides in the electorate, redrawn the political map, and which lay behind the 2016 referendum result. Johnson perhaps grasped the nature of these changes better than his political opponents, skilfully made the right moves, and reaped the rewards.

Delivering for Johnson's cross-class voter coalition of more affluent 'True Blue' Tories from Southern shires and affluent suburbs, and socially conservative blue-collar workers – groups united not by economic experience or interests but by values and identity issues, and by support for Brexit – was always going to raise obviously difficult issues about economic management, taxation, borrowing and public spending after a decade of austerity and in the context of the adverse economic effects playing out from the 'hard' and 'thin' Brexit trade deal, prioritising a mythical 'sovereignty', reached at the end of 2020. However, Johnson never really resolved the strategic tensions and policy contradictions built in to his political coalition, with deep divisions on the economy in his party and many

Conservatives MPs still supporting further neo-liberalism and market deregulation, though a small-state, libertarian, hyper-Thatcherite approach is not what lower-income, working-class voters in the former 'Red Wall' seats of the Midlands and the North of England appear to want. Johnson himself may have had little economic understanding, but he certainly understood the political need to make 'levelling up' more than a slogan to consolidate his new electoral support.

In the immediate aftermath of the general election Johnson seemed master of the political scene, but then the coronavirus pandemic struck and completely changed the context of his political leadership. The government's handling of the crisis frequently seemed chaotic, incompetent and inconsistent. Major policy and administrative failings on the part of the state machine became apparent, while Johnson himself failed multiple tests as a steady and timely decision-maker, communicator and crisis leader, which hugely damaged his political standing and personal ratings, though the successful vaccine rollout gave him a temporary poll bounce. The massive costs and economic fallout from the pandemic also made the issues and problems the government faced about policy, delivery and strategy in the run-up to the next election all the more challenging. And coinciding with this, and making things even harder for Johnson and the Tories, Labour's Keir Starmer quickly established himself as a much better opposition leader, and more competent, credible and popular, than his far-left predecessor.

There had been boasts after the election landslide that Johnson would govern for a decade. In fact he was on the ropes just two years after that victory, and pushed out of office altogether by his party after clocking up only three years in the job. Moreover, he was undone not because of arguments over policy and strategy - though by the final stages there was little sense of coherence there, and a feeling that Johnson had wasted his chance to reshape the country after Brexit and his big election win - but by his own behaviour, attitudes and impropriety: by debasing the office of prime minister through the contempt for the rules, precedent, order and stability that critics had warned in advance he would display. This was very visibly demonstrated through the whole succession of scandals involving sleazy MPs and lockdown partying in Number 10 (that saw Johnson become the first PM in history to be found guilty of breaking the law in office), and the associated lies, incompetence, and botched or misfiring 'fight-backs' and responses - all laying bare the arrogance, hypocrisy, lack of integrity and poor judgement of Johnson and his inner circle and supporters. Johnson was revealed to be a rogue figure, more disdainful of (and a danger to) the conventions and norms of the constitution than any other prime minister, and failing to meet the basic personal ethical standards expected of someone holding his office (Blick and Hennessy 2022). Damaging by-election defeats, Johnson's collapsing personal ratings (worse than Theresa May's - and, crucially, behind Starmer's), and the Labour Party's opinion poll lead all convinced enough MPs that the magic had long worn-off and that he was a liability not an electoral asset for the party. Though the war in Ukraine looked like it might give him some respite, the end actually came quickly, with party vote of confidence in June 2022 in which 41 per cent of his MPs voted against him (a 211 to 148 result), leaving him fatally wounded, and then his government almost literally falling apart as over 60 members quit in a 36-hour period in early July, forcing him to announce his resignation (Payne 2022).

Conclusion

Boris Johnson has been a politician with an inimitable style but that has not stopped commentators looking for parallels and comparators as they seek to understand him. Johnson's own favourite comparison with Churchill hardly works, when one considers the Great Man's seriousness, realism, honesty and integrity. As a maverick leader, some were struck by the case of Disraeli, another unscrupulous adventurer and mountebank, who also demonstrated great abilities at showmanship, flexibility, exploiting opportunities and infuriating self-righteous opponents (Economist 2021). Others talked about a Trump-style populism, partly based on their professions of mutual admiration, with both leaders stoking the flames of a mendacious 'people versus the elite' politics, hostile to and resentful of checks and criticism, and flouting the established norms and constitutional rules. But there were some important policy differences between the two, and they faced different constitutional and institutional structures and cultures, with party constraints on Johnson much stronger than in the US – and ultimately the arbiter of his tenure and fate as leader.

Much of Johnson's background and path to power was a triumph of style over substance, but he could never be underestimated as a tough and astute politician who repeatedly seemed to be a vote-winner, with two terms as London mayor, the 2016 referendum, and the 2019 landslide under his belt. The European issue had tormented and defeated previous Tory leaders and divided the party – he resolved it, albeit by effectively making the Conservative Party into the English Nationalist Brexit Party, though many other serious questions about the party's and the country's politics, strategy and identity remained unresolved. His successor, Liz Truss, clearly aimed to steer a different and more ideologically-driven course to him but her premiership imploded in an extraordinary fashion and she resigned after just seven weeks as prime minister, to be succeeded in turn by Rishi Sunak (whom Johnsonites despised, believing he had brought about their hero's downfall). The collapse of his attempt to run again for the leadership in October 2022 highlighted the ludicrous extent to which Johnson and his backers were in denial about the reasons for his failure and resignation in disgrace as prime minister in the first place. Johnson claimed to have enough nominations to make it on to the ballot paper but withdrew, as it was obvious he could not unite the party and would probably provoke further turmoil and instability.

Johnson has been described as 'a leader of rare gifts' (Fawcett 2020: 436) and his style labelled 'idiosyncratic and unconventional' (Flinders 2020: 226), but the erratic trajectory of his premiership suggests that the skills, strategies and approach required to become prime minister, to campaign and to win elections are not the same as those needed to be prime minister, to provide sustained and disciplined political leadership, and to govern effectively. 'Boris Johnson was a disaster waiting to happen', as Tim Bale (2022) put it: 'the longstanding doubts about his integrity proved well-founded, and he was only interested in being prime minister, not in what prime ministers are actually there to do.' The style and strengths that took Johnson to the top became weaknesses that drove him from power. Having no settled aims or principles, a seat-of-the-pants approach, and displaying an opportunistic ruthlessness over methods and an egoistical disregard for convention and constraints, may have paid off in terms of political gamesmanship and campaigning, but the lesson of the Johnson years was that approach and style was no basis for longer-term policy success, effective and respected leadership, and competent government.

References

Applebaum, A. (2020). *Twilight of Democracy*. London: Allen Lane.

Ashcroft, M. (2022). *First Lady: Intrigue at the Court of Carrie and Boris Johnson*. London: Biteback.

Bale, T. (2022). 'The Damned Disunited? Will the Conservative Party fall apart under Rishi Sunak?' [https:// ukandeu.ac.uk/the-damned-disunited-will-the-conservative-party-fall-apart-under-rishi-sunak/]

BBC (2016). 'Boris Johnson: His rise, fall, rise, fall and rise.' https://www.bbc.co.uk/news/uk-politics-36789123

Bermann, S. (2022). *Au Revoir Britannia*. (English translation). Edinburgh: Luath Press.

Blick, A. and Hennessy, P. (2022). *The Bonfire of the Decencies: Repairing and Restoring the British Constitution*. London: Haus Publishing.

Bower, T. (2020). *Boris Johnson: The Gambler*. London: WH Allen.

Bush, S. (2020). 'Boris Johnson yearns for the time when, as London mayor, he was popular. But those days are gone.' *New Statesman*, 20-26 November.

Colville, R. (2020). 'This government was born of rebellion, so it will have to   get used to   scrappy backbenchers.' *Sunday Times*, 11 October.

Dommett, K. (2015). 'The oratory of Boris Johnson', in R. Hayton and A. Crines (eds). *Conservative Orators from Baldwin to Cameron.* Manchester: Manchester University Press.

Economist (2020). 'Bagehot: The imperial prime minister.' *The Economist*, 22 February.

Economist (2021). 'Bagehot: Dizzy rascal.' *The Economist*, 27 March.

Elliott, F. (2019). 'Jeremy Hunt profile: don't be fooled by the Theresa-in-trousers tag', *The Times*, 20 June.

Fawcett, E. (2020). *Conservatism.* Princeton NJ: Princeton University Press.

Finklestein, D. (2019). 'Cavalier Johnson must curb his wild side.' *The Times,* 18 June.

Flinders, M. (2020). 'Not a Brexit Election? Pessimism, Promises and Populism "UK-Style"', in J. Tonge et al (eds). *Britain Votes: The 2019 General Election.* Oxford: Oxford University Press.

Ford, R., Bale,T., Jennings, W., and Surridge, P. (2021). *The British General Election of   2019.* London: Palgrave Macmillan.

Forsyth, J. (2021). 'Johnson is the master of chaos and confusion.' *The Times*, 28 May.

Gimson: A. (2016). *Boris: The Making of the Prime Minister.* London: Simon & Schuster.

Gimson, A. (2022). *Boris Johnson: The Rise and Fall of a Troublemaker at Number 10.* London: Simon & Schuster.

Guardian (2019). 'A question of character? Boris Johnson by those who know him.' *The Guardian,* 22 June.

Hardman, I. (2020). 'May's ghost is hovering above No.10. Only a full reboot will exorcise it.' *Sunday Times*, 15 November.

Jenkins, S. (2019). 'There is hope: Boris Johnson's big majority could   unleash the social liberal within.' *The Guardian*, 13 December.

Johnson, B. (2013), 'The 2013 Margaret Thatcher lecture.' Centre for Policy Studies. [https://cps.org.uk/events/post/

2013/the-2013-margaret-thatcher-lecture-boris-johnson/]

Johnson, B. (2014). *The Churchill Factor*. London: Hodder & Stoughton.

Kettle, M. (2020). 'Boris Johnson is floundering, and his majority may not save him.' *The Guardian*. 3 September.

Keynes, J.M. (1933). *Essays in Biography*. London: Macmillan.

Mair, J. (ed) (2022). *Boris Johnson: Media Creation, Media Clown, Media Casualty?* Oxford: Mair Golden Moments.

Moore, C. (2020). 'With Dominic Cummings gone, Boris himself is dangerously exposed.' *Daily Telegraph*, 13 November.

Parker, G. (2020). 'Boris Johnson creates new teams to oversee coronavirus recovery'. *Financial Times*, 3 June.

Parker, G. and Bounds, A. (2020). 'Brexit: will Boris Johnson reverse Thatcherism?' *Financial Times*. 30 January.

Payne, S. (2022). *The Fall of Boris Johnson: The Full Story*. London: Macmillan.

Purnell, S. (2012). *Just Boris: A Tale of Blond Ambition*. London: Aurum Press Ltd.

Richards, S. (2020). *The Prime Ministers: Reflections on Leadership from Wilson to Johnson*. London: Atlantic Books.

Shrimsley, R. (2021). 'Making Britain great again'. *Financial Times*. 5 January.

Stewart, R. (2020). 'Lord of Misrule'. *Times Literary Supplement*, 6 November.

Sullivan, A. (2019). 'Boris's Blundering Brilliance.' *New York Magazine*, 9 December.

Syal, R. (2020). 'Dominic Cummings calls for "weirdos and misfits" for No.10 jobs', *Guardian*, 2 January.

Sylvester, R. (2020). 'How Right-Wing is Boris Johnson?' *Prospect*, 7 January.

Worthy, B., Bennister, M., and Stafford, M. (2019). 'Rebels Leading London: the mayoralties of Ken Livingstone and Boris Johnson compared.' *British Politics*. 14 (1): 23-43.

Chapter 17
Evaluating British Prime Ministers

Reviewing the British prime ministers from Churchill and Attlee through to Boris Johnson, it seems obvious that there are multiple ways in which prime ministers approach the job, operate in government – and succeed or fail. We might be able to formulate the basic leadership or governing tasks that a prime minister has to undertake (or should attempt) – in statecraft terms, winning elections, party management, dominating political debate or setting the political agenda, and governing competently; in Greenstein's terms, communicating and mobilizing public opinion, organizing government, showing political skill, providing a strong policy vision, handling the cognitive, decision-making and emotional stresses of office (Theakston 2007). But prime ministers do these things in different ways, with different outcomes. They are different from each other (sometimes they may have got the leadership precisely because they were different from their predecessor), and it is not really possible to identify a set of character traits or a personality type, skills or qualities that would apply across the board and make for success in all situations. Some prime ministers are clearly more successful than others. We can compare them and analyse the ways in which they handled the problems of politics, policy and government they faced. But we cannot assume that other approaches, or another leader, would have been more – or less – successful in the context and with the challenges they faced.

Historian Ben Pimlott once argued that 'lack of distinction has been the rule, and high achievement the exception, among British prime ministers.' Dominic Sandbrook, agreed: 'For every giant who walked through the famous black door [of Number 10], there have recently been all too many political pygmies', he said in 2010. 'So many of our modern prime ministers have been . . . ineffectual.' The best prime ministers, *The Times* political team once argued are those who 'really swung history', were the great war leaders, successfully handled 'a big national crisis', changed the country with 'important and radical domestic achievements', or 'transform[ed] the political landscape, as opposed to just holding office' (see: Theakston and Gill 2011: 78). Many of the prime ministers featured in this book, assessed by these standards, had mixed records at best, may have promised a lot but left office unfulfilled, and often faced adverse political circumstances.

In his comparative analysis of Westminster system prime ministers (in the UK, Australia, Canada and New Zealand), Patrick Weller (2018: 23-25, 239-247) takes three measures of prime-ministerial success: tenure in office (a simple test of longevity and electoral record); control over party and government (as assessed through dominance of decision-making processes in government or party revolts, etc.); and policy achievement (do they have an agenda, introduce new programmes and push through the changes they want see?). As Weller says, the first yardstick is measurable and precise; the second can be assessed with reasonable but not complete certainty; but the third is 'absolutely contingent and contestable' (Weller 2018: 23) and dependent on many factors outside the control of prime ministers and their governments, and in addition prime ministers usually have chequered records – a mixture of policy successes and failures during their time in office. Measures of success, Weller (2018: 246) concludes, are in the end 'subjective and relative'.

Over the years there has developed a veritable cottage industry of prime-ministerial evaluation, using methods ranging from historically-informed qualitative judgements, through mass public opinion surveys, to targeted group surveys tapping the views of political elites or academic experts. Typical of the first approach are the exercises done by the statesman and biographer Roy Jenkins and the historian Peter Hennessy. Jenkins (ranking Britain's prime ministers in 1999) rated Churchill as pre-eminent in the 20th century with Asquith in second place in the 20th century, above Lloyd George in third place, on the grounds that he was 'a more constructive and consistent statesman' although admitting that he was not a good war leader. He ranked Thatcher's as a 'major premiership' on the grounds of her length of office, 'forthrightness of style', and as the first woman to hold the post. Attlee ('signally' in his view), Macmillan and Baldwin ('on balance') he judged as having achieved 'successful terms of office'. Heath was 'not in general a success', but was picked out for his achievement in taking Britain into Europe. Major's ranking as a 'failure', Jenkins claimed was largely as a result of bad luck, something that he described as 'necessarily always a substantial element in political success or failure' (see: Theakston and Gill 2006: 195).

Peter Hennessy (2000: 527-533), in his taxonomy of post-1945 prime ministers from Attlee to Blair, described Attlee and Thatcher as the 'very top flight' post-war prime ministers (Churchill would have been in this category if his two premierships were treated in combination and account taken of his wartime achievements). These were the 'two great "weathermakers" of the postwar years', he judged, setting the political agenda and transforming British politics, though he suggested that Thatcher could be ranked highest as she 'forged her new consensus' while Attlee 'refined his' as 'the beneficiary of a new weather system' created during the second world war. Described as 'below' those top two was the category of 'nation- or system-shifters', prime ministers who were 'remaker[s] of the country in a significant, substantial and almost certainly irreversible fashion'. Heath was in this category because of British entry to Europe and Blair because of his government's constitutional reforms. Described as 'a kind of obverse to the scene-shifters' were the 'seasoned copers but not transformers' - Churchill (on the basis of 1951-55) and Callaghan. Macmillan and Wilson, assessed as frustrated would-be modernisers, were placed in the 'promise-unfulfilled' category. Douglas-Home (a 'punctuation mark' between Macmillan and Wilson) got high marks for decency. Writing in 2000, the bottom two prime ministers in Hennessy's league table were Major and Eden. Major was ranked as 'overwhelmed' ('he succumbed to the political weather rather than made it'), while Eden was described as falling into 'a catastrophic category of his own'.

For his part, prime-ministerial biographer and historian Anthony Seldon (2021: 315-319) places prime ministers into six categories, depending on achievements and legacy. First, there are the 'agenda-changers' who rose to the historic challenges of their periods in power, won notable generals elections, changed the course of the country, and whose influence and impact was felt for many years after them. Attlee and Thatcher were the most modern examples of this group. Second were the 'major contributors', who had a very decisive influence but were often sui-generis or without the long-lasting mark on policy of the agenda-changers. Seldon put Wilson, Heath and Blair in this category. These still made more of a lasting impact than the group of 'positive stabilisers' - a group including Callaghan, Major, Brown and Cameron - who provided competent leadership or steadied the ship, often in turbulent or challenging periods. The 'noble failures' were Seldon's fourth group - prime ministers who tried to do the right thing, were principled and dedicated, but were overwhelmed by events - not surprisingly, he places Theresa May, defeated by the challenges of Brexit, in this category. The most modern example of the 'ignoble failures' category (who, he argues, lacked basic moral seriousness or leadership ability, or both) he gives is Eden, brought down by the Suez disaster. Finally, there is the group of prime ministers 'left on the starting line', as he describes them, whose premierships were too short to judge their performance, most recently Douglas-Home, in office for just under a year in 1963-64.

Turning to examples of mass public opinion rating of prime ministers, a YouGov poll (of 1692 people) in August 2016 indicated that a third of the public at that point thought that David Cameron was a good or great prime minister, but he was still viewed negatively overall (**Table 17.1**). Despite his premature exit from Number 10 following the EU referendum, Cameron was still apparently seen in more favourable terms than any other prime minister since Margaret Thatcher. Gordon Brown was judged the most harshly in this poll, with a majority (55%) of people rating his tenure negatively and fewer than one in ten (9%) thinking it was a success. John Major comes across as a middling PM, with 36% of people saying he was an average PM

– more than judged him either positively or negatively. Margaret Thatcher is the only prime minister who was judged by the public in overall positive terms, with a net score of +13%. She is a polarising figure though, with only 12% considering her an 'average' prime minister – the majority of voters in this survey considering her to have either been good/great (43%) or poor/terrible (30%). There were some interesting partisan differences in these ratings. Overall, those who voted Conservative in 2015 were on balance more positive about their party's PMs, with net ratings of +73% for Thatcher, +52% for Cameron and +1% for Major from those voters. By contrast, 2015 Labour voters were more negative about their party's PMs, with a net rating of -6% for Blair and -25% for Brown. Labour voters rated all these recent PMs negatively overall, it should be pointed out and were even harder on the Conservative ones, while Conservative voters rated only Labour PMs negatively overall.

In a later Ipsos MORI poll of 1,111 adults in August 2022, asking whether prime ministers since 1945 had done a 'good job' or a 'bad job' (**Table 17.2**), Johnson, May and Cameron occupied the bottom three slots in a league table calculated on the basis of net scores (just counting 'good' minus 'bad' ratings) of -16, -13 and -8 respectively, with Churchill (+53), Macmillan (+16), Attlee (+11) and Wilson (+11) rated by the public as the top four prime ministers on this measure. But the picture looks more complex when account is taken of those saying the PMs did 'neither a good nor bad' job, the 'don't knows' and the 'never heard of them' category (this last group alone measuring 10-18% for pre-Thatcher PMs).

The well-established American tradition of polls of academic experts rating and ranking US presidents has now spread to several other countries and political systems, including the UK. The ones focused on here are the Theakston and Gill series of surveys of university academic experts in British politics and/or modern British political history, conducted first in 2004 (with 139 respondents) ranking all 20th century PMs, then on post-1945 PMs only in 2010 (with 106 respondents), 2016 (with 82 respondents) and 2021 (with 93 respondents) (see: Theakston and Gill 2006, 2011, 2021; Theakston 2016). In each poll, respondents were asked to indicate on a scale of 0 to 10 how successful or unsuccessful they considered each prime minister to have been in office (with 0 being completely unsuccessful and 10 highly successful). A mean score for each prime minister was then calculated and the league table of 'performance' worked out. As with the US presidential polls, the standard was not 'lifetime achievement' over the full political/ministerial career but performance in the top job, in Number 10 Downing Street. Not defining or specifying the criteria for evaluating prime ministerial performance also followed the practice of the US academic surveys; respondents were left to decide for themselves.

As in the previous surveys, Labour's Clement Attlee was rated in 2021 **(Table 17.3)** as the most successful post-war prime minister with a mean rating of 8.3. Margaret Thatcher received a score of 7.8 and Tony Blair received 7.7. Sir Anthony Eden at 2.3 (destroyed by the Suez crisis) and Sir Alec Douglas-Home at 3.5 (PM for only a year) languished on the bottom rungs of the 2021 prime-ministerial league table, as in the previous surveys. They were now joined by Theresa May on 2.3 who was rated as even less successful than David Cameron on 3.6. Churchill received a rating of 5.1 in the 2021 survey, placing him 'mid-table' position, as these evaluations are based on his 1950s administration only. The great war leader (1940-45) was seen by respondents as less successful as a peacetime leader, 1951-55; but in the 2004 survey of all 20th century prime ministers, Churchill came out second overall.

Reputations do go up as well as down **(Table 17.4)**. Gordon Brown's rating, for example, has improved from 3.9 in 2010 (when he was the third-worst ranked prime minister since the war) to 4.6 in 2016 and 5.5 in 2021, placing him now in the top half of the league table. And John Major also improved from a 3.7 score in 2004 to 5.5 in 2016 before dipping slightly to 5.1 in 2021. David Cameron's score has fallen from 4.0 in the survey conducted just after he left office in 2016 to 3.6 five years later. These movements perhaps show how the failures and successes of later prime ministers, and the passage of time and the later development of events, can change perspectives.

For comparison, Members of Parliament's evaluations of postwar prime ministers were captured in a survey carried out in 2014 (with 158 respondents) **(Table 17.5)** (Royal Holloway Group PR3710 2015). MPs ranked Thatcher above Attlee and put Brown at the very bottom of the league table, with some of the other mid-table PMs shifting slightly compared to the academic rankings. But there is a broad agreement between the two groups – academics and practicing professional politicians – about the best and worst of the post-war PMs.

Data from the 2021 academic survey shows how UK prime ministers over the last few decades are rated in terms of their positive or negative impact on a range of policy areas **(Table 17.6)**. The 'net score' in the table indicates the proportion rating each prime minister's performance as 'positive' minus those who say 'negative'. David Cameron and Theresa May are the only two of these prime ministers to be rated negatively, on balance, across all five areas. Mrs May scored particularly badly in terms of her perceived impact on Britain's foreign policy and role in the world (-78), on her own party (-78) and on British democracy and the constitution (-72) – under all three of those headings getting the worst net scores of any of any prime minister in the last four decades. The other four prime ministers receive more mixed ratings – sometimes seen as overall positive on one or more aspects, but negative on others. Mrs Thatcher, for example, has the most negative rating of all six prime ministers for her impact on British society, but is rated most positively for her impact on Britain's role in the world.

Leaders with multiple terms of office may be considered more or less successful in their different administrations, as the different scores for Churchill noted earlier suggest. The 2010 academic survey gave respondents an opportunity to rate the different terms of Thatcher, Major and Blair as well as giving those prime ministers an overall score (Theakston and Gill 2011: 73-74). Thatcher's second term (1983-87) was judged her most successful (6.7), compared to her first term (1979-83: 5.3) and her third (1987-90: 4.0). Both Major's (1990-92: 5.1) and Blair's (1997-2001: 6.9) first terms were regarded by respondents as their most successful, followed in each case by a decline (Major's second term 1992-97 score of 3.6 was lower than Douglas-Home's; Blair's scores fell to 5.0 for his second term 2001-05 and 4.1 for his short third term 2005-07, though he was still ahead of Gordon Brown). Similarly, when that exercise was repeated **(Table 17.7)** and respondents were asked in the 2016 survey to rate David Cameron's two terms as prime minister – the first as leader of the Conservative / Lib Dem Coalition, 2010-2015, the average rating the academics gave him was 5.6, which would put him on par with John Major overall and in the top half of the league table (Theakston 2016). It was Cameron's record as the leader of the Conservative majority government that accounted for his overall poor rating. When asked specifically to evaluate Cameron's performance as prime minister between 2015 and 2016, the academics gave him a rating of 2.1. That would have placed him at the bottom of the league table – as a worse prime minster than Anthony Eden as the biggest post-war failure in Number 10. It is likely that for all his achievements as a successful coalition prime minister, David Cameron's reputation and place in history seems destined to be defined by Brexit and his calling and losing the referendum. Fully 86 per cent of the academics answering a question in the 2016 survey asking 'what do you consider to be the single greatest failure of David Cameron as Prime Minister?' cited the EU Referendum.

Academic surveys and ranking exercises like these are sometimes dismissed as only pseudo-serious or as merely parlour games. They have, one critic argued, 'no systematic, objective or scientific basis' (Theakston and Gill 2011: 79). Questions can be asked about the yardsticks, the criteria and the measures of success; there will always be arguments about what constitutes greatness in political leaders. Can success or failure in office be boiled down to a simple score out of ten or a three or four-point scale ('great', 'near-great', 'average', 'failure')? Are we comparing the non-comparable? Moreover, a range of factors can feed into academic opinions and judgements about political leaders, including differences in knowledge and information, trends in recent scholarship and fashions in interpretation, the current atmosphere, and – to some degree – partisan factors. For instance, of the academics responding to the 2021 prime-ministerial survey who volunteered a party allegiance, 60 per cent were Labour, 13 per cent Conservative and 13 per cent Liberal-Democrat. That was also a heavily 'Remain' cohort, with 86 per cent of those answering saying they voted Remain compared to only 14 per cent who voted Leave in the EU referendum. The extent to which these factors, and particularly views on Brexit, influenced the ratings for David Cameron and Theresa May is open to debate, though equally this same group of academics also rated Margaret Thatcher as one of the post-war greats.

Trying to get at what lays behind the academic rankings, there seems to be a correlation between tenure in office and prime-ministerial rankings. As with the US presidential ratings, greatness and longevity in office usually go hand in hand. Roy Jenkins always insisted it was 'essential to have a cumulative period in office of at least five years in order to rank as a prime minister of major impact. No-one of the last hundred years [he wrote in the 1980s] who does not fulfil this criterion has achieved the front rank' (Jenkins 1988: 204). All of the top five prime ministers in the 2021 poll served for six or more years in Number 10, while only one of the bottom five clocked up over five years, and three of the bottom five served as prime minister for only three years or less. Similarly, the cumulative tenure in Number 10 of the top five postwar prime ministers in the 2021 survey was 41 years, compared to 16 years clocked up by the bottom five premiers between them. But the mid-table ratings of John Major (seven years as PM) suggest that a durable period in office is a necessary but not sufficient condition for having an impact, leaving a policy legacy and enhancing a prime-ministerial reputation.

A track record of election victories is obviously related to this factor. Winning even one general election is hard enough (ask Brown or Callaghan), and getting re-elected is an achievement in itself – 'those who win three or four elections are indeed exceptional', as Patrick Weller (2018: 23) notes. The top five postwar prime ministers in the 2016 survey between them won 13 of the 20 British general elections between 1945 and 2017, the bottom five PMs winning only five elections in total (counting both 2010 and 2015 as a Cameron victories, and 2017 as a May victory). Moreover the top three prime ministers (Attlee, Thatcher and Blair) won the big postwar landslide victories – something also associated with high rankings in the US presidential polls. But winning multiple elections is not a guarantee of joining the ranks of the 'great' prime ministers, as Wilson's ranking shows (he won more general elections – four – than Thatcher or Blair).

Related to this, the results of the 2021 survey confirm the notion that 'takeover' prime ministers – those who first enter Number 10 following the resignation of their predecessor and an internal party leadership process, rather than by winning a general election victory and becoming PM after being leader of the opposition – have, on average, less time in office, less successful tenures, and are generally rated as worse-performing (Worthy 2016). Of the group of 14 prime ministers up to and including Theresa May, eight were 'takeover' leaders, while six won general elections to become prime minister. The average rating for the first group was 4.37 compared to 5.25 for the second group.

Expert surveys tap subjective judgements and evaluations – albeit 'informed' ones, though subject to different knowledge levels and perhaps the ebb and flow of established reputations influencing responses - but can we actually identify 'objective' measures of performance? **Table 17.8** represents an attempt at ranking postwar prime ministers (up to and including Cameron) according to a range of political and economic indicators: tenure in office, cumulative or aggregate seat gain (or loss) at all the general elections they fought as party leader, cumulative percentage vote change across those same general elections, net public satisfaction with the PM, and then average (mean) percentage figures for unemployment, inflation and economic growth for the years they were in Number 10. Reading across the table the high rankings of Attlee, Thatcher and Blair on the electoral (vote/seat) indicators is obvious – and is something clearly tied in to their high scores in the academic expert surveys. But Cameron's strong performance in terms of seat gain and vote change should also be noted. Against a background of the public perhaps becoming more critical about politics than they were in the first couple of postwar decades, the low net satisfaction ratings in opinion polls for all prime ministers from Wilson onwards stand out, with Major and Brown plumbing the depths of public dissatisfaction. But Eden's rankings in terms of seat/vote gains and public popularity are very different from his academic ranking, suggesting that the critical expert survey ratings (and historical reputations) are perhaps based on wider (non-quantitative?) judgements about a prime minister's political achievements and legacy. The dismal vote and seat records of Douglas-Home, Brown and Major underline the difficulties faced by 'successor' prime ministers coming into office in the last phases of multi-term governments. On the economic side, the data hints at the more favourable economic context of the prime ministers of the 1950s and early 1960s – years of growth, low unemployment and low inflation – compared to the economic 'hard times' experienced by those in office during the 1970s. It is striking, however, that Thatcher features in the bottom half of the league table for all three economic indicators (and in last place for unemployment) taking her 11 year tenure overall, with the post-financial crash PMs Brown and Cameron in the bottom four on two indicators (growth and unemployment). Despite that, Thatcher consistently figures as one of the very top-ranked PMs in survey rankings, suggesting political achievements ultimately trump economic ones in those historical/political science exercises.

Just as the US rankings are topped by the wartime and/or 'activist' presidents so are the British prime-ministerial league tables. The great prime ministers 'make a permanent shift in the direction of the country' it has been argued. 'They must not only weather the storms, but change the climate' (Rawnsley quoted in Theakston 2013: 231). Over the twentieth century as a whole (as seen in the 2004 survey), wars and international crises can make and unmake premierships and prime-ministerial reputations, as is clearly the case both with the war-winners (Churchill and Lloyd George) and with the failures (Chamberlain and Eden). Meanwhile controversies around the Iraq war have probably damaged to some extent Blair's overall ratings. Association with major and lasting domestic policy achievements, and with a transformation of the framework of politics and the political agenda, has brought consistently high rankings for Attlee and Thatcher but not for Heath (where his achievement in securing entry into Europe is offset by a fairly short tenure, economic setbacks and election defeat).

Daniel Finkelstein (at one time an adviser to John Major) argues that ranking exercises involve a systematic bias 'favour[ing] big ideas and great acts over quiet moderation', elevate the 'dramatic' over the 'mundane', and downplay the achievements of those who 'govern quietly and competently' and of those who 'resisted bad changes' and avoided problems rather than carried through big reforms (Theakston 2013: 232). In the 1990s Major consolidated and entrenched Thatcherism, but in the prime-ministerial league table the low-key transactional political-manager is likely to always stay well below the conviction politician and radical transformational leader who preceded him. In a similar vein, Philip Ziegler has put a case for Wilson, a prime minister often written-off as preoccupied with short-term tactics and party unity above all else, putting off the big problems or botching much-needed reforms. 'A succession of Wilsons as leaders would doom any nation to decline', argued Ziegler (1993: 517); 'a Wilson from time to time to let the dust settle while the demolition squads of the radicals gather strength for the next enterprise can be positively beneficial.' The point is that some prime ministers may have ambitious policy agendas and it is legitimate to ask if they successfully make the big changes they want, while others may be satisfied if they just run things efficiently and manage to find a way through the crises that come along.

The importance of contextual factors – that no two incumbents are dealt the same hand and they confront different situations and events, problems, constraints and opportunities – is obvious. 'Are we measuring good fortune, success or survival?' it has been argued. 'Where would Anthony Eden have ranked without Suez?' it has been asked (Theakston 2013: 234). 'Bad luck' is often pleaded in mitigation for the lower-ranking prime ministers. One Eden biographer (Thorpe 2003: 606) has labelled him 'the unluckiest of twentieth-century prime ministers' and Heath has also been described as 'exceptionally unlucky' (Campbell 1993: xix). His biographer, John Campbell (1993: xix) indeed argued that 'five years earlier or ten years later, with all his shortcomings, Heath might have been a great prime minister.' But leaders have to be rated on how well they understand and react to their context and the challenges they face. A favourable match of skill and context makes major achievements possible; accomplished statecraft in an unfavourable context may make the difference between political survival and disaster; misjudgements, a lack or a loss of feel for the situation, or ineptness can aggravate problems and make a difference for the worst (and *that* – not 'bad luck' – was Eden's problem). Reviewing the thirty years from 1970 to 2000, Dennis Kavanagh and Anthony Seldon (1999: 327) argued that only for about one-third of the time in all were the different prime ministers in control of events and able to hold the initiative, as opposed to being battered by events or having to react to over-determining external circumstances, reducing their scope for significant and legacy-enhancing policy achievement.

Prime-ministerial (and presidential) rankings undoubtedly have their subjective aspects, but they are not meaningless. They tie in to judgements about what has gone wrong and what has gone right in a country's history and in its politics. And they provoke and stimulate reflection on the skills, qualities and abilities political leaders have – or should have – and on what the prime minister's job is, or should, or can be. There is at least as much to be learned from the failures and limitations of leaders as from their successes and strengths, as Fred Greenstein argued. There are, in that sense, positive lessons that may sometimes be taken from leaders ranked low in the ratings scale and negative lessons that can be derived from the so-called 'greats' at the top of the league tables. We need to study, therefore, both the successful and the unsuccessful prime ministers: not just an Attlee, Thatcher or Blair, but also an Eden, Heath, Brown or May – and, ideally, we need to take a long view and compare a range of prime ministers, not just look at one in isolation.

References

Campbell, J. (1993), *Edward Heath: A Biography.* London: Jonathan Cape.

Hennessy, P. (2000). *The Prime Minister, the office and its holders since 1945.* London: Allen Lane.

Jenkins, R. (1988). *Gallery of Twentieth Century Portraits.* London: David & Charles.

Kavanagh, D. and Seldon, A. (1999). *The Powers Behind the Prime Minister.* London: HarperCollins.

Royal Holloway Group PR3710 (2015). 'British MPs on British PMs: parliamentary evaluations of prime ministerial success', *Politics.* 35   (2): 111-127.

Seldon, A. (2021). *The Impossible Office? The History of the British Prime Minister.* Cambridge: Cambridge University Press.

Theakston, K. (2007). 'What Makes for an Effective British Prime Minister?', *Quaderni Di Scienza Politica.* 14 (2): 227-249.

Theakston, K. (2013). 'Evaluating prime ministerial performance: the British experience', in: Strangio, P., 't Hart, P. and Walter, J. (eds) *Understanding Prime-Ministerial Performance: Comparative Perspectives.* Oxford: Oxford University Press.

Theakston, K. (2016). 'Academics rate David Cameron among worst post-war prime ministers.' *The Conversation.* 13 October. [https://theconversation.com/academics-rate-david-cameron-among-worst-post-war-prime-ministers-66780]

Theakston, K. and Gill, M. (2006). 'Rating 20th Century British Prime Ministers', *British Journal of Politics and International Relations.* 8 (2): 193-213.

Theakston, K. and Gill, M. (2011). 'The Postwar Premiership League', *Political Quarterly.* 82 (1): 67-80 .

Theakston, K. and Gill, M. (2021). 'Theresa May joint worst post-war prime minister, say historians and politics professors in new survey.' *The Conversation.* 6 July. [https://theconversation.com/theresa-may-joint-worst-post-war-prime-minister-say-historians-and-politics-professors-in-new-survey-163912]

Thorpe, D. R. (2003). *Eden.* London: Chatto & Windus.

Weller, P. (2018). *The Prime Ministers' Craft.* Oxford: Oxford University Press.

Worthy, B. (2016). 'Ending in failure? The performance of "takeover" prime ministers 1916-2016', *Political Quarterly.* 87 (4): 509-517.

Ziegler, P. (1993). *Wilson: The Authorised Life.* London: Weidenfeld & Nicolson.

Table 17.1: Public ratings of good/bad prime ministers (2016)

	(a) A great or good PM	(b) A poor or terrible	Net rating (a) - (b) %	An average PM %
Thatcher	43	30	13	12
Major	14	31	-17	36
Blair	20	48	-28	23
Brown	9	55	-46	24
Cameron	32	34	-2	26

Source: YouGov 2016.
https://yougov.co.uk/topics/politics/articles-reports/
2016/08/10/cameron-best-prime-minister-since-thatcher

Table 17.2: Public ratings of prime-ministerial performance (2022)

		Good job %	Neither good nor bad %	Bad job %	Don't know %	Never heard of them %
1	Winston Churchill	62	15	9	13	1
2	Margaret Thatcher	43	16	32	8	1
3	Tony Blair	36	21	35	7	1
4	Boris Johnson	33	15	49	4	-
5	Harold Wilson	31	22	15	22	10
6	Gordon Brown	31	27	31	8	3
7	David Cameron	30	25	38	6	-
8	John Major	29	31	26	10	4
9	Theresa May	28	25	41	5	-
10	Harold Macmillan	26	23	10	30	11
11	Clement Attlee	24	19	11	30	16
12	Edward Heath	22	24	21	23	10
13	James Callaghan	21	27	16	23	12
14	Anthony Eden	21	21	12	29	17
15	Alec Douglas-Home	17	22	12	31	18

Source: IPSOS UK 2022.
https://www.ipsos.com/sites/default/files/ct/news/
documents/2022-08/ipsos-political-pulse-polling-past-prime-
ministers-august-2022.pdf

Table 17.3: League table of postwar prime ministers (2021 academic survey)

Ranking	Mean score	Prime Minister
1	8.3	Clement Attlee 1945-51
2	7.8	Margaret Thatcher 1979-90
3	7.7	Tony Blair 1997-2007
4	6.5	Harold Wilson 1964-70 and 1974-76
5	6.1	Harold Macmillan 1957-63
6	5.5	Gordon Brown 2007-10
7=	5.1	John Major 1990-97
7=	5.1	Winston Churchill 1951-55
7=	5.1	James Callaghan 1976-79
10	4.6	Edward Heath 1970-74
11	3.6	David Cameron 2010-16
12	3.5	Alec Douglas-Home 1963-64
13=	2.3	Anthony Eden 1955-57
13=	2.3	Theresa May 2016-19

Source: Theakston and Gill (2021).

Table 17.4: Changing prime-ministerial academic rankings 2004-21

Ranking	2004 survey	2010 survey	2016 survey	2021 survey
1	Attlee (8.3)	Attlee (8.1)	Attlee (8.5)	Attlee (8.3)
2	Churchill (7.9)	Thatcher (6.9)	Thatcher (7.2)	Thatcher (7.8)
3	Thatcher (7.1)	Blair (6.4)	Blair (6.7)	Blair (7.7)
4	Macmillan (6.5)	Macmillan (6.3)	Macmillan (6.4)	Wilson (6.5)
5	Blair (6.3)	Wilson (5.9)	Wilson (6.3)	Macmillan (6.1)
6	Wilson (5.9)	Churchill (5.3)	Major (5.5)	Brown (5.5)
7	Callaghan (4.7)	Callaghan (5.1)	Churchill (5.4)	Major (5.1)
8	Heath (4.4)	Major (4.6)	Callaghan (5.1)	Churchill (5.1)
9	Major (3.7)	Heath (4.4)	Heath (4.8)	Callaghan (5.1)
10	Douglas-Home (3.3)	Brown (3.9)	Brown (4.6)	Heath (4.6)
11	Eden (2.5)	Douglas-Home (3.7)	Cameron (4.0)	Cameron (3.6)
12		Eden (2.3)	Douglas-Home (3.8)	Douglas-Home (3.5)
13			Eden (2.4)	Eden (2.3)
14				May (2.3)

Sources: Theakston and Gill (2006, 2011, 2021); Theakston (2016).

Table 17.5: MPs' ranking of post-war prime Ministers (2014)

Ranking	Mean score	Prime Minister
1	7.4	Thatcher
2	7.3	Attlee
3	6.8	Blair
4	6.5	Churchill
5	6.1	Macmillan
6	5.8	Wilson
7	5.3	Major
8	4.4	Callaghan
9	4.4	Heath
10	4.0	Douglas-Home
11	3.7	Eden
12	3.3	Brown

Source: Royal Holloway Group PR3710 (2015).

Table 17.6: Impact of PMs on policy areas (2021 academic survey)

(Net score: positive impact minus negative impact)

	British society	British economy	Foreign policy/ Britain's role in	Their own political party	British democracy/ constituti
Thatcher	-67	6	36	26	-48
Major	-17	-13	14	-56	-17
Blair	64	70	-17	29	30
Brown	27	51	29	-27	9
Cameron	-48	-55	-59	-43	-62
May	-38	-47	-78	-78	-72

Source: Theakston and Gill (2021).

Table 17.7: Rating PMs' different terms of office (2016 academic survey)

Thatcher	1979-83	5.3
	1983-87	6.7
	1987-90	4.0
Major	1990-92	5.1
	1992-97	3.6
Blair	1997-2001	6.9
	2001-05	5.0
	2005-07	4.1
Cameron	2010-15	5.6
	2015-16	2.1

Source: Theakston (2016).

Table 17.8: 'Objective' measures of performance?

	2016 Academic Survey	Longevity in office	Cumulative seat gain	Cumulative % vote change	Public net satisfaction with PM %	Unemployment (average) %	Inflation (average) %	Growth (average) %
1	Attlee 8.5	Thatcher 11 years, 208 days	Attlee +225	Attlee +12.9	Eden +28	Attlee 1.5	Macmillan 2.4	Douglas-Home 5.2
2	Thatcher 7.2	Blair 10 years, 56 days	Cameron +133	Thatcher +6.5	Macmillan +19	Eden 1.7	Douglas-Home. 2.7	Churchill 3.8
3	Blair 6.7	Wilson 7 years, 279 days	Thatcher +99	Cameron +4.5	Churchill +13	Churchill 1.8	Blair 2.8	Callaghan 3.3
4	Macmillan 6.4	Macmillan 6 years, 281 days	Blair +84	Eden +1.7	Douglas-Home / Callaghan +7	Macmillan 2.4	Cameron 3.0	Macmillan 3.2
5	Wilson 6.3	Major 6 years, 155 days	Wilson +61	Blair +0.8		Douglas-Home 2.7	Brown 3.1	Heath 2.9
6	Major 5.5	Attlee 6 years, 92 days	Eden +24	Macmillan -0.3	Attlee +5	Wilson 3.0	Major 4.0	Blair 2.8
7	Churchill 5.4	Cameron 6 years, 63 days	Macmillan +20	Callaghan -2.4	Wilson +2	Heath 3.7	Eden 4.7	Eden / Thatcher 2.7
8	Callaghan 5.1	Heath 3 years, 259 days	Heath -27	Wilson -4.5	Blair -1	Callaghan / Blair 5.5	Attlee 5.1	
9	Heath 4.8	Churchill (post-war) 3 years, 160 days	Callaghan -50	Churchill -5.3	Heath / Cameron -13		Churchill 5.5	Major 2.0
10	Brown 4.6	Callaghan 3 years, 29 days	Douglas-Home -61	Douglas-Home -6.0		Brown 6.6	Thatcher 8.1	Cameron 1.9
11	Cameron 4.0	Brown 2 years, 318 days	Brown -97	Brown -6.2	Thatcher -14	Cameron 6.9	Wilson 8.8	Wilson 1.8
12	Douglas-Home 3.8	Eden 1 year, 279 days	Churchill -108	Heath -7.6	Major -25	Major 8.7	Heath 9.6	Attlee 1.1
13	Eden 2.4	Douglas-Home 363 days	Major -211	Major -11.6	Brown -26	Thatcher 9.3	Callaghan 13.5	Brown -0.8

Chapter 18
Afterword on Liz Truss (2022)

Holding the office from 6 September until 25 October 2022 - just 49 days in total - Liz Truss was widely described by commentators as the shortest-serving prime minister in British history when she stepped down. She was said to have eclipsed the previous record, held by the unfortunate George Canning, who had died in office in 1827 after 119 days as prime minister.

In fact, things are a little more complicated. If we look at the records on *terms of office*, as opposed to *total length of service* as prime minister, there were 18 prime ministers before Truss who had a stint in Number 10 lasting less than one year. Twelve of these were multi-term prime ministers who clocked up longer spells in the office at other times (including some big names such as Robert Peel, William Gladstone, Benjamin Disraeli and Stanley Baldwin). On this basis, Truss could perhaps be measured against Lord Rockingham, whose second term as prime minister in 1782 was only 96 days (cut short by his death in office), or the Duke of Wellington, whose second term was as a sort of caretaker or acting prime minister (holding the fort as literally a one-man government) for 22 days in 1834, until Robert Peel, who was abroad, could travel back to the UK and take up the reins as PM - Peel going on in turn to serve in that first term of his for only 119 days (Englefield et al 1995: 410; Theakston 2010: 38, 62-3). The difference is, of course, that Truss, unlike them, was a one-term PM (and seems very unlikely ever to be able to return to Number 10).

There was another difference between events in 1834 and 2022. Wellington's three-week spell in temporary charge was marked, one biographer says, by 'no appointments, no decisions, no policy, no legislation' (Longford 1972: 303). It might have been better if Truss had stuck to that pattern too.

The upheavals and instability in Downing Street, with Truss taking over from Boris Johnson and then being supplanted by Rishi Sunak, meant that 2022 was inevitably described as 'the year of three Prime Ministers' (Bogdanor 2022: 571). But nor was this unique in British prime-ministerial history, with the calendar years 1782, 1783, 1827, 1852 and 1868 also each seeing three different prime ministers, and with 1834 actually qualifying as the year of four prime ministers (Englefield et al 1995: 411-12). Against this background, we can see that divided, unhappy and mutinous parties, factionalised politics, political crises and leadership failures are not exactly new in British politics and British history, though the dramatic self-destruction of the Truss premiership perhaps sets new benchmarks for hubristic self-confidence, ideological zealotry and political incompetence.

Liz Truss actually spent longer campaigning for the leadership of her party and country than she did as prime minister. There were 57 days from her campaign launch on 10 July 2022 to her being declared the winner of the Conservative Party's leadership contest on 5 September; she announced her resignation after 44 days in Number 10 before leaving office five days later.

As yet another 'takeover' prime minister - the tenth since Winston Churchill in 1940 - the odds were always somewhat stacked against her. Such mid-term successors - as we have seen in this book - often have relatively short and difficult tenures, inheriting serious problems and crises, struggling with divided parties, and also facing dilemmas about their personal mandate and authority, the scope and space they have for new initiatives, and whether or not to call a general election (Worthy 2022). The constraints and challenges can be even tougher when a leader takes over after their party has already been in office for several terms - as the experiences of Alec Douglas-Home, John Major and Gordon Brown suggest - with plentiful signs of 'governing degeneration', breakdown and decline accumulating by 2022 (Roe-Crines 2022).

In some ways Truss seemed, by modern standards, an experienced pair of hands, having been an MP for 12 years and a Cabinet minister for 8 years, under three prime ministers and in five different departments. David Cameron had made her Environment Secretary in 2014, while under Theresa May she

279

had been Justice Secretary and then Chief Secretary to the Treasury, before serving as International Trade Secretary and then Foreign Secretary under Boris Johnson. But her record had been patchy one, and she had often seemed more interested in burnishing her party, public and political profile, and her social media image, than in the hard grind of government administration and substantive policy achievement (Cole and Heale 2022).

Moreover, she won the leadership without strong backing within the Conservative parliamentary party. Rishi Sunak led in all five rounds of MPs' voting, with Penny Mordaunt in second place until the fifth ballot when Truss edged ahead of her, winning 113 votes (32 per cent) to Mordaunt's 105 (29 per cent) and Sunak's 137 (38 per cent). Though Sunak had supported Brexit in 2016 while Truss had been a remainer back then, she won the backing of the fanatical Brexiteers of the European Research Group (ERG). Truss was the party grassroots' favourite, with Sunak being seen as 'disloyal' by resigning from Johnson's Cabinet and precipitating his downfall, and with Truss steering a path to winning the leadership by telling Conservative party members - a dwindling group, decidedly unrepresentative of the wider public in terms of age, social backgrounds and policy views - what they wanted to hear on issues like taxation, Brexit, and the economy. Even so, it was hardly a landslide result, Truss eventually beating Sunak by 81,000 (57.4 per cent) to 60,000 (42.6 per cent) in the members' votes. Truss won the premiership with an essentially 'boosterish' and ideological pitch to a narrow party 'selectorate'. But her shallow basis of support from Conservative MPs and the strong reactions of the electorate (expressed through public opinion polls) to her policies and actions in office counted for more when it came to holding on to, and then losing, the premiership.

Truss was an unusually ideological prime minister. A strong free-marketeer, a social liberal and an economic liberal, she had long associations with the right-wing think-tank world of groups like the Institute of Economic Affairs. A politician with a strong agenda around competition and free enterprise, growth, deregulation and low taxes, she knew what she wanted and was a self-styled 'disruptor in chief' and 'on the side of the insurgents', willing to take risks and with something of a bull-dozing attitude to what she saw as vested interests, bureaucratic obstructions and opponents of her 'reforms'. She once said she wanted 'a more robust conservatism' and an end to 'trimming' (Cole and Heale 2022). At the same time, she appeared to critics to have little in the way of self-doubt, to dislike dissent, and to be reluctant to acknowledge possibly inconvenient evidence. She also seemed, to some observers, almost to revel in controversy from her earliest days on the political stage. Dominic Cummings called her the 'human hand grenade', suggesting she was a dangerous menace - though Truss herself apparently regarded the label as a compliment (Cole and Heale 2022).

In terms of her political beliefs, personality traits and leadership approach, Truss goes a long way to fitting the models of the 'fiasco prime minister' (Brummer 2016) and the 'hubris syndrome' (Owen and Davidson 2009). Although these notions were originally developed and applied in the context of leadership failings and foreign policy disasters, they seem clearly also to have a broader application, including to the self-inflicted economic and political disasters of the Truss premiership. The root of the problem, according to these theories, can be traced back to a combination of excessive self-confidence and self-belief on the leader's part; ignoring (even contempt for) information, advice or the views of others contrary to their own opinions; a conflictual (as opposed to a more consensual) approach to politics; a predisposition to acting quickly and radically that can spin over into recklessness or impulsiveness; a focus more on their broad vision than on practicality and costs. That Truss was a politician in a hurry who, according to her biographers, charged into situations, was eager to flaunt her radical convictions and define herself against whatever seemed to be the conventional wisdom, had 'no time for critics' and would not listen to counter-argument, and combined 'arrogance and impatience' (Cole and Heale 2022) almost set her up from the start to stumble and fail as a hubristic 'fiasco leader' (see also: Parris 2022).

It is hard to escape the conclusion that Truss lacked the political, managerial and leadership skills to do the job of prime minister successfully. She was not a strong communicator, 'incapable of giving a convincing interview or making a more than pedestrian speech' (Finklestein 2022). She wanted to work through people she trusted but her Number 10 team was relatively inexperienced and underpowered. She instigated a major clear-out and reorganisation of officials and advisers, culling Johnson's team, reducing the number of special advisers and drastically cutting the size of the prime minister's Policy Unit, bringing in a new principal private secretary and also changing the National Security Adviser. Elsewhere in Whitehall the veteran Treasury permanent secretary, Tom Scholar, was unceremoniously sacked on day one of the new government - a deeply symbolic move in her war on 'Treasury orthodoxy', but she (and her Chancellor) would have been better off listening to, rather than sidelining, such expert advice when developing the policies that destroyed her government.

It is not necessary to completely go along with one MP's description of 'a Cabinet of minnows' (Cole and Heale 2022) to recognise that Truss's decision to appoint a Cabinet largely of loyalists (18 out of 23 Cabinet ministers had supported her leadership campaign), to leave out some notable Tory 'big beasts' and exclude Sunak supporters did little for party unity or executive competence. The parliamentary party had been hard enough to manage and keep in line under Johnson, and Truss's appointment of a new and, frankly, clueless Chief Whip only made things worse. Amazingly, two of the holders of the 'Great Offices of State' other than the premiership - Chancellor of the Exchequer Kwasi Kwarteng and Home Secretary Suella Braverman - lasted an even shorter time than Truss herself, 38 days and 44 days respectively before being dismissed. Truss's power was draining away by the time Jeremy Hunt (definitely not a Truss-ite) became Kwarteng's successor at the Treasury, and he, of course, outlasted her, continuing as Chancellor in the Sunak government.

In spite of the brevity of her tenure Truss became the first prime minister since Winston Churchill (in 1952) to serve in

Number 10 under more than one monarch. Queen Elizabeth died just two days after Truss was appointed prime minister and King Charles took the throne, the ten days of official state mourning and preparations for the royal funeral perhaps disrupting the new government's formation and early activities. 'Normal' politics was paused for a while, but the political and policy turmoil and tumult that then followed was anything but normal.

In future university courses and textbooks on political economy the Truss government will doubtless feature as a case study of 'government versus the markets', with the markets winning. It was not the first time that prime ministers had faced intense economic crises and storms in the financial markets - as the experience of previous governments with devaluation of the pound in the 1960s, the IMF crisis in 1976 and 'Black Wednesday' in 1992 shows - but the speed with which economic disaster triggered political meltdown in 2022, and forced the PM from office, was unique.

In recruiting personal aides, Truss apparently had the habit of testing interviewees with mental arithmetic questions (Cole and Heale 2022); however, the problem in 2022 was with the budget arithmetic. Rishi Sunak had warned about Truss's 'fairytale' economic plans during the leadership campaign and that was a good description of the 'mini-budget' that Truss and Kwarteng dreamt up and forced through - ignoring significant internal and external checks and scrutiny in the process. The economic situation Truss had inherited was a difficult one, but she made it worse. A gigantic package of tax cuts, financed by hugely increased government borrowing, designed in 'shock and awe' style to stimulate growth instead triggered turmoil in the financial markets, crashed the pound, forced Bank of England intervention and was condemned by the IMF.

In a blisteringly fast 'U-turn', Truss was forced to ditch her Chancellor, one of her closest political allies, and watch on impotently as his successor reversed most of the tax cuts and ended the 'Trussonomics revolution' (Cole and Heale 2022). Labour's existing lead over the Conservatives in the opinion polls increased dramatically and Truss's personal poll ratings collapsed to below what Johnson's had been when he was forced out (Worthy 2022: 722). Tory-supporting newspapers turned savagely on her, and with Conservative MPs firing off letters of no-confidence to the chair of the 1922 Committee her position quickly became untenable and she jumped, as it were, before she could be pushed out in a formal leadership vote.

Liz Truss's premiership has been rightly labelled a 'debacle' (Worthy 2022: 570), 'disastrous' and a 'deep personal humiliation' (Times 2022). There were no significant achievements in office, other than the political and economic chaos she left behind. Future prime-ministerial ranking and rating surveys of the sort discussed in chapter 17 of this book may require a special 'nul points' category for her or may perhaps need to extend the 'scoring' range to take in negative scores. Truss has earned an unenviable place in the prime-ministerial records books and in the history of the office.

References

Bogdanor, V. (2022). 'Choosing the Conservative Leader: a View from History.' *Political Quarterly*, 93 (4): 564-575.

Brummer, K. (2016). '"Fiasco prime ministers": leaders' beliefs and personality traits as possible causes for policy fiascos.' *Journal of European Public Policy*. 23 (5): 702-717.

Cole, H. and Heale, J. (2022). *Out Of The Blue: The inside story of the unexpected rise and rapid fall of Liz Truss.* London: HarperCollins.

Englefield, D., Seaton, J., and White, I. (1995). *Facts About the British Prime Ministers.* London: Mansell.

Finklestein, D. (2022). 'Truss is a lesson for the Tories, if they'll listen.' *The Times*, 21 October.

Longford, E. (1972). *Wellington: Pillar of State.* London: Weidenfeld & Nicolson.

Owen, D. and Davidson, J. (2009). 'Hubris syndrome: an acquired personality disorder? A study of US Presidents and UK Prime Ministers over the last 100 years.' *Brain.* 132 (5): 1396-1406.

Parris, M. (2022). 'La-la-la I'm not listening! Why Liz was born to fail.' *The Times*, 5 November.

Roe-Crines, A. (2022). 'The Degenerative Tendencies of Long-Serving Governments . . . 1963 . . . 1996 . . . 2009 . . . the Conservatives in 2022?' *Political Quarterly.* 93 (2): 336-341.

Theakston, K. (2010). *After Number 10: Former Prime Ministers in British Politics.* London: Palgrave Macmillan.

Times (2022). 'Bleak Legacy' (Leading article). *The Times,* 21 October.

Worthy, B. (2022). 'Will Truss's Time end in Failure? Assessing Prospects of the latest "Takeover" Prime Minister.' *Political Quarterly.* 93 (4): 717-722.

Printed in Great Britain
by Amazon